D0140199

ELITES IN FRENCH SOCIETY

ELITES IN FRENCH SOCIETY

The Politics of Survival

EZRA N. SULEIMAN

PRINCETON UNIVERSITY PRESS
Princeton, New Jersey

For
my Mother and Father

Things being as they are, there is only one way to avoid what is called the death of a state or a nation, one of those periods of acute crisis, that is, which sometimes cause or enable a type of civilization to disappear, to the unutterable woe of the generations that witness them. That way is to provide for a slow but continuous modification of ruling classes, for a slow but continuous assimilation by them of new elements of moral cohesion that will gradually supplant the old. In this case, probably, as in others, the best results in practice are obtained by a sound balance between two different and opposite natural tendencies, between the drift toward conservatism and the urge for innovation. In other words, a political organism, a nation, a civilization, can, literally speaking, be immortal, *provided it learns how to transform itself continually without falling apart.*—Gaetano Mosca, *The Ruling Class*

Image fréquente: celle du vaisseau Argo (lumineux et blanc), dont les Argonautes remplaçaient peu à peu chaque pièce, en sorte qu'ils eurent pour finir un vaisseau entièrement nouveau, sans avoir à en changer le nom ni la forme.—Roland Barthes, *Roland Barthes par Roland Barthes*

CONTENTS

Contents

LIST OF FIGURES AND TABLES

ACKNOWLEDGMENTS

IN the course of preparing this study for publication I relied on the help and generosity of many people on both sides of the Atlantic. I can only hope that the sum of their expertise as reflected in this book bears some resemblance and does justice to the individual parts of which I was the beneficiary.

Many of those who provided me with the material on which the study is based can only be thanked anonymously. This is the case with the nearly two hundred top-level political, industrial, administrative, financial, and academic officials who granted me interviews. Despite their onerous work schedules, none was ever in a hurry to terminate an interview. It is a source of some regret therefore that I have to observe here the principle of confidentiality as rigorously as I have adhered to it in the study. It could not be otherwise, and it is the only means that an author has of returning the confidence placed in him by his interlocutors.

Much of the library material I consulted was not easily accessible, and without the assistance of several people, numerous important documents might have escaped my attention. M. René Mayer facilitated access to the archives of the Ecole Nationale des Ponts et Chaussées, and M. De Lannurien helped locate much material there. My research in the library of the Ecole Polytechnique and in the Bibliothèque de la Documentation Française was aided by a very welcoming staff. Over the years, I have grown accustomed to relying on the wealth of material housed in the Bibliothèque Nationale and, for different purposes, in the Bibliothèque de la Fondation Nationale des Sciences Politiques in Paris. It was a pleasure to work in the library of the Maison des Sciences de l'Homme, in large part because I could always count on the cheerful efficiency of Mme. Maud Espérou and her colleagues.

The genesis of the study owes a great deal to Juan Linz, for had it not been for our numerous discussions—spanning several years —of the seminal writings of the great European social theorists on whose works this study is largely based, I might possibly not have undertaken this work. From these discussions I learned that social theory can best be made to come alive and prove its relevance when it is combined with empirical research.

A substantial part of the empirical data in this work is based on a questionnaire which benefited from the advice of Guy Michelat, Annick Percheron, and members of the Groupe de Sociologie des Organisations. I wish also to thank Deborah Millican, Béatrice Moine-Roy, and Martha Zuber for their work as research assistants at different times.

Several people read an earlier version of the manuscript in its entirety, and their comments and suggestions were of inestimable help. I am grateful to Giuseppe Di Palma, Robert D. Putnam, Dean Savage, and Steven Englund. I had the good fortune to discuss the development of my research over an entire year in Paris with James Scott, whose reading of the completed manuscript saved me from many rash conclusions. If this book is relatively free of factual errors, I owe it to Roger Errera's erudition and his meticulous reading of the manuscript on two occasions. Stanley Hoffmann read the manuscript in two different versions and each time brought to bear on his comments his unparalleled knowledge of French society. Several parts of the study were reworked, sometimes as a result of a single comment he made. For this I owe him very special thanks.

A number of institutions provided the financial assistance without which this study could not have been carried out. A Fellowship from the American Council of Learned Societies allowed me to spend fifteen months in Paris in 1973-1974. Another award from the ACLS permitted me to return to France for three months in 1975 to complete the research. The Ford Foundation, the American Philosophical Society, and the Senate Research Committee of the University of California, Los Angeles, provided additional financial assistance for research, travel, data analysis, and the writing of the book. A Fellowship from the John Simon Guggenheim Memorial Foundation in 1977-1978, awarded for work in progress on the problem of the autonomy of the state in modern industrial societies, made it possible for me to rework Chapters 8 and 9.

This is the second book that Sanford Thatcher of the Princeton University Press has worked on with me. Both experiences have been a pleasure because of his extraordinary dedication and skill as an editor.

Acknowledgments

All the work on this study was carried out in France, which meant that my family had to cross the Atlantic far more times than they would like to remember. This occupational hazard is now a normal part of our lives, and it is not without its compensations, for the book was written over two summers in a bucolic setting (albeit under a monastic regime) in southwestern France. My most stringent and devoted critic throughout was my wife, Susan. The hours she gave up to a book that she read, discussed, and criticized several times are too numerous to count, and it is to her that I feel most indebted. My children, Michael and Daniel, did all they could to prevent me from working, and for this they earned only my love. The dedication of this book to my parents speaks for itself.

Ezra N. Suleiman
Paris, May 1978

ELITES IN FRENCH SOCIETY

INTRODUCTION

WHY do some elites endure whereas others die? This is a question to which historians and social theorists have addressed themselves in trying to explain the severe conflicts that have plagued particular societies. It is, of course, a truism that certain societies are more prone to conflicts and to instability than others. But even within such societies there often lies, beneath the all-too-evident turbulence, a considerable stability of certain groups and institutions. The changes that occur in the wake of crises often distribute their impact on different sectors of society so unevenly that they completely bypass, or are successfully resisted by, certain groups. The result is that some groups and institutions manage to preserve their dominant positions and their privileges even while the society as a whole is experiencing crises, instability, and change.

France has often been seen as a classic example of a society that is at once static and turbulent. Crises are seen as leading merely to previously established patterns; the society remains, therefore, in a condition of perpetual stalemate. Like all sweeping explanations, this one is neither wholly true nor wholly untrue. It does not take account of either the scope or the nature of institutional change. The important question that needs to be asked is why political change, either gradual and peaceful or sudden and violent, affects certain institutions more than it does others. Change, in other words, needs to be viewed as involving two interacting components: the change that takes place in society as a whole and the change that takes place within various institutions in reaction to the transformation of the society. The ability of particular institutions to survive will depend largely on their capacity to change and to adapt to an evolving social, political, and economic environment.

France has experienced profound economic and political changes over the past century and a half. Economically, it is one of the wealthiest and most technologically advanced societies.

Politically, it is one of the few democratic societies of the contemporary era. Yet, the gradual democratization of the society has scarcely affected the ways in which the society's elites are selected, the nature of the elites' organizations, and their dominant position in the society. The post-aristocratic ruling groups, as we will see, have managed to preserve themselves and their institutions and to remain singularly unaffected by the profound transformations that have been making their mark on the society. The coexistence of democracy and elitism constitutes the underlying concern of this study.

This, then, is a study not of the turmoils that have characterized French society but of the stability and endurance of elitist institutions in the face of the democratic surge. It is the study of an elite that has refused to consign itself to what Pareto called the "graveyard of aristocracies." We need to keep in mind that we are dealing with a democratic society, but that it is the elitism, or elitist aspect, of this society that we are most concerned with. By "elitism" I mean the creation and maintenance of a small number of institutions wth extremely restrictive entrance requirements, institutions which grant lifelong membership, and which have the responsibility for defining and certifying excellence.

All societies are governed by elites[1] and every society has some means of producing its elites. But few societies have succeeded in *institutionalizing* their elite-forming mechanism to quite the degree that France has. One needs to demonstrate considerable competence before one can acquire membership in France's elite institutions. But once that competence has been demonstrated at an early age, it is never again called into question. Furthermore, for a wide spectrum of key positions in the society the system does not make much allowance for any recognition or reward of competence that has not been certified by the elite institutions. Merit, then, is recognized and legitimized only when it is certified by a restricted number of institutions. This phenomenon becomes more comprehensible and allows for comparisons with other societies when it is placed within a theoretical context.

---

[1] This is, of course, a tautological statement since by definition all those who occupy positions of authority are part of the elite. It is entry into and exit from the elite, as well as the unity of and conflict within the elite, that constitute the crucial aspects of elites and that serve to distinguish the different kinds of elites.

THEORY

There are, to be sure, widely differing theories of the rise, evolution, and disappearance of ruling groups. I have not relied exclusively on any one theory to analyze the bases for elite survival in France. I have had recourse to different theories, because to have relied exclusively on any one would have necessitated the tailoring of the findings to that theory. My work was largely inspired by the writings of Mosca, Tocqueville, Pareto, Mannheim, Weber, and Schumpeter. Some of these social theorists had a good deal to say about the rise and decline of ruling groups, and while their theories have been much commented upon, they have seldom been put to any kind of empirical test. For Mosca and Pareto, the survival of elites was a, if not *the*, central question that permeated their writings, and one wonders why it has received so little attention in the genre of elite studies. Pareto, for example, has been condemned to see even the source of his fame among social scientists[2]—the "circulation of elite" theory—largely misunderstood. For the circulation of elites does not refer to the way in which elites "circulate" or create interlocking directorates through different sectors of society, but to the way in which elites are able to transform themselves in a manner that ultimately ensures their survival. This problem is also at the heart of the second, and less well-known, essay in Schumpeter's *Imperialism and Social Classes*, another of the studies that form the theoretical underpinning of this book.

It will be evident even from a casual glance that this is an empirical study and not a purely normative one. It attempts to explain and to analyze, without applauding, an incontestable phenomenon: the dominance and stability of France's governing elites and their institutions.

To maintain that this is not a normative study does not mean that it will not be seen to have—perhaps with some justification—certain political implications. There is no escaping the fact that the subject itself could not, by its very nature, be devoid of ideological considerations. To explain why some particular condition or phenomenon exists may seem to be another way of justifying its existence. It is difficult, for example, to attempt to explain English working-class deference or the vote of workers for the Conservative

[2] The source of his fame is different for economists, who know Pareto largely for his "optimality theory."

Party without seeming to justify the class structure of British society or, at the very least, to downgrade its class antagonism. Similarly, the attempt to explain the survival of an elite might be seen in this light. This would be a grave error, for I have tried to explain the manner in which the elite has maintained itself in as much detail as possible, which also means that I have often laid bare the tactics and strategy of this elite, as well emphasizing the inegalitarian consequences of the elitist system. Survival, however, also implies a certain amount of dexterity and competence, so that we inevitably maintain the same kind of ambivalence to an elite that has survived as we do to Sièyes who, when asked what he had done during the French Revolution, replied: "I survived." The important point is that, despite the prevalence of crises and political turbulence, certain institutions and groups endure, and this endurance is a phenomenon that calls for examination. As Charles Maier has noted in his historical account of the continuity in and the stability of European societies after World War I, "In an era of upheaval, it is continuity and stability that need explanation."[3]

This is, then, an analytical and empirical study of the transformation of an elite. The problem of transformation has been well stated by Mosca: "The comprehensive and generic demonstration that a ruling class necessarily exists has to be supplemented . . . with an analytical study. We must patiently seek out the constant traits that various ruling classes possess and the variable traits with which the remote causes of their integration and dissolution, which contemporaries almost always fail to notice, are bound up."[4] If I have found it helpful and even necessary to lean on the analyses of Mosca and Pareto, two theorists scarcely known for their dedication to democracy, I feel no need to apologize for this. The questions they raise are highly legitimate and they are questions that have at various times been raised by theorists as different as Tocqueville, Marx, and Schumpeter. Thus Schumpeter could state the matter of class survival in the following terms:

> Class structure is the ranking of such individual families by their social value in accordance, ultimately, with their differing aptitudes. Actually this is more a matter of social value,

[3] Charles S. Maier, *Recasting Bourgeois Europe: Stabilization in France, Germany, and Italy in the Decade After World War I* (Princeton: Princeton University Press, 1975), p. 3.

[4] Gaetano Mosca, *The Ruling Class* (New York: McGraw-Hill, 1939), pp. 336-337.

once achieved, becoming firmly established. This process of entrenchment and its perpetuation constitutes a special problem that must be specifically explained—at bottom this is the immediate and specific "class problem."[5]

Schumpeter is preoccupied with the same sorts of questions that constitute the bulk of Mosca's and Pareto's writings. That Mosca and Pareto were, as has often been noted,[6] profoundly influenced by the prevailing economic and political transformations of Western societies is clear. Their writings ultimately reflect the fears which socialism and the emerging working classes inspired, as well as the disenchantment with what they referred to as the "myths" of democratic organizations. But they were not mere ideologues, for if they had been, their writings would probably not have survived the test of time. Consequently, even though both Mosca and Pareto are acknowledged foes of democracy and even though they are generally regarded as "reactionary" theorists, I have tried to make most use of those aspects of their writings that have especial analytical and explanatory value. The normative and ideological bases of the theories are of little concern to the present study.

PROBLEMS

In an earlier study of the interaction between politics and administration in France,[7] I dealt exclusively with the French administrative elite. It seemed to me at the time unfortunate that the study had to be circumscribed by the elite's role in a narrow sector, for it was clear that this was not merely an "administrative" elite, but rather an elite that had made successful incursions into other sectors. This "imperialistic" phenomenon led to a more general question that I did not discuss in my earlier study: what accounts for the entrenchment and endurance of this elite in French society? The imperialism of this elite may itself be one of the key factors that explains the endurance of the French elite. As Schumpeter has observed: "Every class that has once enjoyed an elevated position

[5] Joseph Schumpeter, *Imperialism and Social Classes* (New York: Meridian Books, 1971), p. 160.

[6] See H. Stuart Hughes, *Consciousness and Society* (New York: Alfred A. Knopf, 1958), and H. Bottomore, *Elites and Society* (New York: Basic Books, 1964), pp. 57-61.

[7] Ezra N. Suleiman, *Politics, Power, and Bureaucracy in France* (Princeton: Princeton University Press, 1974).

is greatly aided in seizing new functions, because the sources and gains of its prior function survive for some time."[8] But Schumpeter is referring here to what is no more than a *potentiality*. Some elites perceive the declining importance of their specialized functions and seize upon other "socially necessary"[9] functions in order to justify their position of dominance. Others may not have the same powers of perception, or if they do, they may nevertheless be incapable of acting upon this perception. In either case, they render their demise inevitable. Schumpeter observed that the inability of a particular group to move beyond its narrow sector of specialization is often what accounts for its demise.

> Hence we encounter the Germanic aristocracy from the very outset in a more sharply circumscribed special function. We need scarcely fear contradiction when we characterize this function as that of military leadership—a leadership, however, that meant not merely the command of forces but, to an increasing degree during the ensuing centuries, the actual execution of combat actions. Nor need we fear contradiction when we assert that this is the primary explanation for the generally enhanced position of the aristocracy, for its association with further functions—presiding at group meetings, leadership in other group concerns. It is plausible that the predominance of the military function, in uncomplicated circumstances and where the group is small in numbers, inhibits the emergence of positions of a different character.[10]

The question that is central to our study is that of *adaptability*. Why do some elites successfully adapt to changing economic and political conditions and so enhance their powers while others do not? The way in which the French elite has adapted to the profound changes experienced by the society is one of the keys for understanding its survival and is one of the major themes of this study. The adaptation of the French elite is especially significant because of the ways in which it appears to have avoided the errors of the defunct aristocracy. One is naturally led to ask whether this capacity for adaptation in the face of large-scale social change is true only of the elites or whether it is equally true of other institutions in the society. The changes that French society has experienced in the past thirty years suggest that French institutions—

---

[8] Schumpeter, *Imperialism and Social Classes*, p. 151.
[9] *Ibid.*, p. 160. [10] *Ibid.*, pp. 139-140.

political, social and professional—have shown far less rigidity and a far greater flexibility than they have usually been given credit for.[11]

In defining the elite that is the subject of this study we are not merely talking about the stability of social composition, for as Robert Putnam has justly noted, "if incumbent and successor are basically similar, so that the social composition of the elite remains constant, we hardly want to speak of elite transformation."[12] A distinction needs to be made, as Putnam notes, between the fate of individuals and that of social groups. This distinction is observed in the present study, for what we are above all concerned with are elites as definable structures and organizations. By dealing with organizations, we avoid a number of pitfalls that plague most elite studies.

First, most elite studies immediately run up against the major problem of defining the elite. None of the three methods used for identifying elites—positional, reputational, or decision-making—has proved wholly satisfactory. Elites imply, to be sure, a certain degree of coherence and self-consciousness about membership in an elite group. But this, in turn, implies organization, for there can be no power without organization.[13]

Second, by concentrating on organizational structures, we avoid reliance on the social background of elite members. We concentrate instead on the *functions, interests*, and *power* of the elite. In fact, this study will have very little to say about the social composition of the French elite, an omission that may seem startling and totally out of keeping with what is expected of elite studies. However, it is a conscious omission, and one that is dictated by the requirements of a study of political power and behavior. While many Marxists study the distribution of power in modern societies by almost exclusive emphasis on the social background of leaders, they seem unaware of the extent to which they have adopted a profoundly un-Marxist approach. For Marx saw society as guided above all by *interests* that derive from one's relationship to the

[11] I develop this argument in a work now in progress, *France: Social Change and the Transformation of a Society* (New York: Alfred A. Knopf, Inc., forthcoming).

[12] Robert D. Putnam, *The Comparative Study of Political Elites* (Englewood Cliffs, N. J.: Prentice-Hall, 1976), p. 168.

[13] See Mosca, *The Ruling Class*, p. 53. See also James Meisel, *The Myth of the Ruling Class* (Ann Arbor, Michigan: The University of Michigan Press, 1962), pp. 37-40.

economic structures of society. He was singularly unconcerned with the biographies of leaders. Moreover, to have chosen to emphasize the background of the French elite would have detracted from our emphasis on the behavior, the interests, and the adaptability of this elite. There is no doubt that studying the social composition of a group is far easier to do than trying to gauge its coherence, its policies, and its strengths for survival. As Ivor Crew has noted of British elite studies: "The British tradition regards the study of elites as an exercise in social arithmetic. [There is an] overwhelming emphasis on elites' recruitment patterns to the exclusion of their ideology, performance, power or relations with other elites."[14]

There is also the question of the extent to which social background determines behavior. I treated this question at length in my earlier study and suggested that, insofar as the administrative elite was concerned, it was probably correct to argue that social background exercised little effect on behavior. The behavior of these officials seemed to be guided more by the positions they occupied than by their social origins. Although I showed at length that the administrative elite was most unrepresentative of the society in terms of geography, education, and class, I concluded that this probably did not have a decisive impact on the behavior of the members of this elite. At the very least, I suggested, greater stress had to be put on factors other than background. This is a view that is not always easy to accept, and yet one sees even someone like R. K. Kelsall, who twenty years ago wrote an excellent book on the social composition of the British higher civil service, arguing today that "It is . . . not unreasonable to ask what difference it makes if the top people in key occupations are predominantly of one kind of social origin rather than another? And the honest answer to such a question must be that the attitudes and behavior of such a group would not necessarily be altered in any particular direction by a change in the social background of the office-holders." Kelsall rightly maintains that, while data on social origins are not without value, they "ought ideally to be supplemented by the much more difficult investigation of how he [the officeholder] behaves when he has reached the top."[15]

[14] Ivor Crew, *British Yearbook of Political Sociology: Elites in Western Democracy* (London: Croom Helm Ltd., 1974), p. 20.

[15] R. K. Kelsall, "Recruitment to the Higher Civil Service: How Has the Pattern Changed?" in Philip Stanworth and Anthony Giddens, eds., *Elites*

Third, the emphasis on organizations permits us to deal with the crucial problem of legitimacy. This is a question that preoccupies all wielders of authority; yet, discussions of it have not figured prominently in elite studies, not only because it is difficult to seize in a concrete way, but primarily because the chief concerns of elite studies have been such as not to assign a primary importance to the problem of legitimacy. But the need for an elite to maintain legitimacy both in its own eyes[16] and in the eyes of society is fundamental in societies where authority does not depend simply on force. As Weber put it, "It is an induction from experience that no system of authority voluntarily limits itself to the appeal of material or affectual or ideal motives as a basis for guaranteeing its continuance. In addition, every such system attempts to establish and to cultivate the belief in its 'legitimacy.' "[17] The fact therefore that the French elite and the institutions that nurture it have continued to exist down to our own day seems to suggest that the elite has managed to maintain its legitimacy even though it appears out of tune with current notions of democratic organization.

DEFINITION

The elite institutions and organizations that we are dealing with are essentially the *grandes écoles* and the *grands corps*. The first are the state institutions that train and nurture the state elite. The second represent the various organized elite structures (Inspection des Finances, Corps des Mines, Corps des Ponts et Chaussées, Conseil d'Etat, Cour des Comptes) whose recruits come almost exclusively from the grandes écoles. A successful academic career in one of the top grandes écoles leads to a career in one of the grands corps, which then facilitates the choice of a number of other possible careers within *and* outside state service.

I have chosen to refer to these elites as *state* elites because they are trained by the state and destined for state service. Had they confined themselves to state service, that function alone would have ensured them a remarkable influence. The importance of

---

and Power in British Society (Cambridge: Cambridge University Press, 1974), p. 171.

[16] The need to be legitimate in one's own eyes, to believe in one's self is, as we shall see in Chapter Five, crucial for elite survival.

[17] Max Weber, *The Theory of Social and Economic Organization* (New York: The Free Press, 1965), p. 325.

these elites, however, transcends the public sector, for their members today dominate—in some instances, monopolize—the key positions in the administrative, political, industrial, financial, and even educational sectors. We are dealing therefore with what can be called state-created elites who are trained, promoted, and legitimized by a highly selective educational system and who use state education and state service as a base from which to launch themselves into other careers. The result of this practice has been to concentrate the key posts in the major sectors of society in the hands of those who are able to make their way through these institutions.

The contours of this study should be spelled out. First, I do not claim to deal with all elites in French society. I am concerned only with the elites who exercise power and who influence decisions in the key sectors of society. If I have not discussed the survival of the judicial or academic or scientific elites, it is because they do not exercise the kind of influence on political or economic decisions that the state-created elites do. In short, this work deals only with governing elites.

Second, I have limited the discussion to only a few institutions. This is especially true in the case of the academic institutions that train the elites. There exist a number of other very important grandes écoles in France, and if this were a study of the grandes écoles, they would surely have received more than a brief mention. I have not dwelt on them because they are not directly relevant to the goals of the study. Similarly, there are a far greater number of corps than the few that I have chosen to deal with. Again, it needs to be emphasized that just as this is not a study of the grandes écoles, neither is it a study of the grands corps as such. I deal with only a small number of corps, and I do not assign equal space to those I deal with. Nor do I seek so much to delineate differences among the various corps as to describe general patterns. The essentials of what is said about one corps apply, *grosso modo*, to the others. What is being described is a system of recruiting, training, legitimizing, and privileging an elite. Those who gain entry into these institutions and reach the summits of different sectors (or, if they prefer, enjoy a sufficient degree of liberty to pursue their own pastimes) owe their status to their membership in a corps. They do not constitute a random collection of the most outstanding elements in the society, an "aristocracy of merit," as they often refer to themselves. Hence, while there are differences among the various corps, these differences pale before the characteristics that they have in common. In sum, I do not aim to cover every facet—history, organization, jurisdiction—of the corps that are discussed.[18] The reason for this is that the study derives from certain theoretical concerns bearing on the transformation of ruling groups.

What distinguishes the elites that are discussed in this work from the other elites (military, religious, intellectual, academic) is that the former's power and influence transcend a particular sector, whereas the latter's importance is confined to a specific domain. The elites that I have concentrated on are only secondarily specialized; that is, despite their control over a particular sector, they come to hold key positions in other sectors.

ORGANIZATION

The data on which this study is based are diverse. They include a survey of 125 members of the organized elites holding top positions in the private sector (presidents and vice presidents of industrial corporations) and in the public sector (ministries, nationalized industries, and ministerial cabinets). The interviews were based on a structured questionnaire and they lasted between two to four hours. In addition, unstructured interviews were conducted with over 50 political, administrative, and academic officials.[19] Finally, data were obtained from internal documents (journals, mag-

[18] For detailed information on the individual corps, see Pierre Escoube, *Les Grands corps de l'état* (Paris: Presses Universitaires de France, 1971); Marie-Christine Kessler, *Le Conseil d'Etat* (Paris: Armand Colin, 1968); Pierre Lalumière, *L'Inspection des Finances* (Paris: Presses Universitaires de France, 1959); Jean-Claude Thoenig, *L'Ere des technocrates: le cas des ponts et chaussées* (Paris: Les Editions d'Organisations, 1973); Pierrette Rongère, *La Cour des Comptes* (Paris: Fondation Nationale des Sciences Politiques, 1963); and André Thépot, *Le Corps des mines* (Paris: forthcoming).

[19] The confidential nature of these interviews has been rigorously maintained, and care has been taken to see that none of the respondents is recognizable. On rare occasions where an official is cited by name, the citation has either been taken from a published source, or prior permission was obtained by the author for the use of the citation. In either case, no indication is given as to whether he was or was not in our sample of interviewees.

azines, commission reports, debates) of the major elite organizations.[20] The last is an extremely important source because it enables us to follow elite opinions, projects, aims, and reactions. If these documents have not been fully exploited thus far, it is partly due to the fact that they are not easily accessible and also because "house publications" are generally regarded as being of interest only to members. I have included only what I have considered important to the subject as it is defined by its theoretical interests, some of which I have already mentioned.

The study is divided into three parts. The first deals with the state institutions that nurture the French elite. After outlining in Chapter One the nature of what I have referred to as "state-created elites," I turn to a detailed analysis of the system of higher education, or rather the parallel system of higher education, on which the entire elite structure reposes. It is scarcely necessary to insist on the importance of the structure of the institutions of higher learning. The chapters in Part One will suggest why a system so vehemently criticized at various periods during the nineteenth and twentieth centuries has endured so well.

In Part Two we shall be concerned with the questions of the organization, legitimacy, and adaptation of the elite and its institutions. We shall emphasize the manner in which these institutions have adapted themselves so as to maintain their legitimacy and to take advantage of new opportunities.

Part Three will deal with some of the policy and political implications of the elitist system. Because the elite we are dealing with was an ostensibly public-service elite but is now also an industrial elite, we will attempt to examine the impact of this cross-sectoral transference on the relationship between business and the state. This is a more complex problem than might appear at first glance because we need first to explain how a public elite traditionally hostile to private-sector interests (profit, investment) could come to embrace industrial development and interests.

[20] All translations from the French are my own.

Part One

❈ ❈

FOUNDATIONS

Chapter One

STATE-CREATED ELITES

A DISTINCTION needs to be drawn between societies that possess elite-creating mechanisms and societies that make no institutional provisions for the creation of their elites. The more established the mechanisms are, the more likely are the elites to be characterized by or grouped into a series of small circles, as well as by a well-regulated system of networks among these circles. Moreover, the offices which these elites occupy are likely to be endowed with considerable prestige, even with a certain degree of charisma.

France has one of the most clearly established mechanisms for the creation of its elites of any Western society. This is principally due to the fact that the state takes it upon itself to form the nation's elites. The state has thus devised a system that is complex and elaborate, tying as it does the professional training of the elites to their corporate organizations. To explain France's elitist structure, we must begin by understanding the organization of the educational system that creates the elites.

BASIS FOR STATE MONOPOLY

The development of secondary and higher education in France, and the ultimate control of both educational levels by the state, were the result of a political philosophy which has lost little of its force over the past century and a half. Ultimately, there was little pedagogical basis for the centralization of the educational system in the hands of the state. Indeed, pedagogy itself came to be seen as a derivative of the political aims of the state. The state's monopoly over the educational system has had two important consequences: it has not allowed the development of institutions that might rival the state's own, and it has meant that the state has taken it upon itself to ensure that the entire responsibility for the training of its leaders would be its alone. Even at the beginning of the nineteenth century, the ultimate purpose was to regulate not only those elites destined directly for state service (military officers, engineers, teachers) but others whose functions were considered necessary for any prosperous, ambitious, and well-ordered society. Hence, the Napoleonic reforms sought to control the training of doctors, lawyers, pharmacists, and other such groups. The aim of this chapter is to outline the bases for the state monopoly over the educational system and the impact this has had on the training of France's elites in the public and private sectors.

"No school, no educational institution can be established outside of the Imperial University."[1] This, in a nutshell, was Napoleon's basic philosophy regarding the control of education in France. It is a philosophy that has shaped the educational foundations of French society and that has scarcely permitted the modifications of these foundations. As Louis Liard, one of the pioneers of the university system, observed:

> Many changes have taken place since then in our higher education—structure, organization, methods, spirit, customs—almost everything connected with it has been modified and transformed. But, in spite of all these changes, the substance of the regulations of the years XI and XII has remained intact.[2]

For Napoleon, the centralization of the educational system[3] in the hands of the state had several distinct purposes. In the first place, it had a political purpose, one that Napoleon spelled out on many occasions. "My principal aim in establishing a teachers' corps," he declared before the Conseil d'Etat, "is to have a means

[1] Cited in J.-L. Crémieux-Brilhac, *L'Education nationale* (Paris: Presses Universitaires de France, 1965), p. 19.

[2] Louis Liard, *L'Enseignement supérieur en France*, Vol. II (Paris: Armand Colin, 1894), p. 34. A contemporary historian of the educational system has observed in a similar vein: "What is astonishing, therefore, is not that secondary education should have been included in the total reorganization introduced by the Consulate and the Empire, but that in this domain the Napoleonic work should have proved equally enduring. In fact, the University received at that time its definitive shape. It was born adult, and if the Second Republic altered some of its traits, for the most part it remained in 1880 what Napoleon had made it." See Antoine Prost, *L'Enseignement en France, 1800-1967* (Paris: Armand Colin, 1968), p. 23.

[3] I refer here only to secondary and higher education. Primary education remained until the advent of the Third Republic mostly in the hands of the church. See Michalina Vaughan and Margaret S. Archer, *Social Conflict and Educational Change in England and France 1789-1848* (Cambridge: Cambridge University Press, 1971), pp. 117-130, and 187.

by which to direct political and moral thought."[4] Liard has expressed very clearly the political aims that underlay Napoleon's reforms:

> The men of the Revolution had envisaged national education above all as a duty of the state toward its citizens. Napoleon saw in it above all the interest of the State and of the sovereign. To him, public education, left to itself and free to dispense its own doctrines, could quickly become a public danger. Its real function and its real *raison d'être* was to serve as a moral support for the power incarnated in and personified by the State.[5]

It was in the interest of political stability that education should be not only controlled by but also put at the service of the state. "I want to create a corporation," said Napoleon, "not of jesuits who have their sovereign in Rome, but of jesuits who have no other ambition than that of being useful, and no other interest but the public interest."[6] The public interest rested on certain fundamental principles which necessitated order and stability, and without which, it was believed, society could not exist as a viable unit. Napoleon's aim was, according to Liard, simple and could be expressed thus: "a nation is a whole; this whole has a bond; this bond is a set of principles; these principles are the maxims from which the State is derived and on which it stands. Whence, the need for the State to have a doctrine, and not only to have it, but to formulate it and to teach it, as a guarantee of its own stability."[7]

For the state schools to play their role in ensuring stability, it was above all necessary that no rival institutions should exist, for these might threaten to undo the work that the state schools were accomplishing. The state therefore had to have *total* control of education so as to assure the training of the young in a manner that conformed to Napoleon's doctrine. As Albert Delfau explained:

> The Emperor, in creating the Imperial University, did not intend to stop at the creation of schools where civil servants would come to inspire in the students a respect for the estab-

[4] Pelet de Lozère, *Opinions de Napoléon* (Paris: Firmin Didot Frères, 1833), p. 167.

[5] Liard, *L'Enseignement supérieur en France*, II, 69.

[6] De Lozère, *Opinions de Napoléon*, p. 163.

[7] Liard, *L'Enseignement supérieur en France*, II, 69-70.

lished regime. Such a creation would not have sufficed to insure the moral unity of France, if outside of and parallel to the official educational system, competing institutions had been allowed to exist and to develop without control. This is precisely what Napoleon would not tolerate. . . . Nothing was to escape his surveillance.[8]

For the founder of the modern educational system, "the university had to be above all an instrument of rulership."[9] But in addition to being an instrument for reigning, a second and clearly related function of a state-controlled educational system was its ability to assure uniformity in the society. The need for uniformity was an important element in all the reforms that Napoleon undertook, for it was bound up with his conception of a society based on order and hierarchy and devoid of squabbles that threatened anarchy. Napoleon was deeply impressed, and his reforms were ultimately influenced, by the manner in which the church transmitted its doctrines. Indeed, it is now recognized that the secular educational system he established was founded on the organizational principles of the ecclesiastic order. Even while seeking to wrench the educational system from the hands of the church, he admired the means by which the church transmitted its doctrines.

> As Napoleon conceived it [wrote Liard], the university teaching corps, open equally to ecclesiastics and laymen, but being essentially civil, secular and public, was a kind of transposition, in accordance with the needs of the new society, of the old type of religious corporations. Like the corporation, it had stability, permanence, a unified set of regulations. Like the corporation, it had also to possess doctrinal unity and unity of action. But, unlike the corporation, it was not a foreign element within civil society; the interests it pursued were not of a supernatural order, and did not direct it to cut itself off from everyday life and from social obligations.[10]

Nor was the need for uniformity incompatible with the task of education, which was conceived in a rather strict sense. The aim of the school was not to educate, as we sometimes understand that term. The school was, above all, an institution whose existence and

---

[8] Albert Delfau, *Napoleon 1ᵉʳ et l'instruction publique* (Paris: Albert Fontemoing, 1902), p. 17.

[9] Liard, *L'Enseignement supérieur en France*, II, 74.

[10] *Ibid.*, p. 73.

loyalty was due to the state. Consequently, rather than to educate, its task was to train and "to train according to the model which best suits the State, which has the right and the duty to decree and to impose. . . . The most important requirement is that citizens be shaped by public education as the sovereign, repository and guardian of public power, thinks that they ought to be; that they think what the State believes they ought to think; and that they desire what the State needs them to desire."[11] For all this, it was necessary to have an organization that mirrored the church, an organization that was "permanent, homogeneous, enveloping like a placenta the young generations and transferring to them through a thousand channels the moral substance that it receives from the state. . . . Such was the basic aim of the University."[12]

The uniformity in curricula and teaching methods was, of course, to become of crucial importance, though not at the outset. For the aim at the beginning was uniformity in organization, which itself would lead to uniformity in behavior and obedience to the state. The organization and regimentation of the *lycée* was an indication of what Napoleon had in mind.

> The school became a copy of the regiment. It was divided into companies, each of twenty-five pupils, with a sergeant and four corporals. The school-life was regulated by drum-signals and in many *lycées* periodic "route marches," to the accompaniment of military music, were a regular feature of the curriculum. The school uniform of the pupils consisted of a green coat with a light blue collar and trimming and metal buttons stamped with the name of the *lycée*. . . . One of the chief school punishments was to deprive the pupil of his right to wear this costume and to substitute for it "un habit d'étoffe grossière. . . ."[13]

This regimentation had a purpose and it foreshadowed what was to follow in the other institutions that Napoleon was to create. The organizational principles of the church and the military, which Napoleon admired so much, were well tailored to achieving the desired goals that Napoleon had set for the French state. However, as Barnard points out, where, as in the school, "everything done to the most trivial details was closely regulated . . . the ultimate

---

[11] *Ibid.*, p. 70.   [12] *Ibid.*

[13] H. C. Barnard, *Education and the French Revolution* (Cambridge: Cambridge University Press, 1969), p. 221.

aim obviously was not to produce free citizens, but to fit boys to serve the state in the Napoleonic armies or administrative posts, and to stimulate military and patriotic enthusiasm."[14]

The third important function of state-controlled education was utilitarian. Indeed, "the ultimate aim of public education is to create professions useful to the society."[15] The state was going to need qualified men to serve it in the spheres that it was going to control, and one of the main aims of the new educational system was to provide these trained people. The idea that education should serve practical and useful goals was not a purely Napoleonic invention. Napoleon was merely to push it to great lengths. As Artz notes, "The purpose of the educators, the scientists, and the legislators of the Revolutionary era was to turn the young away from the study of God, of men, and of the past and to direct their attention to nature and to science, to the state, to what was believed to be socially useful, and to the practical."[16] French scientists, believing in practical application and wishing to eliminate church control of the school system, came to welcome state control of education.[17] The principle that was to influence Napoleon most—that of practicality and usefulness—can perhaps best be understood by citing the chemist Hassenfratz, who felt that the national festivals that were suggested by all the educational proposals for reform were an absurdity. "Let us be careful," he said, "lest while we are busy organizing our festivals, our neighbors may organize their industry, and destroy our manufactures and commerce. It was not with festivals that the English have been able to acquire a great preponderance over the political balance of Europe. It was not with festivals that the United States of America became a flourishing people. . . . The most beautiful festival which we can give the French people is to organize education for arts and trades, and to give great stimulus to national industry."[18]

It is difficult to exaggerate the utilitarian function that Napoleon ascribed to French education; and, as we shall see in the following chapters, it is this function that is the basis of elite formation in

[14] *Ibid.*, p. 222.

[15] Liard, *L'Enseignement supérieur en France*, II, 100.

[16] Frederick B. Artz, *The Development of Technical Education in France, 1500-1850* (Cambridge, Mass.: The M.I.T. Press, 1966), p. 180.

[17] Joseph Ben-David, *The Scientist's Role in Society: A Comparative Study* (Englewood Cliffs, N. J.: Prentice-Hall, 1971), p. 96.

[18] Cited in Artz, *The Development of Technical Education in France*, p. 120.

France today. The practical aim of education has had many critics, none more uncompromising than Taine, who bitterly criticized the Napoleonic system of education on the ground that it was utilitarian, concrete, and unconcerned with art and literature. "When Napoleon made himself some jurists, it was to have people to execute his orders, not to criticize them; his Faculties would provide him with men capable of applying his laws, but not of judging them."[19] The only people who were useful to society were those who performed specific functions, not the "erudite man or the philosopher."[20] Renan, on the other hand, was willing to recognize that both the "useful" and the "erudite" had a place in society, and he maintained that the training of the first was the responsibility of the state. He distinguished between *l'instruction*, which involves the acquisition of a given body of knowledge and its application, and *l'éducation*, which makes *"le galant homme, l'honnête homme, l'homme bien élevé.* It is clear that it is the latter which is the most important. The first is the responsibility of the state, the other is not."[21]

The emphasis on the utility and practicality of knowledge may seem at odds with the proverbial view that "culture" and "theory" have been accorded a certain mystique, if not sanctity, in France. Indeed, some have even seen fit to criticize the abstract preoccupations of French education and to suggest that it ought to be more closely associated with reality. Marc Bloch, in his *L'Etrange défaite*, argued just such a case. "An old tradition," he wrote, "impels us to love intelligence for itself, like art for art's sake, and to place it apart from what is practical. We have great scholars, and no technicians are less scientific than ours. We read, when we do read, to cultivate ourselves, which is fine. But we do not sufficiently realize that we can, and that we should, use our culture to help us when we act."[22]

How is one to reconcile the views of those who see French education as being excessively preoccupied with practicality and usefulness and those who see it as being excessively divorced from the

[19] Hippolyte Taine, *Les Origines de la France contemporaine*, Vol. 2 (Paris: Hachette, 1894), p. 206.

[20] Ernest Renan, *La Réforme intellectuelle et morale* (Paris: Michel Lévy, 1871), p. 326.

[21] *Ibid.*

[22] Marc Bloch, *L'Etrange défaite* (Paris: Albin Michel, 1957), pp. 194-195. This book was first published in 1946.

real world? In effect, it is possible to see both principles at work because, as will become clear, two systems of higher education have come to coexist in France. One (the grandes écoles) is oriented almost exclusively toward providing a technical or professional training, while the other (the universities) is more preoccupied with theoretical and intellectual concerns. This is, to be sure, an oversimplification because the universities have always provided their share of professional training. Doctors, lawyers, and pharmacists have always received their training in Faculties that were attached to universities. On the other side, the Ecole Normale Supérieure, one of the more illustrious of the grandes écoles, has been concerned solely with intellectual matters, its primary function having been to train teachers for secondary and higher education. Nevertheless, the contrast between the universities and the grandes écoles is striking because the latter are almost exclusively technical or professional schools, while the vocational mission of the former has tended in the recent past to diminish. We shall return to this problem in the chapters that follow. For the moment, it is only necessary to note that the consequences of this parallel system of higher education, perhaps more sharply divided today than in the past, have been profound and far-reaching. And it is this educational system that underlies not only the formation of elites in France, but also their organizational structures.

DIVERSIFICATION OF STATE ELITES

Although the Napoleonic reforms gave the state a predominant role in shaping and controlling the educational system, the purpose was not to exclude nonstate or private schools from playing a part in education. The new system was merely a "method of surveillance, both of the religious schools and of the church, which Napoleon regarded as at best an unreliable ally."[23] There was little doubt, however, that the system was intended to have, and did indeed come to have, a monopoly over one crucial area: the training of elites. This was merely another side to the utilitarian emphasis of the educational system: the elites are the ones who put their training to practical endeavors on behalf of the state. This explains why I have chosen to refer to the French elites—political, administrative, and industrial—as state-created elites. The state today,

[23] John E. Talbott, *The Politics of Educational Reform in France, 1918-1940* (Princeton: Princeton University Press, 1969), p. 5.

more than ever, is responsible for the training, organization, and experience not only of the elites that directly serve it, but even of those in the nationalized and private sectors.

It may seem a little perplexing to an Anglo-Saxon reader to be informed that even the financial and industrial elite is trained in France under the aegis of the state. This was not intended to be the case in the early part of the nineteenth century when the private sector did not loom very large and when the Napoleonic state was beginning to make inroads into all activities in the society. Today, there are no private schools that compare with the Ecole Polytechnique, the Ecole des Arts et Métiers, or the Ecole Nationale d'Administration (ENA) and whose purpose is to train managers for the private sector. The Ecole Centrale and the Ecole des Hautes Etudes Commerciales, both of which train their students for the private sector, are no longer strictly private institutions. Indeed, the Ecole Centrale came under the control of the Ministry of Education between 1946 and 1959, after which date the school regained its "civil and autonomous personality." Nevertheless, neither of these schools, important as they are in the training of middle-level industrial managers, competes with the Ecole Polytechnique or with the ENA in the creation of the mobile elite with which this study is concerned. The state has been concerned to enhance the prestige of its own schools—the grandes écoles—to such an extent that the graduates of these schools are practically omnipresent in the key posts in the society. The administrative, financial, and industrial elites are today drawn from among the graduates of schools whose task has always been, and continues to be, the training of those destined to serve the state.

To be sure, the state continues, perhaps even to a greater extent than in the nineteenth century, to train its own public service elite. But since this elite spills over into the private sector, it also follows that the state today has taken upon itself the task of supplying the private sector with its leaders. It did this also to some extent in the nineteenth century, though at that time this was perhaps more a by-product than a mission of the state institutions. In the course of the twentieth century, however, the diversification of the state's elite came in response to the expansion of the nationalized and private sectors and to the curtailment or diminishing importance of other sectors that had been under the state's tutelage. In sum, the state educational institutions which had previously been endowed with the sole responsibility of training the elite for particular sectors within the public domain now responded to a new calling.

Now, this new mission of certain state institutions (the specialized schools that fall outside of the university system) has had profound consequences for the educational system as a whole, and for the relationship between the state and the private sector. We shall have occasion in the course of this study (Part Three) to examine in detail some of the consequences. Suffice it to say here that the concept of the state as a distinct entity which stands above society's divisions and encompasses an interest transcending that of its constituent parts has undergone considerable modification. Moreover, the state has willingly accepted its new role of training the private sector elite, so that an added interest has arisen in maintaining the parallel system of higher education. Finally, the traditional hostility that characterized the relationship between the state and the private sector has, to a very considerable extent, given way to a new type of relationship.

We are concerned in this part of the study with the educational institutions in which the state trains the future holders of the key posts in society. The educational system fashioned by Napoleon has endured remarkably well despite the changes that have been instituted during the past century. The reason for this endurance is not trivial: the system was throughout supported both by republicans and by conservatives.[24] We have already examined some of the factors that led to the state's control of the educational system. Subsequent to the establishment of this control, theoretical justifications were offered which tended to buttress the actions of the republicans. Durkheim, for example, justified the monopoly of the state in regulating education on the grounds that it contributed to the cohesiveness and stability of the society, arguments that neither conservatives nor republicans could fault. "If, as we have tried to show," he wrote, "education has, above all, a collective function; if it aims to adapt the child to the social milieu where he is destined to live, it is impossible for the society not to take an interest in such an undertaking. How could society remain indifferent, given that it provides the criterion according to which education has to model itself? It is therefore up to the society to remind the teachers unceasingly what ideas and sentiments it is necessary to impress on the child in order to place him in harmony

[24] Prost, *L'Enseignement en France, 1800-1967*, p. 9.

with the milieu in which he must live."[25] For if the state was not always "present and vigilant" to direct education toward "un sens social," this would lead to dividing the nation's soul and, hence, ultimately to divisive conflicts. No school, Durkheim maintained, can "claim the right to give with full freedom an antisocial education."[26] It is therefore up to the state to outline the main principles that are common to everyone in society—respect for reason, for science, and for the ideas that underlie democratic morality—and to ensure that they are taught in schools and respected by all.[27] Diversity is, of course, necessary, according to Durkheim, but the task of education is to form a "social being," for only then is a cohesive society possible.[28]

If the state has maintained its strong grip over the educational system, then, this has been due—as Napoleon's reforms and Durkheim's arguments make clear—to the need for cohesiveness within the society, to the fear of competing particularisms, and to the need for a trained cadre to serve the state. All these factors are as important today as they were in the nineteenth century. It is possible to see the state's educational policies as merely a part of its centralizing predilection. But it would be unfortunate to view it entirely in this way because it then becomes very difficult to analyze and disentangle the educational, pedagogic, social, and political impact of the institutional structures within which education is carried out. Writing after the outbreaks of May-June 1968, Alain Touraine noted the impact of the state in the area of education:

> If the university can be accused of being bourgeois, it is not because it spreads knowledge, ways of thinking, and social attitudes favorable or necessary to the defense of the capitalist economy. The link between the university and society is not that direct. It passes through the State which transforms and sometimes reverses it. The State has given the university its uniformity but it also assures teachers of national status, lifelong jobs, and protection against local pressures. It is the State that organizes teaching personnel on all levels, defines programs, the spirit behind them, and methods of controlling knowledge. Finally, the State, in its administration and in its

[25] Emile Durkheim, *Education et sociologie* (Paris: Presses Universitaires de France, 1966), pp. 58-59.
[26] *Ibid.*, p. 60.   [27] *Ibid.*   [28] *Ibid.*, p. 120.

schools, assures career openings for many students, who are thus removed from economic activities.[29]

The role that the state plays in education in France is, to be sure, all-encompassing. And yet one must not conclude that centralization has implied total uniformity, for centralized as the educational system has been in France, the state has nonetheless been careful to make very definite distinctions among the various institutions of higher learning. It has in the past placed, and it does so today, by far the greater reliance on the grandes écoles to the detriment of the universities, so that the division within the higher educational system—between the grandes écoles and the universities—has in fact widened. It is the grandes écoles that have the primary responsibility for training the French elites. We shall see in Chapter Four the extent to which the various elites in French society are in fact recruited not from the universities but from the grandes écoles. But we shall first have to examine the basis for this double system of higher education, which has a logic of its own and which found sympathy, despite the rhetoric, on both the Left and the Right.

That higher education in France has experienced a remarkable growth in the past 25 years is evident. But this fact becomes less important the moment we recognize that those who occupy the key positions in French society are not graduates of the universities. The remarkable expansion in enrollments in universities has been paralleled by the static nature of enrollments in the grandes écoles.[30] This serves to underscore the twin policies that are followed with respect to the two sets of institutions of higher learning in France, policies that have remained basically unchanged despite all the demands for reforms that have been made over the past century.

At this point, we need do no more than point to some of the consequences of this double-track educational system, whose primary aim remains that of assuring social stability. Depending on the path that one chooses to follow in the higher education system —the universities or the grandes écoles—one enters two different realms of training, expectations, and employment prospects. The university churns out its graduates at an ever-increasing rate, with the result that diplomas are devalued and employment opportuni-

[29] Alain Touraine, *The May Movement: Revolt and Reform* (New York: Random House, 1971), p. 90.

[30] See Chapter Three below.

28

ties are diminished. The grandes écoles continue to restrict the number of their graduates, with the result that competition among these graduates becomes, if anything, less severe. In comparison with university graduates, they are more desirable to employers and the fact that they can choose between the public and private sectors widens their opportunities even further.

The point to be stressed is that there exists in France a double-track, or parallel, system of higher education. Entering a university requires no more than the possession of the *baccalauréat* (the diploma granted at the termination of secondary-level studies); entering a grande école requires post-baccalauréat preparation (usually two years) for and the passing of highly competitive national examinations. Now, this parallel system of higher education that has existed for so long in France and that shows no sign of crumbling is important because it is the foundation on which rests the elite structure of French society. Consequently, no discussion of the distribution of power, of social mobility and opportunities, and even of the policy-making process can ignore the structure of higher education in France. Without this system, we would not find the elite organizations that exist in France.

The grandes écoles have a direct link to the major corporate organizations of the elites: the grands corps. These corps, which will be discussed in greater detail in the course of this study, are institutions that carry out functions on behalf of the state. At the same time, they are institutions, or clubs, that group together an elite that is united by a common educational background, common career horizons, and common corporate interests. How does one enter a grand corps? By graduating at the top of one's class in the appropriate grande école. Thus, to enter the Corps des Mines or the Corps des Ponts et Chaussées, one must graduate at or near the top of the Ecole Polytechnique. Similarly, to enter the Inspection des Finances, the Cour des Comptes, or the Conseil d'Etat, it is necessary to graduate within the top 20 percent of one's class at ENA. Hence, the educational system is tied in an unambiguous way to the society's elite structures. To be sure, the link between the grandes écoles and certain corps was not always indispensable, for some grands corps did exist in the past without having a direct link to a grande école.[31] Nevertheless, the situation today is such

[31] This was notably the case with the Inspection des Finances, the Conseil d'Etat, and the Cour des Comptes which, before the creation of the Ecole Nationale d'Administration in 1945, recruited their own members. But even

that the grandes écoles train the French elites and take an active part in their organizations, which in turn reciprocate by supporting the institutions that provide them with the best recruits.

Enough has been said so far to indicate that the role of the state in the training and recruitment of the society's elites is not a negligible one. Indeed, we need at this point to recognize that the very use of the term "state," which so far has perhaps been unduly abstract, can now begin to take on a more concrete meaning. Since the grandes écoles are state institutions and since they have what amounts to an exclusivity on the training[32] of elites, who in turn run the state, we begin to see who forms educational policy. This not only renders the use of the term "state" less abstract but allows us to understand the rationale that governs the type of educational system that exists in France. Whether we accept this rationale should in no way obscure the fact that it unquestionably exists. This explains why it is so difficult to find in France today an "opposition" policy toward education, for even the Left has not been able to repudiate this rationale, which has been seen as crucial to the whole process of governing in France.

---

then, these corps had a more than tenuous link to the Ecole Libre des Sciences Politiques since nearly all their recruits came from this school.

[32] Some have preferred the use of the term "production" of elites, a term that is becoming more and more common. But this is a term that I have avoided, because elites are always small in number and they are usually carefully trained, groomed, and nurtured, which seems to suggest a craft trade rather than an assembly line.

❧ Chapter Two ❧

THE BASIS OF ELITE FORMATION: THE UNIVERSITIES VS. THE GRANDES ECOLES

THE analysis of the recruitment and training of elites has understandably emphasized the degree of openness of the educational system both in quantitative terms and in the degree of representation of society's social classes in the student population. Invariably, regardless of the type of political system that prevails, it has been found that those who attain the diplomas conferred by higher education and who gain entry into the various elites are usually endowed with economic and social advantages that are not available to those who do not attain these positions. This is evidently as true of France, Britain, and the United States as it is of the Soviet Union and India.[1]

In the case of France, the social background of those who gain access to higher education has been the starting—and often the finishing—point of studies of elite recruitment, as well as of elite ideologies and behavior.[2] The extent to which access to higher education fulfills or short-circuits the requirement of equality of opportunity is still open to debate, though in recent years there has appeared a certain disenchantment with the belief that the path to opportunity lies through education.[3] Bourdieu and Passeron showed some years ago that social origin constituted the greatest

[1] For cross-national data on the backgrounds of elites, see the summary in Robert D. Putnam, *The Comparative Study of Political Elites* (Englewood Cliffs, N. J.: Prentice-Hall, 1976), pp. 20-70.

[2] See Edmond Goblot, *La Barrière et le niveau* (Paris: Presses Universitaires de France, 1967); this book was first published in 1925; Luc Boltanski, *Prime éducation et morale de classe* (Paris: Mouton, 1969); Alain Girard, *La Réussite sociale en France* (Paris: Presses Universitaires de France, 1961); and J.-A. Kosciusko-Morizet, *La "Mafia" polytechnicienne* (Paris: Editions du Seuil, 1973).

[3] It is more common now to talk of equality of "results" rather than equality of "opportunity." See Christopher Jencks, *Inequality* (New York: Basic Books, 1973).

influence on academic success.[4] Their study was regarded at the time of its publication as extremely important, not so much for its political conclusions, of which there were almost none, but for its laying bare the means by which higher education restricted the drive toward equality. Raymond Boudon, in an extremely sophisticated study that can be read as a response to *Les Héritiers*, argues that there is no single relationship between inequality of educational opportunity and inequality of social mobility since there are great variations in the status of people having the same education, as well as in the impact of educational qualifications on income.[5] Others have argued that it is false to concentrate on the university, or on education in general, as a means of democratization, because such a question is irrelevant. Those who take this view argue that the school system is simply a reflection of the capitalist system. Baudelot and Establet write that "education is, from the point of view of the bourgeoisie, already democratic. But this democracy has no other meaning, in a capitalist society, than the cleavage between two antagonistic classes, and the domination of one of these classes by the other."[6] They argue that education in France has two paths, one that they call "secondary-higher," the other "primary-professional."[7] The function of these two distinct paths is as follows:

> There are two opposing networks of education because the social division of labor, which is most often presented as a purely technical division of "functions" and of "competence" or of "qualification," is in reality directly determined by the division of the society into antagonistic classes, by the need for the exploitation of labor in the production process and, outside of the production process proper.[8]

That education is a mere reflection of the division of labor in a society and that it serves to reproduce the prevailing class structure of a society are themes that have received a great deal of

[4] Pierre Bourdieu and J.-C. Passeron, *Les Héritiers* (Paris: Editions de Minuit, 1964).

[5] Raymond Boudon, *L'Inégalité des chances* (Paris: Armand Colin, 1973), now translated as *Education, Opportunity and Social Inequality* (New York: John Wiley & Sons, 1974).

[6] Christian Baudelot and Roger Establet, *L'Ecole capitaliste en France* (Paris: Maspéro, 1971), p. 18.

[7] *Ibid.*, p. 42.   [8] *Ibid.*, p. 118.

attention in recent years.[9] Our purpose in this chapter is to move away from this controversy, not because we do not consider it important but rather because the abstract nature of the debate will scarcely help us resolve the controversy. Moreover, if one accepts the view that society is organized along more complex lines than is indicated by the existence of two classes, one must then accept that educational institutions, like other institutions, can serve the interests of groups that belong neither to the class that owns the means of production nor to the one that owns only its labor. This is suggested by the fact that the school system has more complex divisions than is indicated by the Baudelot and Establet dichotomy. If we take, for example, the "secondary-higher" path, we find that the divisions within it are perhaps greater than those between it and the "primary-professional" category. For if the products of the "primary-professional" are destined to be the fodder of the capitalist system, it is possible to argue that the products of the university system ("secondary-higher") have a comparable, if not at times worse fate in comparison with the graduates of the grandes écoles (also "secondary-higher"). My purpose in underlining the serious division between the universities and the grandes écoles is not to emphasize the differing interests that divide the bourgeoisie. I am simply attempting to show that the system has serious implications for the society insofar as pedagogy and equality are concerned. From certain points of view, it is also endowed with rationality.

This is not to deny, however, that the educational structure serves certain interests. Trying to decipher just what these interests are is a complex problem and one that can be resolved only by patient analysis of the structure itself and of its historical bases. Moreover, it is equally important to understand why the system as it was originally constituted continues to exist in our own day; why, in other words, it has survived so many different epochs and regimes.

If we bear these preliminary remarks in mind, we will be led to adopt a cautious, not to say skeptical, approach to the theory ac-

[9] See Pierre Bourdieu and J.-C. Passeron, *La Reproduction* (Paris: Editions de Minuit, 1971); and Pierre Bourdieu, "Reproduction culturelle et reproduction sociale," *Informations des sciences sociales*, Vol. 2, No. 10. See also Samuel Bowles and Herbert Gintis, *Education in Capitalist America* (New York: Basic Books, 1976).

cording to which the educational system is merely a creation and an indispensable part of the capitalist mode of production. We shall see that the system that we are about to analyze has existed for over a century and a half and that it has, on the whole, been supported by both the Left and the Right. This fact alone indicates that reality is at variance with the theory; or, alternatively, one has to conclude that the Left itself has been a tool of the bourgeoisie.

The answer to the question of why the educational structure and the elite institutions which it fostered and now supports have survived for over a century and a half raises a more general question that is of both theoretical and practical importance: why do some groups or institutions survive while others die? This is not an easy question to answer, but one that is crucial for understanding the continuity of France's elites and their institutions.

THE GRANDES ECOLES

In 1871, Emile Boutmy wrote the following in a letter: "Privilege has gone, democracy cannot be halted. The higher classes, as they call themselves, are obliged to acknowledge the right of the majority, and they can only maintain their political dominance by invoking the right of the most capable. Behind the crumbling ramparts of their prerogatives and of tradition the tide of democracy must encounter a second line of defense, constructed by *manifest* and *useful* abilities, of *superior qualities* whose prestige cannot be gainsaid. . . ."[10] Boutmy, basically an opponent of the grandes écoles, made in this letter the clearest arguments for the schools that would train "useful, superior and prestigious" elites, and his words are cited partly because he himself was an opponent of elite schools and partly because they show how widespread, consciously or otherwise, the hankering for specialized schools was.

The grandes écoles were not, strictly speaking, Napoleon's creation. Some had been created in the aftermath of the Revolution and some, like the Ecole Nationale des Ponts et Chaussées, had even been created under the *ancien régime*. Yet, if they came to be central institutions in the formation of elites, this was in large part owing to Napoleon who recognized that the *écoles spéciales*,[11] as

[10] Cited in T. B. Bottomore, *Elites and Society* (New York: Basic Books, 1964), p. 82. My italics.

[11] For a clarification of the origins of this term, see A. Aulard, *Napoléon Ier et le monopole universitaire* (Paris: Armand Colin, 1911), p. 130.

they were called and as they are often called today, could be an important instrument for his reign. As Delfau noted:

> Thus when Bonaparte appeared, only the grandes écoles had been able to rise above the ruins of the Revolution, and only they appeared destined for a durable and brilliant future. In fact, these grandes écoles could not, either by their aims or by their characters, do harm to Napoleon. In the realization of his public education projects, Bonaparte at no moment found them an obstacle. On the contrary! Was he not to find in them powerful supporters—at the Ecole Polytechnique, officers for his armies, at the Ecole Normale, professors for his lycées?[12]

Far from doing away with the grandes écoles, Napoleon saw in them the complement to his reforms of secondary education, which is what he was most concerned with and which bears his stamp today. Least of all was he concerned with the *facultés*. It is important to emphasize that the reform of the educational system concerned the university, as we know it today, very little. Indeed, the university suffered as a result of the importance attached to and the attention accorded both the lycées and the specialized schools (the grandes écoles). "The abysmal state of French universities in the nineteenth century," notes John Talbott, "was in part both cause and consequence of the attention lavished on secondary education."[13] Subsequent reforms did not alter the structure that Napoleon had established. This was to be the case for the universities also. "The Revolution had abolished the twenty-two universities of the Old Regime; it gave up the idea of the university as an institution encompassing the whole of human knowledge. In place of the university, separate institutions—the Ecole Polytechnique, the Ecole normale supérieure and other Grandes Ecoles—were founded to provide professional training in specialized subjects."[14] The facultés were relegated to secondary importance throughout the nineteenth century, to such an extent that it was possible for one observer to remark in 1875 that there was no higher education in France.[15] If the current state of the French university is generally

---

[12] Albert Delfau, *Napoléon Ier et l'instruction publique* (Paris: Albert Fontemoing, 1902), p. 29.

[13] John E. Talbott, *The Politics of Educational Reform in France, 1918-1940* (Princeton: Princeton University Press, 1969), p. 6.

[14] *Ibid.*   [15] *Ibid.*

seen to be less than ideal, this was no less the case in the nine-teenth century.

Napoleon was, as were those who came after him, primarily concerned with creating qualified elites that would serve the state with incontestable dedication and loyalty. The lycées and the grandes écoles were the chief vehicles for this purpose. "To form a leadership elite [*élite dirigeante*], such is the role of secondary education,"[16] said Alexandre Ribot in his committee's report on secondary education. No less was this true of the grandes écoles, which embodied the utilitarian view of education that was consid-ered so important. Because of the emphasis on usefulness, it was possible to look at these schools from two vantage points: either as indispensable institutions for the fulfillment of society's ambitions, or as institutions reflecting an unusual degree of philistinism.[17] Taine took the second view and became a vehement critic of the grandes écoles.

> According to this principle [he wrote], the State instituted its *écoles speciales*, and by the indirect monopoly which it conferred on them, filled them with students. It was these schools which would henceforth give the youth of France its higher education. . . . From the outset, as a logician, with his usual lucidity and precision, Napoleon decreed that they would be strictly professional and practical schools. "Make me regents," he said one day of the Ecole Normale, "and not *litterateurs*, sensitive souls or scholars and creators in some field of knowledge" [*sic*]. Always the same subordination of science to art, the same desire for immediate or almost imme-diate applicability, the same utilitarian direction leading to a public post or a private career.[18]

It was in the areas of teaching, science, and the military that the most prestigious grandes écoles were first established and upon which Napoleon subsequently came to rely for the achievement of his aims. The Convention created the Ecole Normale Supérieure, and a decree of 1808 reestablished this school and made of it an institution for the training of teachers. Napoleon, in reconstituting

[16] Cited in *ibid.*, p. 7.

[17] There were, of course, other criticisms made of these schools. We will examine them presently.

[18] Hippolyte Taine, *Les Origines de la France contemporaine*, Vol. 2 (Paris: Hachette, 1894), p. 204.

the school, imposed on the candidates rigorous requirements for admission. In 1813, a circular declared that it was no longer permissible to become a teacher without passing through one of the écoles normales that were created for this purpose.[19]

But there is only one Ecole Normale Supérieure, and to get into it, one must follow a long and arduous road that culminates in the grueling *concours*. "One is a *normalien*," wrote the normalien Georges Pompidou, "as one is a prince by blood."[20] One does not become a normalien, said Pompidou, one is born a normalien. By this he meant that nothing but extraordinary intelligence earned one a place at the school. The same, of course, may be said of a number of other grandes écoles. The Ecole Normale, however, differs from other grandes écoles in one important respect: it is not a professional or vocational school in a narrow sense. The two cultures—science and humanities—coexist within the school, and although scientific research of a high order is carried out in the laboratories of the school, Normale is known for the politicians, philosophers, and men of letters that it has produced over the years.

Normale has always provoked ambivalent feelings in the powers that be. Its accomplishments are undisputed and it is recognized as the queen of the academic system. What has often (as in May 1968) troubled the men in power is that most normaliens possess an abundance of (as one normalien politician put it) *esprit critique*, which has usually placed the school in opposition to all non-Left governments. According to Raymond Aron, Leftism has always characterized the school, though the nature of Leftist thought and action has varied. In the 1920s, the Leftists were generally socialists and pacificists; in the 1930s and 1940s they were Marxist-Leninists and Stalinists; today they are Maoists and Trotskyists, profoundly influenced by Louis Althusser, the famous "structuralist" interpreter of Marx who is a teacher at the school.[21] But although Normale is firmly associated with the Left, one must not forget that it has also produced illustrious men of the Right.

---

[19] See Mortimer d'Ocagne, *Les Grandes écoles de France* (Paris: J. Hetzel & Cⁱᵉ, 1887), pp. 350-351; Antoine Prost, *L'Enseignement en France, 1800-1967* (Paris: Armand Colin, 1968), p. 72; and Delfau, *Napoleon Iᵉʳ et l'instruction publique*, p. 58.

[20] Georges Pompidou in Alain Peyrefitte, ed., *La Rue d'Ulm: chroniques de la vie normalienne*, 2nd ed. (Flammarion, 1964), p. 9.

[21] Raymond Aron, cited in *L'Express*, May 31, 1971.

There is no doubt that Normale is now going through a major crisis. The school's traditional *raison d'être*—the training of lycée professors—is more and more being questioned. Gone, it seems, are the days when graduates of the caliber of a Bergson or a Sartre were content to spend many years as lycée professors. Normaliens no longer want to become secondary school teachers; they would rather be university professors. Admittedly, they have a distinct advantage even here over the non-normaliens, but they are not *guaranteed* a good post. The waiting line for university posts now stretches longer than it ever did, and a normalien often has to bide his time in a job (whether in research or in a lycée) that he longs to leave.

The present crisis at Normale has not diminished its intellectual prestige. It is still much easier to become a university professor or to get a research job when one is a normalien. But the school no longer produces as many major political figures as it once did, and those that it does produce have usually gone directly into the Ecole Nationale d'Administration upon graduation from Normale. It no longer seems questionable that with respect to the training of France's governing elites, Normale has now ceded its place to the Ecole Polytechnique and ENA.

Just as "The original Ecole Normale . . . was conceived to satisfy an immediate need—the training of a corps of republican teachers who would instruct other teachers in the departments"[22]— so other grandes écoles were created to meet specific needs. The oldest of the grandes écoles, the Ecole Nationale des Ponts et Chaussées, was founded in 1747. The engineers trained in this school have since had a monopoly on the construction of roads, canals, and railways.[23] In effect, as is the case for the Ecole des Mines de Paris, the Ecole Nationale des Ponts et Chaussées is among the most restrictive of the grandes écoles, for its student body is largely composed of those who graduate near the top of their class at the Ecole Polytechnique. Both the Ecole des Mines and the Ponts et Chaussées are what are known as "schools of application," that is, the application of concrete knowledge to specific activities, and both, according to Artz, "take rank as the

[22] Robert J. Smith, "*Normalien* of the Rue d'Ulm: An Elite of the Third Republic," unpublished manuscript, p. 7.

[23] See Jean-Claude Thoenig, *L'Ere des technocrates: le cas des ponts et chaussées* (Paris: Les Editions d'Organisations, 1973).

first well-organized schools of civil engineering in the modern world."[24]

Under the ancien régime, there were two kinds of engineers, military and civil; the first were trained at the Ecole de Mézières, a small institution reserved for nobles, while the second were trained at the Ecole des Ponts in Paris, a larger and less restricted school in terms of its composition, but existing largely to train its own future teachers. In 1793 an evident lack of engineers posed a danger for national defense. The Committee of Public Works, run by Carnot, Robert Lindet, and Prieur de la Côte-d'Or, was impatient with the Committee on Public Instruction. It created forthwith a school to train engineers, the school that was to become the Ecole Polytechnique,[25] and whose launching constituted, according to Artz, "The greatest achievement in the field of technical instruction, and in some ways the most significant advance in the whole history of higher technical education in Europe."[26] Aside from its contributions to scientific developments, the school was created to fulfill a specific need in a moment of crisis, and the men who created it did so "with as much rapidity and precision as they organized an army and formulated a battle plan. They created it to fulfill a specifically determined need, without for a moment being concerned about a general plan of higher education which, in any case, did not exist except as a series of controversial projects."[27] A decree of 1804 turned the Ecole Polytechnique into a school for the training of military officers,[28] and ever since it has remained under the direction of the Ministry of Defense.

The Ecole Polytechnique was thus charged with a mission: the training of military officers. The Napoleonic armies were to need well-trained officers capable of leading as well as training others. That the school itself was actually imbued with the Napoleonic

[24] Frederick B. Artz, *The Development of Technical Education in France, 1500-1850* (Cambridge, Mass.: The M.I.T. Press, 1966), p. 110.

[25] On September 1, 1795 (15 fructidor An III), the Convention changed the name of the Ecole Centrale des Travaux Publics to the Ecole Polytechnique. This school was then placed under the authority of the Minister of Interior. See D'Ocagne, *Les Grandes écoles en France*, pp. 107-108.

[26] Artz, *The Development of Technical Education in France*, p. 151.
Armand Colin, 1894), p. 260.

[27] Louis Liard, *L'Enseignement supérieur en France*, Vol. II (Paris:

[28] See G. Pinet, *Histoire de l'Ecole Polytechnique* (Paris: Librarie Polytechnique Baudry, 1887), p. 50.

mission can be seen from the extent to which those who gained entry into the Ecole Polytechnique identified with Napoleon's ambitions. Here is an extract from a letter that the students at the school sent to Napoleon in 1803:

> The students of the Ecole Polytechnique ardently transmit to you their burning desire to participate in a prompt military expedition against England. Their talents and their arms are as of this moment at the service of the Nation. They all envy the fate of the brave soldiers who will be the first to see the coast. But if such good fortune cannot be the lot of everyone, history will say one day: *under the Consulat of Bonaparte, the students of the Ecole Polytechnique were always devoted to the national cause.*[29]

In addition to fulfilling a specific utilitarian function, the Ecole Polytechnique and the other grandes écoles also had a political mission. In the case of Napoleon, it was allegiance to a specific person and a specific regime; in the case of the other regimes, it was an allegiance to the state. The state had to *rely*, in precisely the way that a battle commander has to rely on his troops, on a cadre that was at once expert and loyal. Napoleon was not always certain of the loyalty of the Ecole Polytechnique. On two occasions, in 1801 and 1808, he expressed a desire to close the school permanently because he was "never completely convinced that the Polytechnicians were politically reliable. In spite of his many precautions to insure the recruitment of students sympathetic to his regime, he continued to fear that the EP was a haven for radical Jacobins intending someday to challenge his authority."[30] Nevertheless, the purpose of the grandes écoles was to bring to them young people who were, as Napoleon and others had said, destined to form the nation's elite and to occupy the top posts in the state. This aim gained strength with subsequent regimes, and, as we shall see, is no less ingrained today than it was during the whole course of the nineteenth century. That Napoleon's innovations, insofar as the grandes écoles were concerned, were to endure be-

[29] Cited in *ibid.*, p. 38. Italics in original.

[30] Terry Shinn, "The Dawning of an Elite: The Ecole Polytechnique and the Polytechnician Circles" (unpublished manuscript, 1973), p. 52. A French version of this study will be published in 1978 by the Presse de la Fondation Nationale des Sciences Politiques.

cause of their appeal to subsequent regimes was made very clear in an official report released by a commission set up under the Restoration:

> We live in a time when only the education of the higher classes can insure the tranquility of the state, by allowing their members to acquire, through their personal superiority in virtue and intelligence, the influence that they must exercise on others for the peace of all. A happy necessity, if one envisages it with a lofty soul, which leads to the justification of rank by merit and of wealth by talent and virtue. As concerns the sciences and all kinds of positive knowledge, the Ecole Polytechnique will provide this generous ambition with all the means necessary for its realization.[31]

A century later, when Michel Debré created the Ecole Nationale d'Administration, he noted in a similar vein: "The training—one need not hide this—also has a moral objective. It is not one of the missions of the school [ENA] to play politics or to impose a particular doctrine. But the School must also teach its future civil servants 'le sens de l'Etat,' it must make them understand the responsibilities of the Administration, make them taste the grandeur and accept the servitudes of the *métier*."[32] The Ecole Nationale d'Administration, created a century and a half after the founding of the most prestigious grandes écoles, was itself modeled on the existing scientific grandes écoles. In fact, the founders of this school took as their specific model the Ecole Polytechnique.[33] The creation of the ENA in 1945 merely represented the culmination of a century of efforts to create a civil service school based on the Ecole Polytechnique model.[34] When, for example, a short-lived Ecole Nationale d'Administration was born in 1848, the decree that brought about its existence stated that "a school destined to recruit for the various branches of the administration, which have heretofore been deprived of preparatory schools, ought to be

[31] Cited in Pinet, *Histoire de l'Ecole Polytechnique*, pp. 426-427.

[32] Michel Debré, *Réforme de la fonction publique* (Paris: Imprimerie Nationale, 1946), pp. 24-25.

[33] *Rapport de la commission d'étude des problèmes de l'Ecole Nationale d'Administration* (Paris: La Documentation Française, 1968), p. 14.

[34] See Vincent Wright, "L'Ecole Nationale d'Administration de 1848-1849: un échec révélateur," *Revue historique* (January-March 1976), pp. 21-42.

established along lines analogous to those of the Ecole Polytechnique."[35]

The model of the Ecole Polytechnique has had a profound impact on the development and structure of higher education in France. All the specialized schools created in its image were intended to fulfill analogous aims. First, they were responsible for creating an elite. Nor was there any reticence about expressing this goal, as Philippe Ariès tells us about the use of the term and its link to the grandes écoles:

> . . . the grandes écoles, where one entered by competitive examination, which became more and more difficult, established within the powerful but fluid divisions of birth and of fortune, a new social category, defined at once by its small size and by its merit. It carried a name, the "elite." The word is of the time. In an older language the word certainly existed, but it was always used as part of a phrase: the elite of the regiment, the elite of the nobility. It became the elite of the nation or the country, and then simply the elite.[36]

The creation of an elite was, of course, not an end in itself, for the grandes écoles all sought an elite that was trained for a specific task, an elite that was "useful." Napoleon fully embraced this principle, which his predecessors had already begun to act upon. Indeed, as Artz observes, John Locke's *Some Thoughts Concerning Education*, which was published in 1693 and argued that the purpose of education should be to fit a person for a practical trade or profession, was the "greatest influence in the educational theorizing of eighteenth-century France."[37] The practical nature of the training that the grandes écoles dispense has always been their *raison d'être* and, as we shall see, it has marked them off from the universities.

The third important function of the grandes écoles was their contribution to political stability and order. So important has this function been that the creation of the grandes écoles may, to some extent, be regarded as a response to the political instability that has characterized French politics since the Revolution. And if this was an element in their creation, it has certainly been an element in

[35] *Ibid.*, p. 23.

[36] Philippe Ariès, "Problèmes de l'éducation," in *La France et les français* (Paris: Bibliothèque de la Pléiade, Gallimard, 1972), pp. 934-935.

[37] Artz, *The Development of Technical Education in France*, p. 62.

their preservation.[38] That the Popular Front government itself gave birth to an Ecole Nationale d'Administration[39] testifies to the political importance of the grandes écoles for those in power, whether of the Left or of the Right.

THE FACULTIES AND THE GRANDES ECOLES

We observed earlier that, centralized as the French educational system is, it nonetheless has important differentiating characteristics. The grandes écoles, few of which come under the tutelage of the Ministry of Education,[40] are one aspect of this differentiation. Indeed, throughout the nineteenth century the universities tended to be considered as only an adjunct of the structure of higher education in France. A group of scholars that met at the Collège de France in 1870 to examine the condition of the universities concluded that "there is no higher education in France."[41] After 1789, the universities that had existed prior to the Revolution were abolished and specialized schools began to be set up. The Faculties were no longer parts of universities, for each Faculty became wholly independent of the other and each had the right to grant degrees. They were poorly housed, had practically nonexistent budgets, and usually had four to six professors whose task it was to cover all subjects.[42]

Throughout the nineteenth century there was a great deal of dissatisfaction voiced about this state of affairs. But, as Zeldin and others have shown, there was not much interest in the question of higher education before 1940 because secondary education continued to be regarded as the most important aspect of the educational system.[43] It was only in 1896, following the tireless work of Liard, that the provincial universities were established. But the Faculties maintained, to a very large extent, their independence within the new university structure.[44] "The war of 1914 postponed

[38] This is discussed in greater detail in Chapter Three.

[39] The outbreak of the war prevented this school from beginning to function.

[40] Now the Ministry of Universities.

[41] Theodore Zeldin, "Higher Education in France, 1845-1945," *Journal of Contemporary History*, Vol. I, No. 3 (July 1967), p. 57.

[42] *Ibid.*

[43] *Ibid.*, p. 56.

[44] One of the aims of the Loi d'Orientation of 1968 was to break down the barriers between the Faculties in the universities.

reform for a generation. . . . On the one hand the country's economic problems made retrenchment a principal objective of suc-
cessive governments. The universities were quickly picked on as
particularly wasteful institutions, over-grown, overlapping, capable
of being pruned without harm; indeed a definite hostility to them
developed. On the other hand, reformers declared that the universities were based on outdated principles."[45] Throughout the
interwar period, the emphasis continued to be placed on primary
and secondary education. The innovations of the Third Republic
in the realm of education lay in the extension of free primary and
secondary education. Even Jean Zay, generally considered "the
most active reforming education minister of the century (1936-
39),"[46] showed little concern with the universities, partly because,
according to Zeldin, "from the social point of view which concerned him most, the universities would never be made democratic
until the *lycées*, which supply them with pupils, lost their class
character."[47] Zay, as the Popular Front's Minister of Education,
was largely preoccupied, from the moment he entered the ministry
in May 1936, in establishing an Ecole Nationale d'Administration.[48] This may seem anomalous, but it is entirely in keeping with
the approach that those in power have taken to the problem of
higher education in France. The point is that higher education was
of concern to Zay and to the Popular Front government in general,
but, following the paths previously traced by their numerous predecessors, neither regarded the universities as central to it: secondary
education and the grandes écoles were the pivots of the entire
educational system. This remained the case until after the war. The
Napoleonic influence remained very strong throughout this period:
the lycées provided the *culture générale*, and the grandes écoles
provided the specialized knowledge—with the result that the universities were not considered central to the educational system. As
Zeldin observes:

> The revival of the universities took place long after an
> active cultural life had already been established in France and

[45] Zeldin, "Higher Education in France," p. 61.

[46] *Ibid.*, p. 63.　　　　　　　　[47] *Ibid.*

[48] See Marcel Ruby, *La Vie et l'oeuvre de Jean Zay* (Paris: M. Ruby,
1969), pp. 224-230. See also Pierre Rain, *L'Ecole Libre des Sciences Politiques, 1871-1945* (Paris: Fondation Nationale des Sciences Politiques,
1963), p. 95, and André Ferrat, *La République à refaire* (Paris: Gallimard,
1965), p. 244.

had found ground in which to grow. The intellectual elite, men of letters, the world of the salons, continued more or less independent of the universities. The progress of knowledge took place largely outside them too. The most specialized forms of education were entrusted to *grandes écoles*, which became major institutions of higher learning outside the university.[49]

Despite the undisputed preeminence throughout the nineteenth century of the grandes écoles, it would be wrong to suppose that few efforts were made to rescue the university from its position as the stepchild of the educational system. The first half of the Third Republic was a period in which various attempts were made to strengthen the university system. As Shinn notes, "During the first and second decades of the Republic the earlier murmurings for change in the *facultés* grew into a massive and articulate demand. Implicit within that demand and subsequent reform efforts was a challenge to the earlier undisputed hegemony of the *grandes écoles*."[50] Indeed the period between 1880 and 1914 was one of intense rivalry between the universities and the grandes écoles. This was a period not unlike that which followed World War II, one in which many reform-minded people expressed disillusionment with the institutions of the previous period and suggested a fresh start. Liard argued unceasingly that the time had come, both socially and politically, to build up the Faculties because the grandes écoles could no longer meet the nation's needs. Other reformers were to argue at the same time that the grandes écoles were anachronistic institutions and that the nation's hopes lay in reviving the universities. The governments of the last two decades of the nineteenth century shared the views of those urging reform and acted to strengthen the universities by substantially augmenting their budgets. In 1890 the budgets of the Faculties were separated from the primary and secondary schools, and in 1896 Emile Combes separated the administration of the Faculties from that of primary and secondary education.[51] These were important measures, destined to upgrade the universities, and they reflected a genuine desire on the part of the reformers of the early part of

[49] Zeldin, "Higher Education in France," p. 69.

[50] Shinn, "The Dawning of an Elite," p. 365. I am very much indebted to this study for what follows on the relationship between the universities and the grandes écoles under the Third Republic.

[51] *Ibid.*, pp. 368-369.

the Third Republic to achieve greater equality in higher education and a more efficient educational system.

In retrospect, we see that such measures also represented a missed opportunity because they were not extended after 1900. This was to a large extent due to the opposition of the grandes écoles. The opposition did not develop immediately after the establishment of the Third Republic, and there is sound evidence to show that the grandes écoles did not consider the development of the universities as a threat during the early part of the Third Republic.[52] This may have been due in part to the timidity of the reform and in part to the feelings of security, superiority, and indispensability with which the grandes écoles were endowed. Following the early reforms of the Third Republic, however, it became clear that if the universities were to become the key institutions of higher learning in France, a challenge to the fortress of the grandes écoles was inevitable.

Starting in the mid-1890s, a massive campaign was undertaken by the universities against the grandes écoles and particularly against the Ecole Polytechnique, which after 1900 organized itself and its graduates to defend itself against its enemies.[53] The grandes écoles were criticized for providing an uninspiring curriculum, for being undemocratic, and for leading to privileged careers. Those who argued for a reform of higher education maintained that, in Shinn's words, "so long as the *Grandes Ecoles* continued to function in accord with the principles of conservative pedagogy and in behalf of the *haute bourgeoisie* there would be an irreparable cleavage in the nation which could only be bridged when the *Grandes Ecoles* accepted the modern curriculum and utilitarian and democratic axes of the *facultés*."[54]

The main target of these criticisms was the Ecole Polytechnique, which trained the scientific and engineering elite. The easy access enjoyed by the graduates of the Ecole Polytechnique to positions in the state administration and in industry placed the scientists trained at the Faculté des Sciences at a serious disadvantage in the search for employment. Those seeking to change the system of higher education continually argued for the reform of this system, which often left the scientists trained in the Faculté des Sciences unemployed. One need only examine the present situation of higher education to see how little was done in the past to rectify this state of affairs, for, sometimes word for word, the same themes reappear today.

[52] *Ibid.*, pp. 370-371.   [53] *Ibid.*, p. 373.   [54] *Ibid.*, p. 380.

That the vehemence of the debate concerning the universities and the grandes écoles continued to grow was due to the profound influence which the grandes écoles exercised on the structure of secondary education. These schools recruited by special examinations (concours) which necessitated specialized preparation in the lycées. In setting the standards for their own entrance requirements, they exercised a remarkable influence on the curricula of the lycées. To shelter the lycées from what many considered the nefarious influence of the grandes écoles, it was necessary to oblige the grandes écoles to accept the secondary system as a given and to tailor their own admissions requirements to this system rather than vice versa.

The story of the Ecole Polytechnique's intransigence, and often its flagrant refusal to comply with government regulations and with the law in regard to the kind of *baccalauréat* that should be accepted as sufficient for admission to the school, is one of the remarkable examples of the power of an institution to defy the constituted authorities.[55] The state required all baccalauréats (the *baccalauréat ès lettres-philosophie*, the *baccalauréat ès sciences*, and the new *baccalauréat ès lettres-rhétorique*) to be treated equally. The Ecole Polytechnique refused to grant the same number of points to those holding the baccalauréat ès lettres-rhétorique because it wished to discourage those holding it from gaining admission. The Superior Council of Public Instruction appealed on several occasions to the Ecole Polytechnique, and on more than one occasion its appeals were simply ignored by the school. In a letter addressed to the head of the school, the Minister of War wrote in 1881 that the Ecole Polytechnique's "past and present refusal to cooperate with the Minister of Public Instruction and the Superior Council of Public Instruction clearly represents the political and social hostility of the school's policymakers to government efforts to permit new groups to enter the *Ecole Polytechnique* and the Schools of Application."[56] The struggle between the governments and the Ecole Polytechnique continued unabated, and in 1910 the national debate focusing on this particular issue obliged the government to act. The Minister of Public Instruction, Gaston Doumergue, wrote to the Director of Studies of the Ecole Polytechnique, claiming "that the position of the Superior Council [of the Ecole Polytechnique] was openly in opposition to the spirit of

---

[55] This entire episode is excellently retraced in Shinn's study, *ibid.*, pp. 305-361.

[56] Cited in *ibid.*, p. 311.

the 1902 Educational Reform Act and also clearly thwarted the will of the Ministry of Public Instruction. He said that the Minister of War agreed that the Superior Council must immediately change its policy. The Ecole Polytechnique must work more harmoniously with the nation's other institutions of instruction."[57] Doumergue's letter went unanswered, and eight months later the Minister of War simply decreed that all cycles of the baccalauréats were to be given equal points. And even then the Ecole Polytechnique did not fully comply.

The public debate over the various baccalauréats and the various cycles was long and complicated. The Republican governments' attempts to implement reforms aimed at improving the quality of secondary and higher education and to democratize the educational system met with only mild success. This also testified to the Ecole Polytechnique's ability to thwart the governments' will, although it may well be argued that the governments did not impose their will with sufficient force. The outbreak of World War I put an end to the entire debate and to the struggle, the results of which are well summarized by Shinn:

> The mood of France's Moderate and Modernist pedagogical reformers was one of gloom on the eve of World War I. Their two-and-a-half decade struggle to achieve sweeping changes in the nation's secondary schools had been successful only in part. Indeed, the reform of 1902 embraced the majority of their aspirations, yet the substance of these reforms had not resulted in the desired impact of the system of *lycée* instruction. The pedagogical Conservatives, although unable to thwart the will of their opponents in the National Assembly, had arranged to block *de facto* implementation of the reforms through the preservation of the EP as a school which only marginally recognized the letter and spirit of the 1902 innovation.[58]

NEED FOR SPECIALIZED SCHOOLS

It is not entirely correct to suggest that the universities were of little concern to the state. The Third Republic certainly made efforts to upgrade them, but at no point, save perhaps on the eve of the outbreak of the First World War, did any government

---

[57] *Ibid.*, pp. 354-355.   [58] *Ibid.*, pp. 358-359.

threaten to integrate the grandes écoles within the universities so that only one system of higher education would exist. The suggestion had been made on many occasions that, at the very least, the grandes écoles should come under the control of the Ministry of Public Instruction. But the Third Republic made no serious attempts in that direction. Undoubtedly, this was due to the fact that no government was strong enough to undertake such a measure. Also, the grandes écoles were, if not allies of the government, certainly neutral in the church-state education struggle that preoccupied the governments of the Third Republic during the last two decades of the century. But there was a more fundamental reason that made governments move cautiously when confronted by the problem of the grandes écoles. This was a belief that despite their faults, the grandes écoles performed critical tasks for the society which the universities did not. Until the universities took their rightful place in the society, the grandes écoles would be needed. All societies needed capable people—elites—and the universities did not produce such people. Hence one could not abolish the institutions that produced them.[59] The creation of the Ecole Libre des Sciences Politiques shows how men opposed on principle to the creation of grandes écoles and favoring the development of the universities came themselves to create a grande école.

The Ecole Libre was created in the aftermath of the Franco-Prussian War and was a manifestation of a profound dissatisfaction with the universities. Like other grandes écoles, it aimed at training an elite, a leadership elite that would possess a *culture générale* and that would be trained in subjects with which the university did not bother—economics, diplomatic history, politics. Renan, who played a large part in the founding of the Ecole Libre, wrote, "One must be blind not to see the French ignorance behind the mad declaration of war which has led us to where we are. . . . We must create the elite which, little by little, will set the tone for the entire nation. Make a new head for the nation—everything leads to this conclusion. . . . France lacks a system of *haute culture* or, if you like, of liberal debate. It must be given one."[60] The task

[59] Despite its evident circularity, for the universities could not develop to a point where they would provide the nation's leaders so long as the grandes écoles attracted the most capable students, this has remained a powerful argument for preserving the grandes écoles. This is discussed in Chapter Three.

[60] Cited in Rain, *L'Ecole Libre des Sciences Politiques*, p. 9.

of creating such a school fell to Emile Boutmy, who, even after he had created the Ecole Libre, could criticize the existence of the grandes écoles, thus implying that eventually, when the universities were reformed, they would be able to absorb the grandes écoles. The possibility that the universities could not take their rightful place in the system of higher education *before* they absorbed the grandes écoles did occur to men like Boutmy. "The closed schools, the Ecole Polytechnique, the Ecole Normale," wrote Boutmy, "will find themselves committed to opening their doors, to let in students from outside and their professors will have occasion to mix with others. In fact, we will never organize a university worthy of the name if these great institutions do not form a part of it; but before annexing them, there is a necessary preparation: the charm which keeps them closed must be broken and they must be accustomed, little by little, to secular life."[61]

The argument that Boutmy and others were making throughout the nineteenth century was that the university could not become the pivot of French higher education unless it attracted the best students, who presently were going to the grandes écoles. So long as preparation for the entrance examination to the grandes écoles was conducted in the preparatory courses in the lycées, the impact of the former reverberated throughout and set the standards for the entire educational system. Nor should it be forgotten that the grandes écoles and the lycées were originally regarded as twins.[62] The top forms of the lycée, notes Zeldin, "the *classes de philo- sophie*, and *mathématiques spéciales*, and the preparatory classes for candidates for the *grandes écoles* . . . worked to a level which could rival that of the *licence*. Some of the teachers in these higher forms, like Alain and Bellesort, provided what was virtually higher education in the *lycée*. . . ."[63] Indeed, the elite lycées in France continue to provide most of the entrants to the grandes écoles.

It was not with the standards set by the grandes écoles that men like Boutmy quarreled; rather, they wanted the universities to exhibit similar standards of excellence. But, as the creation of the Ecole Libre suggests, men like Taine, Boutmy, and Renan believed that the university in France was incapable of providing the nation

[61] Emile Boutmy, *Quelques observations sur la réforme de l'enseignement supérieur* (Paris: Librarie de Germer Baillière, 1876), p. 24.

[62] It was not until 1847, for example, that the Ecole Normale moved into the buildings in the rue d'Ulm, where it still is today. Until then, it had been an appendage of the lycée Louis-le-Grand. See Zeldin, "Higher Education in France," p. 71.

[63] *Ibid.*, p. 69.

with what it needed; they argued that the university had succeeded in carving a niche for itself outside, or at least on the sidelines, of society. But, as we noted earlier, the politicians of the Third Republic did not show much inclination to reform the universities in a drastic way. By their passivity and lack of foresight, they encouraged the universities to remain outside the mainstream of higher education. The reforms they introduced were "tackled in a very piecemeal manner, so that they [the universities] never became the true apex of the educational system."[64]

The need for universities and the importance of having the universities absorb the grandes écoles was a prevalent point of view throughout the nineteenth century. It was a view shared often by those who themselves attacked the universities and who thought it essential to create a specialized school for a particular national activity. Renan, who was one of the earlier champions and creators of the Ecole Libre, was categorical when it came to the question of the role of the grandes écoles in the system of higher education. He believed that they must eventually give way to the universities, and it is worth quoting the argument he set forth in his *La Réforme intellectuelle et morale*:

> There must be created in France five or six universities, independent of one another, independent of the towns where they are located, independent of the clergy. At the same time, we must abolish the specialized schools, the Ecole Polytechnique, the Ecole Normale, etc., which are useless institutions when a good university system exists and which prevent universities from developing. These schools, in effect, do no more than rob the universities of their best students. . . . We complain that the Faculties of Letters, of Sciences, do not have brilliant students. Why is this surprising? Their natural students are at the Ecole Normale, at the Ecole Polytechnique, where they receive the same education, but without participating in any of the beneficial movement or in the community of minds created by the university.[65]

If men like Boutmy and Renan, who themselves had been responsible for creating a grande école,[66] were critical of the grandes

[64] *Ibid.*, pp. 68-69.

[65] Ernest Renan, *La Réforme intellectuelle et morale* (Paris: Michel Lévy, 1871), pp. 101-102.

[66] The Ecole Libre was created with private funds and remained, until its nationalization and incorporation into the University of Paris in 1945, a

écoles and of the role they played in French higher education, why were their efforts not directed toward the universities? Why did they seek to create another select institution outside the university? The answer tells us a good deal about the rationale that underlay the creation of the grandes écoles. The element of expediency always played an important role. If Boutmy, Renan, and Taine, who wished to see the grandes écoles abolished so that the university would become the center of higher education, created a grande école, it was because they believed that such a school was needed there and then. Just as Napoleon had found it more expedient to maintain the specialized schools created by the ancien régime and the Convention and refashion them rather than build wholly new ones, so it was more feasible in the aftermath of the French defeat at the hands of the Prussians to create a new institution in an old mold than to radically transform the Faculty of Law. That there was a contradiction in the position—and certainly in the actions—of men like Boutmy, Taine, and Renan is clear, for by creating the Ecole Libre, they made the transformation of the Faculty of Law a virtual impossibility. Had not these men expressly recognized that the creation of grandes écoles made the flowering of the universities impossible? Perhaps this was a long-range problem, for what mattered above all in 1871 was that France needed to begin training an elite dedicated to state service, an elite trained in diplomacy, history, economics and capable of applying their knowledge to the problems, domestic and external, that confronted the state. This task could not wait for radical changes to take place within the university. Hence a new school was needed. Among the guiding principles of the school were practicality and utility, and to that end it was thought necessary that all the teachers should be professionals—diplomats, lawyers, businessmen, bankers—rather than academicians.

The moment the "indispensability" of the grandes écoles was avowed, for whatever reason, it was not difficult to justify, as the founders of Ecole Libre were to do, a preeminent position for the grandes écoles. It would appear, then, that the creation of the grandes écoles was always in response to a pressing need: the need for engineers, for military officers, for teachers, for diplomats, for civil servants. And because they were created to meet specific

---

private institution. It has remained, however, an institute separate from the university. Consequently, I have felt it justifiable to refer to it as a grande école.

needs, they could quickly become indispensable in their individual areas, which in turn would encourage their emulation in other areas. The university could not hope to attract the best students; nor could it attract greater funds, either from industry or from the state, as was the case with the grandes écoles. Most importantly, it could not have the political impact that the grandes écoles could always marshal so easily as a result of their organizations and the placement of their graduates in key positions.

There is another factor that should be stressed about the creation of the grandes écoles, one that points to their insertion into the practical world and that is also central to this study. This is the fact that, apart from the Ecole Polytechnique, the Ecole Normale, and the Ecole d'Arts et Métiers, all of the other grandes écoles were created at the time of the industrial revolution to fulfill the needs of emerging industries. Sometimes a specialized school was created by a group of industrialists and then later taken over by the municipalities, as was the case, for example, of the first Ecole de Chimie de France, founded in Mulhouse; at other times, schools were founded by the Chambers of Commerce.[67] In all cases, the grandes écoles became schools that were responsible for supplying the nation with the men who kept industry and the state machine functioning. Much as the neglect of the universities was regretted by some, they could not deny that the facultés were incapable of fulfilling this task, so that even those who seriously called for the abolition of the grandes écoles, men like Boutmy and Renan, ultimately came to see in them overriding advantages.

A vicious circle was thus set in motion, one that was hard to stop and that has continued to this day to plague the educational system. On the one hand, the independence and autonomy of the facultés, the narrow and often outdated knowledge they transmitted, and their incapacity for self-reform led to the creation of parallel institutions of higher learning that were in no way connected with the universities and that fulfilled distinct functions. On the other hand, the creation of these specialized institutions—the grandes écoles—relegated the universities to second-class status so that reform, whether from within or from without, came to be regarded as not a pressing matter. Once this process had been set in motion, in the early part of the nineteenth century, it seemed to gather momentum, with the ultimate result that the "reform" of

---

[67] Pierre Papon, "Le Problème des grandes écoles," *Esprit*, Special Number (May-June 1964), p. 1,050.

the universities, as this has been defined, has not precluded the creation of other specialized schools which were in no way connected with the universities.

It is important not to exaggerate the differences between the grandes écoles and the universities insofar as the type of education that each provided is concerned. The grandes écoles did not have a monopoly on training people for specific vocations. The Faculties of Law, Science, Medicine, and Pharmacology all trained their graduates for practical careers. Furthermore, the quality of the vocational training provided by the universities was no lower—and often was higher—than that provided by the grandes écoles. On the other hand, the highest diplomas granted by the universities— the *Agrégation* and the *Doctorat d'Etat*—opened the doors to a teaching career, so that there was a much greater academic bent to the training offered by the universities than there ever could be in that offered by the grandes écoles. It was, to a large extent, the size of the specialized schools that helped keep intact their vocational mission. The small size of each school meant that its training never had as its purpose "self-reproduction," which is what the universities have generally been accused of. Even those who maintained that the universities could in fact provide the same training that the grandes écoles dispensed were willing to recognize that the specialized schools did serve a purpose. However, Marc Bloch argued that this purpose—utility—should always be secondary.

> Let us simply say, in two words [he wrote], that we ask for the reconstitution of real universities, divided from now on not into rigid Faculties which see themselves as separate nations, but into flexible disciplinary groups; then, along with this great reform, the abolition of the specialized schools. In their place should be created a few institutes of technical application allowing for the final preparation for certain careers —after, however, an obligatory passage through the universities. In order to allow for the training of a particular category of engineers, the Ecole des Ponts et Chaussées for example, is indispensable. The general scientific preparation belongs to the university, and there is no reason to leave it to a school enclosed within impenetrable walls, like Polytechnique.[68]

[68] Marc Bloch, *L'Etrange défaite* (Paris: Albin Michel, 1957), pp. 255-256.

In describing an historical situation, we have also, to a very large extent, as will be seen in the following chapter, described the contemporary situation that prevails in French higher education. Alain Touraine, for example, rightly observes that the fundamental problems posed by the universities in France have never elicited much interest. "What is most striking in the recent history of the university system," he writes, "is that French society has no interest in the problems raised by its transformation. . . . Neither the government nor the opposition was ever able to express itself except in numbers. For the former, the growth was admirable; for the latter, insufficient. They spoke often of money and square feet, almost never of pedagogy or employment, much less of the role of the university system or of the general culture needed in our society."[69] Touraine is, of course, correct in emphasizing the preoccupation that political leaders have had with the problem of "numbers," for in a society that for so long restricted higher education to a small percentage of the population, the expansion of the university system became important in its own right. It was only later that the increase in numbers was seen to pose more problems than it actually solved.[70]

The reason for this is that policies concerning the universities have always been seen as being, at least in part, a function of existing policies concerning the grandes écoles. There has not been a general policy that has encompassed the entire higher educational system. Two different sets of policies have been applied. They have, as we will see, often been incompatible, but they have often served specific goals. Consequently, the proposals that call for an increased importance of the universities without making allusion to the grandes écoles miss one of the chief reasons for the present state of the French universities.[71] It is simply not possible

[69] Alain Touraine, *The May Movement: Revolt and Reform* (New York: Random House, 1971), p. 110.

[70] See the arguments developed in Raymond Boudon, "The French University Since 1968," *Comparative Politics*, Vol. 10, No. 1 (October 1977), pp. 89-120.

[71] An important O.E.C.D. report, prepared by Stanley Hoffmann, Wassily Leontief, and Henry Tajfel, makes a number of serious proposals for upgrading research in the French universities. The authors firmly believe that "a policy which did not make them the effective centers of research would be doomed to failure." They also believe that it is possible for the universities to be upgraded independently of what happens to the grandes écoles. See Committee for Scientific and Technological Policy, *Social Science Pol-*

to discuss higher education in France without taking into account the dual nature of the system, which we will explore in the following chapter.

We shall have to deal more explicitly with the question of why the grandes écoles have exhibited such staying power. It need only be noted here that this has been a remarkable feat, for while the grandes écoles have had as their primary task the training of engineers, teachers, technicians, and civil servants to serve the state, they have also supplied the private sector with technicians, industrialists, and executives. Because of their utilitarian and practical bent, these schools have always been linked in some way to the private sector. Indeed, when certain of the state functions for which a grande école may have been created lost their importance or became outdated, the school often began to train its students for the private sector, claiming that serving the state implied not merely the state apparatus, but rather serving in any endeavor that contributed to the nation as a whole. In this way, the schools—and we shall see that this was particularly the case with regard to the Ecole Polytechnique—were able to readapt to changing conditions, preserve their legitimacy and their *raison d'être*. This was no mean accomplishment, considering that the bases for their "indispensability" had all but disappeared.

---

icy: France (Paris: O.E.C.D., 1975), pp. 265-266 and pp. 277-278. This report underscores the very serious division in France between teaching and research. For more details on this, see the excellent discussion in Robert Gilpin, *France in the Age of the Scientific State* (Princeton: Princeton University Press, 1968), pp. 85-123.

❧ *Chapter Three* ❧

THE SANCTITY OF THE GRANDES ECOLES

THE parallel system of higher education that exists in France is as entrenched today as it was in the past. The system has innumerable detractors, but even among these, few would tamper with a system that is only half bad, or, depending on how one views the matter, half excellent. As had rarely happened in the past, the events of May 1968 brought the problem of higher education into the realm of public debate in which most people could participate. This was not the case with the debate that preceded World War I, which was confined for the most part to the intellectual journals and magazines and, despite its political content, often contained long discussions of a technical nature. In 1968, things were altogether different because the debate was initiated by a crisis and because the number of those directly affected by the educational system had grown to proportions unimagined by the participants of the Third Republic debate.

The events of May 1968 were therefore important in focusing attention on problems in the educational system that had since World War II been obscured by the rapid expansion of the university system, but that had never been solved. A deluge of criticism was heaped on the entire educational system, and one of the most widely proposed (or demanded) solutions included not only the reform of the universities, but also the abolition of the grandes écoles or their integration into the universities. There could be no equality either in education or in the society, it was argued, so long as the double system of higher education continued to exist. Given the persistence of this problem in French history, it is hardly surprising that the criticisms directed at the grandes écoles in 1968 should have represented scarcely more than an echo of those that had been heard since the early years of the Third Republic. The grandes écoles were attacked for draining the universities of the most capable students, for being elitist and undemocratic, and for serving the bourgeois class that supported them.

Despite all the criticisms that have been made of the grandes écoles, during and after 1968, the idea of a truly serious reform has not been envisaged by any government in recent years. One must add that the events of 1968, while they served to reopen the whole question of the role of the grandes écoles and momentarily threatened these schools, in no way jeopardized their position. On the contrary, far from being weakened and threatened with extinction, the grandes écoles have, since 1968, reinforced their position in French society and augmented their importance in the system of higher education. This is certainly paradoxical, given the scope of the 1968 events and the fever with which reforms were being undertaken, or at least discussed. Moreover, the events of 1968 appeared to have indicated to those in power that unless structural reforms were undertaken in the educational system, the future consequences would turn out to be even more serious. Why, then, have the grandes écoles been able to reinforce their position to such an extent that it is probably more solid today than it was even prior to 1968? This seeming paradox can be explained by four factors: 1) the disenchantment with, or the fear of, the universities; 2) the importance of the grandes écoles in ensuring social and political stability; 3) the successful lobbying of the grandes écoles; and 4) the self-reforming capacities of these schools, which contrast markedly with the inertia and paralysis that have characterized the university. This chapter bears largely on the first three factors; the fourth will be taken up in Part Two.

THE UNIVERSITIES SINCE 1968

The Loi d'Orientation of 1968 entailed substantial changes for the French universities. The law came in the wake of the student outbreaks of May 1968 and it was a response to the centralization of the higher education system, to the compartmentalization of the disciplines within the universities, and to the hierarchical nature of institutional and personal relations. It granted a substantial degree of administrative and financial autonomy to the universities. With the abolition of the Faculties and their replacement by the UER's (Unités d'Enseignement et de Recherche), the universities were now encouraged to undertake interdisciplinary teaching and to combine teaching and research. They were also free to determine their own curricula and program needs.[1] Coupled with the

[1] Jacques Fomerand, "Policy Formulation and Change in Gaullist France: The 1968 Orientation Act of Higher Education," *Comparative Politics*, Vol.

reorganization of the French universities went the creation of new ones and the increasing access to higher education.

Despite all these changes in the structure, autonomy, and number of universities, it remains a matter of considerable debate whether the universities have undertaken the kind of transformation that would be required to redefine their relationship to the larger society.[2] In his analysis of the May 1968 outbreaks, Boudon noted the exclusive concentration of the universities on culture ("education") to the detriment of "training."[3] This is an important point and one that was, as we have seen, raised incessantly during the nineteenth century. It raises, in effect, the whole question of the relationship between institutions of higher learning and society.

The universities in France have not traditionally shunned the training of students for specific functions, but they have been seen as being far more concerned, to use Renan's terminology, with "education" than with "instruction." As a consequence, the university has not been preoccupied with training its students for employment; this became even more marked as the size of the universities increased. Thus, the failure or dropout rate has been extremely high, as can be seen from Table 3.1.

Closely related to the training of university students is the problem of employment, which is merely another side of the training coin. Writing of the pre-1968 period, Boudon observed that "It was even, up to a certain point, frowned upon to raise the problem of job openings."[4] He suggests that behind all the issues that provoked the May-June 1968 outbreaks—attacking the mandarinate, the absence of contact between students and professors, the examination system, the consumer society—there lay one problem that was central to the university outbreaks: the problem of employment. The I.F.O.P. survey undertaken in September 1968 bears out Boudon's point (Table 3.2). Consequently, the very concep-

---

8, No. 1 (October 1975), pp. 59-89. See also Fomerand, "The French University: What Happened After the Revolution?" *Higher Education*, No. 6 (1977), pp. 93-116.

[2] On this point see the discussion by Raymond Boudon of the consequences of the Loi d'Orientation: "The French University Since 1968," *Comparative Politics*, Vol. 10, No. 1 (October 1977), pp. 89-120.

[3] Raymond Boudon, "La Crise universitaire française: essai de diagnostic sociologique," *Annales*, Vol. 24, No. 3 (May-June 1969), p. 746.

[4] *Ibid.*, p. 745.

TABLE 3.1

Rate of Success after Three Years of *Licence* (Paris)

(percent)

Discipline	Received Diplomas	Noncompletion				Partial Success
		No Diploma After 3 Years	Dropped Out After 2 Years	Dropped Out After 1 Year	Total	
Letters (classical)	47	11	7	3	21	32
Philosophy	41	11	14	2	27	32
Geography	37	10	12	10	32	31
Spanish	33	8	14	11	33	34
Letters (modern)	29	10	18	14	42	29
Psychology	29	5	30	12	47	24
History	26	11	22	18	51	23
English	26	12	22	11	45	29
German	25	13	17	10	40	35
Sociology	17	15	26	18	59	24
TOTAL	30	11	19	11	41	39

Source: Boudon, "La Crise universitaire française," *Annales*, Vol. 24, No. 3 (May-June 1969), p. 742.

TABLE 3.2

Reasons for Student Anxiety[1]

(percent)

	1st Choice	2nd Choice	3rd Choice
Anxiety regarding the possibility of finding a post related to one's chosen field of study	56	33	8
Rejection of the consumer society	7	10	8
The inability of the university (in terms of curricula, teaching methods, material means) to adapt to current requirements	35	54	8

[1] The question posed to students in September 1968 by I.F.O.P. was the following: Here are three reasons that might explain the troubles of May and June with respect to the students. Please rank them in order of importance, putting first the one that played the most important role.

Source: Boudon, "La Crise universitaire française," p. 745.

tion of the traditional role of the university, whose task had merely been to confirm one's social rank, was now radically changed. As Boudon put it:

> The fundamental element of this analysis seems to me to reside in the passage from the ideal type of the "bourgeois" university to that of the "moyenne" university. In the former case . . . the university does no more than confirm the social rank of the family, and one's professional choice depends essentially on this rank. The "bourgeois" university is therefore part and parcel of a social system in which the mechanisms of career orientation are essentially taken care of by the family. In the latter case, the role of selection and of social differentiation assumed by the family tends to disappear. The result of this is that this function is more and more largely the province of the educational system and particularly of the university. The university assumes therefore a totally new role: in a society where social rank is more and more determined by one's profession, the university becomes—or tends to become—the essential mechanism of social mobility, upward as well as downward.[5]

[5] *Ibid.*, p. 763.

The analysis which Boudon gives of the causes of the university outbreaks also tells us, though indirectly, a great deal about the entire higher educational system of which the universities represent only a part. For if the universities have accepted a dropout rate that in some instances has exceeded 50 percent, and if they have been unconcerned about the eventual employment prospects of their graduates, this has served to single out the grandes écoles still further. The graduation and employment rate of grandes écoles students is over 95 percent.[6] This discrepancy between the universities and the grandes écoles not only indicates that each has seen its role vis-à-vis the society in wholly different terms, but that these self-perceptions have *political* consequences. The society takes the functions which both the universities and the grandes écoles perform as a given and proceeds to act accordingly.

Thus, there is little doubt that the elite holds the view, which is translated into policy, that the society needs to rely to an ever-greater extent on the institutions that conceive of their task as being linked to the specific needs of the society. In effect, the elites in both the private and the public sectors have come to regard the universities with what can only be characterized as contempt. Table 3.3 shows that these elites are strongly in favor of maintaining the grandes écoles. While some members of the elite believe that certain reforms are in order—mostly having to do with democratization—they very largely hold the opinion that the universities are neither equipped nor willing to train their students in accordance with society's needs. They maintain that "the universities are run

TABLE 3.3

Elite's View of Parallel System of Higher Education[1]

	Very Good		Quite Good		Quite Bad		Very Bad		Don't Know			
	%	No.	%	No.	%	No.	%	No.	%	No.	Total	N
Public sector	46.6	27	41.1	24	8.6	5	0.0	0	3.4	2	100.0	58
Private sector	42.9	24	39.3	2	10.7	6	3.6	2	3.6	2	100.0	56

[1] Question: France is one of the few countries where a parallel system of higher education (consisting of the universities and the grandes écoles) exists. All things considered, do you believe this to be a good or a bad thing?

[6] O.E.C.D., *Rapport sur la politique d'enseignement en France* (Paris: La Documentation Française, 1971), p. 28.

by and for professors, who only want to train other professors";
or "the universities teach only theory; they live in an abstract
world that has little to do with reality"; or, "if the universities were
to begin training their students for employment, then the grandes
écoles would lose their importance." Undoubtedly, there is something of an antiintellectual bias in the views of the elite, but this
would not be sufficient reason for dismissing their views outright.
Even Marc Bloch asked the question, "What is a Faculty of Letters, if not, above all, a factory for producing professors, much
as Polytechnique is a factory for producing engineering and artillery officers?"[7]

The view is widely held by the elite that the way out of the
present dilemma is for the universities to take a different view of
themselves and to begin seeing their role as that of fulfilling society's needs.[8] It is argued that the universities did not seize the rare
opportunity to diminish the importance of the grandes écoles that
was offered them by the 1968 reform. This opportunity was provided by the creation of the Instituts Universitaires de Technologie
(I.U.T.), whose aim has been to provide a vocational type of
training.[9] If the university is overcrowded, if it incurs the disdain
of the elite in power, if many of its students do not complete their
studies, and if those who obtain their diplomas are unable to find
employment, the conclusion is that the university has *chosen* to
cut itself off from the rest of society by refusing to reform itself.
Few would deny the elements of truth this view contains, and
countless have been those—*universitaires* and critics of the grandes
écoles—who have attacked the bureaucratization and rigidities of
the universities themselves. Now as in the past, the critics of the
grandes écoles have felt obliged to emphasize one fact: the efficacy
of these schools. At the end of the nineteenth century, Louis Liard,
whose service in behalf of the university has been unequaled, could
deplore the monopoly exercised by the grandes écoles and yet go
on to observe: "Would they not continue to attract and retain the
elite of the young, leaving to the future universities only the less
good, the rejects? Moreover, such were the services they had ren-

[7] Marc Bloch, *L'Etrange défaite* (Paris: Albin Michel, 1957), p. 254.

[8] For a balanced view of the university held by the elite, see the opinion
of François Bloch-Lainé, *Profession: fonctionnaire* (Paris: Editions du
Seuil, 1976), pp. 149-158.

[9] On the impact of this reform, see Boudon, "The French University
Since 1968," pp. 96-100.

dered that no one could think of abolishing them or reducing their role."[10] And Ludovic Zoretti, who maintained that "the specialized schools are one of the fortresses of the capitalist class,"[11] could also conclude, "Let us try to pose clearly the question of recruitment into the grandes écoles and into the institutes. No one thinks of strangling the Ecole Polytechnique. . . . The grandes écoles have their autonomy of which they are justly very jealous: we cannot impose anything on them. They will maintain the method of recruitment which they choose."[12]

The emphasis placed on the "efficacy" and "usefulness" of the grandes écoles entails, of course, a certain view of education, one that involves *service* rather than the posing of theoretical questions. In a society that has experienced serious ideological conflicts, the former type of education is one that is most likely to contribute to stability. The "contact with reality" is often seen as an end in itself, but it has an unmistakable political content. The grandes écoles ensure acceptance of the social order, belief in stability, and an abhorrence of agitation and *contestation*. As one former graduate of the Ecole Polytechnique noted in the alumni journal:

> But it is blindingly evident that France has more and more of an imperative need of an elite that does not allow itself to be contaminated by certain viruses and that is hungry to serve, to serve in a way which, in the final analysis, gives the only real and durable satisfactions. Thank God, I know a number of *camarades* who are inspired by this desire. X [Ecole Polytechnique] cannot continue to claim the right to train elites if it is not imbued with this notion of service. If the young prefer the independence of individualism, nothing obliges them to enter X; there are other schools where their temperament can freely find expression. We cannot reduce the problem of the School to the mere acquisition of a diploma or of an enviable title; *noblesse oblige*, a magnificent maxim which is all too often forgotten.[13]

[10] Louis Liard, *L'Enseignement supérieur en France*, Vol. II (Paris: Armand Colin, 1894), pp. 348-349.

[11] Ludovic Zoretti, *Education: un essai d'organisation démocratique* (Paris: Plon, 1918), p. 57.

[12] *Ibid.*, p. 275.

[13] René Perrin, "En marge de la réforme de l'enseignement: de l'utilité

This is not merely an isolated view, for a reading of the journals and magazines of the schools and of the elite organizations shows how prevalent is the idea that the grandes écoles represent the best guarantee for the preservation of the social order. This view became, as will be seen presently, critical in 1968, and it influenced in a crucial way the elaboration of the Loi d'Orientation. Writing after 1968 of the difference between the universities and the grandes écoles, the then president of the organization which groups the Corps des Ponts et Chaussées and the Corps des Mines (PCM),[14] noted that we have arrived at the "absurd" situation where those who lay claim to the advantages of society are the same ones who question the principles and functioning of this society. This was, according to him, mostly the case with the universities.

And if the grandes écoles also experienced the consequences of this absurdity, we cannot fail to note that the agitation had nothing in common, neither in force nor in length, with that which continues to trouble the university. This is without a doubt because the grandes écoles are institutions of higher learning which maintain in France concrete contact with the society. Their professors are professionals, in contact with reality. They function in conjunction with the administrative and economic sectors. Their students participate systematically in these sectors, by means of training programs. They can therefore judge for themselves the world in which they are going to work, and if they have to criticize it, at least they will do so based on real knowledge rather than on some preconceived ideas.[15]

Insofar, then, as the universities are seen as being singularly unconcerned with the needs of society and as continually questioning the structure of society, it follows that the grandes écoles are the

---

de la formation polytechnicienne," *Bulletin de l'association des anciens élèves de l'Ecole Polytechnique*, No. 68 (July 1957), p. 14.

[14] The members of this organization are almost all former graduates of the Ecole Polytechnique, and they are *all* graduates of either the Ecole Nationale des Ponts et Chaussées or the Ecole des Mines. Consequently, the organization maintains a link among its members regardless of the sector they work in.

[15] Discours du President, Assemblée Générale de l'Association Professionnelle des Ingénieurs des Ponts et Chaussées et des Mines, *Bulletin de PCM*, No. 66 (July 1969), p. 20.

beneficiaries of this state of affairs. They are able to preserve their autonomy, remain subject to little control, and obtain favored employment opportunities for their graduates.

THE QUESTION OF NUMBERS

The view that is taken today by both defenders and detractors of the grandes écoles is that one cannot tamper with institutions which, whatever their defects, fulfill certain crucial functions for the society, functions which no other institutions can fulfill. Consequently, it was still possible to write in 1963, as did the Director of Studies of the Ecole Polytechnique, in these unambiguous terms:

> The education of the grandes écoles is an education *de luxe* from which an elite must benefit. It is one of the rare cases where France has succeeded in escaping from the formula of equal treatment for all, which does not allow the best to develop. It must be preserved, but reserved for those who are worthy of it. Getting through an educational selection process should not be considered sufficient for meriting such an elite training. One must have moral qualities: desire for work, acceptance of a body or rules, and confidence in those who have the responsibility of applying them.[16]

Now, it is believed that one way to preserve the special character of these institutions is to distinguish them in size from the universities, among whose chief problems has been their unchecked growth (Figure 3.1). The response to the question of whether the number of entrants into the grandes écoles should be increased (as shown in Table 3.4) indicates that the general belief of the elite is that the size of these schools should not be increased; at most, the increase should be determined by society's needs. In other words, if the society needs more engineers, then the grandes écoles should take it upon themselves to train more engineers. But the view was also expressed that it is highly preferable to maintain the relatively small size of these schools. Although this may be a mere indication of snobbery and elitism, it also reflects a desire not to see these institutions turn into universities. The latter is the more logical explanation, as the government's policy has been to increase the

[16] R. Cheradame, "Les Méthodes d'enseignement dans les écoles scientifiques," *Cohesion* (November 1963), p. 29.

Figure 3.1   Number of Students Enrolled in Universities, 1934-1975

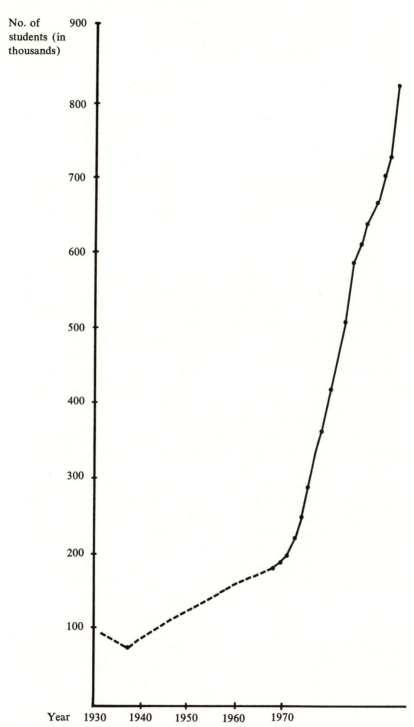

TABLE 3.4

Increasing the Size of Grandes Ecoles[1]

	Public Sector		Private Sector	
	%	*No.*	*%*	*No.*
It should be greatly increased	10.2	6	23.2	13
It should be increased moderately	30.5	18	16.1	9
It should not be increased	25.4	15	32.1	18
It depends on need	33.9	20	28.6	16
TOTAL	100.0	59	100.0	56

[1] Question: Do you think that the enrollment in the grandes école should be increased?

number of grandes écoles rather than the size of existing ones. Tables 3.5 and 3.6 show that the number of entrants to the engineering grandes écoles is very small. More importantly, this number has remained small. Indeed, the school that has the largest number of entrants, the Ecole Polytechnique, has not increased the size of its student body since the beginning of the Third Republic (Table 3.7). There have been many proposals to increase considerably the size of the Ecole Polytechnique's student body, but the size of each class has tended to remain at around 300 for the last century. Nor is this an isolated case: during the same period, the size of the Ecole Normale Supérieure, which increased slightly, has also remained very small in absolute terms (Table 3.8). Table 3.9 shows that the number of students admitted to the Ecole Nationale d'Administration has also remained relatively small.

That the grandes écoles have remained relatively small in size has a good deal to do with the fact that this is an important means for setting them apart from the universities, which are seen as large bureaucracies that cannot train students or shape them. Moreover, the individuals in these vast institutions, left to themselves and given no guidance, naturally develop "individualist" traits rather than those of duty and discipline. But the limited size of the grandes écoles is important not only for distinguishing these institutions from the "politically ridden" and alienated universities, but also for preserving them as elite institutions, which provide the recruits for the grands corps, the other elite institutions whose size remains extremely restricted, and about which we shall have more

TABLE 3.5

Number of Places Available for Entry
into the Grandes Ecoles[a]

Schools	Number of Places
1. Engineering schools in Paris[b]	
Ecole Centrale des Arts et Manufactures	275
Ecole Supérieure d'Electricité	120
Ecole Supérieure d'Optique	20
C.E.S.T.I.	40
Total (Paris)	455
2. Engineering schools in provinces	
E.N.S.I. (11 schools)	455
Ecole Centrale Lyonnaise	120
Total (provinces)	575
3. Other[c]	
Ecole Polytechnique	300
Ponts et Chaussées, Génie Maritime, Télécommunications, Supérieure Aéronautique	170
Mines (Paris, Saint-Etienne, Nancy)	190
Ecole du Service des Statistiques	50
E.N.I.C.A. Toulouse	35
I.D.N.	120
E.N.A.C.	20
Total	885
TOTAL	1,915

[a] Refers to engineering schools recruiting from the preparatory classes A.
[b] Schools falling under the jurisdiction of Ministry of Education.
[c] Schools falling under the jurisdiction of other ministries.

Source: Adapted from *La Jaune et la rouge*, No. 223 (February 1967), p. 31.

to say in subsequent chapters. The restriction in size is a matter of conscious policy on the part of the state. Writing of the Corps des Ponts et Chaussées, Thoenig notes:

The corps functions according to the conception of an elite based on rarity. The individual's competence and prestige are inversely proportional to their numbers. There cannot, for example, be within each educational generation more than fifteen to thirty young Frenchmen who are sufficiently talented to become members of the corps. Beyond a very low demo-

TABLE 3.6

Number of Places Available for Entry
into the Grandes Ecoles[a]

Schools[b]	
1. Engineering schools in Paris	
Ecole Supérieure d'Electricité	40
Ecole Supérieure d'Optique	20
E.N.S. Chimie de Paris	60
Ecole Physique et Chimie de Paris	45
Total (Paris)	165
2. Engineering schools in provinces	
E.N.S.I. de "Mécanique Physique" (5 schools)	215
E.N.S.I. de Chimie (south, 5 schools)	219
E.N.S.I. de Chimie (north, 5 schools)	152
Institut de Chimie Industrielle de Rouen	60
Total (provinces)	646
TOTAL	811

[a] Refers to engineering schools recruiting from preparatory classes B.
[b] All these schools fall under the jurisdiction of the Ministry of Education.
Source: *La Jaune et la rouge*, No. 223 (February 1967), p. 32.

TABLE 3.7

Number of Students Admitted to
the Ecole Polytechnique, 1850-1969

Year	*Number*	*Year*	*Number*
1850	90	1930	255
1860	143	1940	202
1872	290	1950	181
1882	250	1960	306
1892	264	1965	307
1900	250	1966	310
1901	180	1968	308
1910	187	1969	309
1920	225		

Source: for 1850-1881, G. Pinet, *Histoire de l'Ecole Polytechnique*; for 1882-1934, *Société amicale des anciens élèves de l'Ecole Polytechnique*; for 1935-1969, *La Jaune et la rouge*, No. 223 (February 1967).

TABLE 3.8

Number of Entrants into Ecole Normale Supérieure,
1890-1967[a]

Year	Number
1890	46
1900	37
1910	65
1920	55
1930	53
1940	52
1950	60
1960	82
1967	91

[a] Includes both Letters and Science

Source: for 1890-1940, Robert Smith "L'Ecole Normale Supérieure in the Third Republic" (unpubished Ph.D. dissertation, University of Pennsylvania, 1966), p. 15; for 1950-1967, Association Amicale des Anciens Elèves de l'Ecole Normale Supérieure, *Annuaire*.

TABLE 3.9

Number of Entrants into ENA by Method of Entry, 1952-1969

Year	Total Candidates Admitted	Admitted through First Concours		Admitted through Second Concours	
		No.	%	No.	%
1952	129	62	48.1	67	51.9
1953	95	53	55.8	42	44.2
1954	80	39	48.7	41	51.3
1955	63	32	50.8	31	49.2
1956	60	32	53.4	28	46.6
1958	60	33	55.0	27	45.0
1959	60	46	76.5	14	23.5
1960	60	43	71.5	17	28.5
1961	78	60	76.9	18	23.1
1962	93	71	76.3	22	23.7
1963	93	70	75.3	23	24.7
1964	81	62	76.5	19	23.5
1965	96	65	67.7	31	32.3
1966	96	67	69.7	29	30.3
1967	99	66	66.6	33	33.4
1968	105	70	66.6	35	33.3
1969	93	62	66.6	31	33.4

Source: Ecole Nationale d'Administration, *Concours d'entrée, statistiques,* 1952-1969.

graphic limit, any increase in the number of persons recruited through the ranking system of the graduating class of the Ecole Polytechnique implies a more than proportional lowering in the level of individuals [belonging to the corps.][17]

The strong support which the graduates give to the grandes écoles (Table 3.10) is not seen as a contradiction of the demo-

TABLE 3.10

Importance of Grandes Ecoles

(percent)

	Non-Commuinst Left	Center Opposition	Majority Parties	Total
1. Maintain the present system of grandes écoles as it is	32	72	80	66
2. Maintain the grandes écoles by profoundly reforming them	64	26	18	30
3. Abolish the grandes écoles and replace their training by that traditionally provided by the universities	4	1	1	3
4. No opinion	0	1	1	1

Source: Les Informations, No. 1,462 (May 1973), p. 61.

cratic precept that education be largely open to all. Indeed, recognizing that it is their grande école education that is largely responsible for their rapid access to elite positions, they are inclined to be strong defenders of the need for such institutions. They view the type of mass education that the universities dispense as being too little concerned with standards. Consequently, the grandes écoles are strongly supported by the elite not only because of the solid education they offer but also because the universities show little concern with standards. Now, by "standard" is meant no more and no less than that the number of those entering the universities is too large. If the universities really were concerned with standards, the elite maintains, they should not open their doors so

[17] Jean-Claude Thoenig, *L'Ere des technocrates: le cas des ponts et chaussées* (Paris: Les Editions d'Organisations, 1973), p. 223.

widely. They ought to end the open-enrollment system and institute a system of *sélection*. As one member of the elite put it: "If
democracy forces us to give a higher education to everyone regardless of aptitude, to anyone that is who desires it, then you
could say that I'm not very democratic because I'm against this."
Another member observed that "I used to be in favor of abolishing the grandes écoles because I considered them narrow, outdated, and undemocratic. Now I find myself very strongly dis-
posed toward them. The reason is that I, like many others, have
come to the conclusion that every society needs institutions to
select and to train people for its needs. Given that the universities
do not do this in France, I think that it would be the height of
irresponsibility—and I consider my earlier position to have been
irresponsible—to want to do away with the grandes écoles." Still
another of our respondents, who also emphasized that all societies
need to select highly trained leaders, noted that "the state cannot
really, no matter what the demands of democracy are, confine the
training of its highest servants to the universities so long as they
remain *contestataire* and irresponsible."

The controversy over "selection," insofar as entry into the university is concerned, has been a highly charged political issue for
over a decade, and its opponents won an important battle in the
wake of the May 1968 outbreaks. The demands for equality, participation, and greater democracy in 1968 precluded the introduc-
tion of any system of selection that would have denied entry into
the university to those who possessed the baccalauréat. This
was considered a political concession on the part of the government, one based on the exigencies of the moment rather than on
any commitment to democracy. Moreover, because it was a political concession, it was totally unrelated to the larger and more
important question: higher education for what? It was, in other
words, a decision that was unrelated to the needs of society or to
the employment opportunities that would eventually be available
to the increasing numbers of university graduates.[18] And because
the government regarded its decision as no more than a reluctantly

[18] François Bourricaud maintains that the original decision to increase
drastically the number of university students (a decision taken in the 1950s
and early 1960s) derived from the belief that "France having decided to
become a great industrial power needed learned men." But even with this
as its basis, the decision was both elitist, since it wasn't tied to secondary
education, and unrelated to the larger needs of society. See Bourricaud's
"La Réforme universitaire en France après 1945 et ses déboires," *Fondation
Européene de la Culture*, Cahier 3, 1977.

granted political concession, it now faces an even greater problem; namely, the existence of the largest number of unemployable *diplomés* that France has so far experienced.

The fact that the opening of the doors of the universities and the creation of new universities after 1968 was a political rather than an educational or social decision has served to strengthen the claim of the grandes écoles that they are the only institutions that are legitimately concerned with competence. If mass higher education is to continue unregulated in the universities, it is argued, all the more reason is there for preserving that part of the educational system that is highly competitive and highly selective in its admission procedures. Some have called this restrictive admission policy "Malthusian"; but, for the elite that these schools produce, the restrictive policy that is based on highly competitive examinations is not only the surest guarantee of "quality," but is seen to be all the more necessary in view of the universities' total abandon to exaggerated notions of "equality." Consequently, to the extent that the universities refuse to accept a system of admissions based on some criteria of merit, the elite has come to attach an even greater importance to the qualities that the grandes écoles have always stood for and defended.

THE LEFT AND THE GRANDES ECOLES

Given the general disenchantment with the universities, it becomes easier to understand why the grandes écoles have not only been able to preserve their structure and to maintain their position, but have even been able to assume greater importance in an era where demands for greater democratization, participation, and access to educational opportunities have become more vigorous. While the existence of such institutions as the grandes écoles, which in turn feed the grands corps, appears to contradict the requirements of democracy, they nevertheless are regarded as being perhaps even more indispensable than they were in the past. One indication of this can be found in the attitude of the Left and the non-Left oppositions to these elitist institutions.

One would expect that the most severe critics of the grandes écoles would come from the Left. This is, in fact, pretty much the case, though some of the critics of these institutions that we have mentioned—Taine, Renan, Bloch—were by no means men of the Left. However, the Left's actions with regard to these institutions suggest that it by no means differs from the Right when it comes to assessing the importance of these institutions in French society. We have already pointed to the Popular Front's creation of an Ecole Nationale d'Administration, a measure that even at the time seemed totally out of keeping with its ideology.

> We saw in the past [wrote Marc Bloch], the Popular Front proposing to do away with the quasi-monopoly of the Ecole des Sciences Politiques as the recruiting ground of our higher civil service. Politically, the idea was sound. A *régime* always has the right not to recruit its agents from a milieu whose traditions are almost totally hostile to it. But what did the men in power think of? They could have thought of instituting a general examination for the civil service similar to the admirable one of the British civil service. . . . They preferred instead to draw up a plan for yet another *école spéciale*: another school of political science [ENA] even more closed than its rival.[19]

Was the Popular Front's policy in the realm of higher education merely an aberration, or does it indicate a more general attitude that is likely to be shared by today's Left? There is little doubt that the Left has, in general, been more critical of the parallel system of higher education and of institutions that are fairly autonomous, that are not open to all, and that have principally served the bourgeois class. This notwithstanding, one needs to be cautious about attributing the desire for reform exclusively to the Left, for despite the Left's severe criticism of the grandes écoles, there is little evidence to indicate that it would effect major changes in the structure of higher education were it to assume power at some future time.

To suggest that the Left would, when in power, be likely to preserve the present structure in the higher education system does not mean that it adheres to the principles of an inegalitarian educational system. That it would not be likely to transform in a radical way this system in the foreseeable future is nonetheless a telling criticism of the Left. One cannot fail to observe that this problem hardly figured at all in the presidential campaign of April-May 1974. The Left had united as never before to back a single candidate—François Mitterrand—who had promised certain far-

[19] Bloch, *L'Etrange défait*, p. 256.

reaching reforms in a number of other areas. Moreover, Mitterrand himself had in the past been a critic of the elite institutions that gave rise to the "technocratic state."[20]

It is difficult to ascribe this omission to the importance of other issues—nationalization, inflation, tax inequalities. Mitterrand was the candidate and representative not only of his own Socialist Party, but of a united Left that included the Communist Party and that had a common program. Mitterrand, in fact, seems to have given the "technocratic" elite that is produced by the ENA sufficient cause for believing that he does not plan to reform, let alone abolish, this school. As one eloquent member of this elite put it in an interview with Maria-Antonietta Macciocchi:

> As far as the union of the Left is concerned, if it were to govern this country, not only would it not change anything, but it would increase the weight of nationalism (in contrast to European bourgeois internationalism). And when ENA students invited Mitterrand to the school and asked him whether with socialism in power, he would preserve ENA, he replied that "the problem was delicate and that he would have to consult his party." When he was asked what reforms could be made with respect to ENA, he continued hypocritically to say that he "would have to consult his party." He meant by that things would remain unchanged. With a "socialist" regime, believe me, there would come out of ENA some highly appreciated state-bureaucrat-apparatchiks, who would still constitute, as they do today, a caste.[21]

As far as the Communist Party is concerned, it too has not evidenced any particular hostility to the grandes écoles. As Lavau has observed, "The PCF is certainly not in favor of technocrats nor of the higher civil service, but it is willing to argue with the technocrats without any undue ill-feeling, and it has never advocated the abolition of the Ecole Nationale d'Administration."[22] In fact, when in 1976 a high-ranking member of the Socialist Party,

---

[20] François Mitterrand, *Le Coup d'état permanent* (Paris: Plan, 1965), p. 147.

[21] Maria-Antoinetta Macciocchi, *De la France* (Paris: Editions du Seuil, 1977), p. 276.

[22] Georges Lavau, "The PCF, the State, and the Revolution: An Analysis of Party Policies, Communications, and Popular Culture," in Donald L. M. Blackmer and Sidney Tarrow, eds., *Communism in Italy and France* (Princeton: Princeton University Press, 1975), p. 100.

Claude Estier, created a scandal by maintaining that examining juries at ENA were biased against those who expressed sympathies with the Left, he found little support from his communist allies. Not surprisingly, the PCF has been seen by *énarques* as "our best spokesman in critical moments."[23] While maintaining that Estier's arguments were an absurdity, Mme Macciocchi's interviewee, himself a strong defender of the status quo, readily acknowledged that "our ENA is an emanation of the bourgeois class, and it's purpose is to extend the power of the class which exercises a hegemony over the lower classes." He went on to observe that "what is most curious about this is that the PCF is our most clever defender and that it profited from Estier's error in order to take its distance [from the socialists] within the opposition . . . and, in effect, to give us a hand."[24]

That the Left has prepared no plans for reforming the system of higher education is evident. It may not be an accident, therefore, that the Common Program of the Left, which devoted a mere one and a half pages to "higher education," had no more to say than the following on the role of the grandes écoles and the universities:

> The restructuring of post-baccalauréat training will occur by stages, as closely linked as possible, which will take account of the specificity of each kind of training and which will utilize all the existing potential. This implies, in particular, that the existing grandes écoles and their preparatory classes will be progressively integrated into higher education, even *while preserving their qualities*. All these changes presuppose that the universities receive the financial means to adapt themselves to their new missions.[25]

It is difficult to imagine a political party vigorously committed to a more egalitarian society having so little to say about what it

[23] Cited in Macciocchi, *De la France*, p. 276.

[24] *Ibid.*, pp. 275-276. The interviewee then cited what *L'Humanité*, the newspaper of the French Communist Party, had to say on the Estier charges. "If there is 'opposition,' it has not placed itself under a single party. Feeling obliged to affirm that members of the PS [Parti Socialiste] are found only beyond a certain rank in the graduating classes at ENA, Claude Estier was speaking only in the name of his party, in the weekly newspaper of his party, which is the Socialist Party" (*L'Humanité*, June 1, 1976).

[25] *Programme commun de gouvernement du parti communiste et du parti socialiste* (Paris: Editions Sociales, 1972), pp. 83-84. Italics added. For an additional explanation, see Ezra N. Suleiman, "La Gauche et la haute administration," *Promotions* (November 1976), pp. 23-25.

regards as one of the chief underlying causes of this inequality. The *Radical Manifesto* of Jean-Jacques Servan-Schreiber goes somewhat further than the Common Program of the Left in its analysis of the educational system. It states that "we propose to begin *building the world of man in opposition to the laws of economic 'fatality'. . . . This undertaking implies a profound transformation of the educational system.*"[26] It goes on to observe that the present educational system denies equality of opportunity and it proposes its abolition.

> The educational process being uninterrupted, the notions of failure and of success will become attenuated. Someone who fails at a certain age or in a particular enterprise will find other occasions, and still others. The barbaric distinctions between the diplomé and the non-diplomé, the polytechnician and the *licencié*, insurmountable barriers which separate destinies forever and which rigidly compartmentalize the society, will be abolished.[27]

The proposed reform of the higher educational system, or rather the little that is said about it in the *Radical Manifesto*, is treated not in a separate and detailed discussion on education, but rather as part of the chapter on "Access to Social Equality." This may have its own logic, but it does not allow for a serious analysis of the future of the universities and the grandes écoles, of access to higher education, and of the problem of training and employment. The *Manifesto* states in a manner so categorical as almost to mask the absence of specific reforms: "We will formulate *two essential propositions* which will serve to concretize and illustrate these themes: an attack on cultural inequalities at the base, that is, well before the current schooling age; replacement of the grandes écoles system in order to expand and renew the recruitment of the country's leaders."[28] How? By what means? Almost as if to retract what had been said earlier, the *Manifesto* goes on to eulogize the grandes écoles:

> The intellectual tradition of our grandes écoles is a precious capital, which must not be destroyed or wasted. Moreover, there is in the desire for public service, with all the material

---

[26] Jean-Jacques Servan-Schreiber and Michel Albert, *Ciel et terre: Manifeste Radical* (Paris: Denoel, 1970), p. 91. Italics in original.
[27] *Ibid.*, p. 92. [28] *Ibid.*, p. 93.

sacrifice that this implies a kind of disinterestedness which does honor to our administration and constitutes the basis of its tradition. This tradition will be maintained.[29]

How is it possible both to maintain the "intellectual tradition" of the grandes écoles and to abolish these institutions? The vagueness of the *Radical Manifesto* with respect to the grandes écoles and to the reform of higher education, like the total absence of a reform in the Left's program, suggests not only that the problem is a highly complex one but also that the present system has a certain rationale, at least in the short run, which is acknowledged by the Left and the Right. This is supported by the survey of grandes écoles—broken down according to political affiliations—cited earlier (Table 3.10).

One needs to bear in mind that the graduates of the grandes écoles have come to play an important role within the opposition political parties. It follows that the programs of these parties with respect to higher education are undoubtedly influenced by people who are themselves products of the grandes écoles and who, perhaps in spite of themselves, feel some degree of attachment to them. Even as concerns the question of democratization, or lack thereof, one sees (Table 3.11) that the graduates of grandes écoles who

TABLE 3.11

Are the Grandes Ecoles Democratic?

(percent)

	Non-Communist Left	Center Opposition	Majority Parties	Total
Very democratic	4	26	30	24
Quite democratic	40	53	54	51
Rather undemocratic	41	19	13	19
Not at all democratic	10	1	2	4
No opinion	5	1	1	2

Source: Les Informations, No. 1,462 (May 1973), p. 61.

belong to the opposition are far from being in agreement on the extent of the undemocratic character of these institutions.

Whatever the allegiance of the members of the elite to the program of the Left, they cannot easily shake off the marks of their

[29] *Ibid.,* p. 105.

socialization into a grande école or a grand corps. Moreover, those who play an active role in the hierarchy of an opposition party are doomed, or have the good fortune (it all depends on one's view) to lead a double existence. They are an integral part of the Left (Rocard, Attali, and Fabius are illustrative examples), but they do not sever their ties to their corps of origin. Indeed, it is their ties to and work within their corps that really make it possible for them to devote their time to their party. It bears emphasizing that the corps continues to pay the salaries of these officials, even if it often employs them in nominal fashion only. When Jacques Attali, an official in the employ of the state, writes an article in *Le Monde*, he does not list his title or occupation as a member of the Conseil d'Etat. He lists himself as "adviser to François Mitterrand." The point is that to a large extent the state in effect subsidizes the political activities, both on the Left and on the Right, of the elite. Is the elite, whether its political sympathies lean toward the Left or the Right, likely to abandon a privileged situation that has no parallel in the Western world? We shall return later in the study to assess the full implications of this phenomenon. For the moment, we need only note the indication this provides of the strength that institutions like the grandes écoles and the grands corps were able to marshal in their attempt to escape inclusion in the Loi d'Orientation of 1968.

The Loi d'Orientation and the Grandes Ecoles

The events of May-June 1968 led to a major reform of the French university system. It was widely hoped that this occasion would be seized to reform not just the universities but the entire system of higher education. The groundswell of attacks directed at French institutions engulfed both the universities and the grandes écoles. Yet, the grandes écoles emerged unscathed and resisted, most successfully, being placed under the jurisdiction of the Loi d'Orientation.

The Loi d'Orientation, then, applies exclusively to the universities and serves to underscore the dichotomous system of higher education. To preserve this dichotomy, so heavily under attack, required a considerable marshaling of forces on the part of the grandes écoles. Edgar Faure, the Minister of Education who was responsible for the Loi d'Orientation, had shown every indication of wanting to bring these institutions under his control. Indeed, at the outset he indicated that to be a true Minister of National Education, it was necessary for him to have jurisdiction over the entire educational system, not just a part of it. He was not unaware of the fact that one of the reasons for the autonomy of the grandes écoles, as well as for the inability of a Minister of National Education to shape educational policy, was that jurisdiction over the grandes écoles was dispersed rather than centralized in a single ministry.

The first draft of the Loi d'Orientation, written by Faure himself, left out the grandes écoles. But in the version dated September 2, 1968, Faure took a much more ambitious stand, for this draft of the bill included *all* institutions of higher learning, not just the universities. It stated that "the National Council will give its opinion regarding the creation of all public institutions of a scientific or cultural nature, even if they are under the jurisdiction of other ministerial departments. . . . Furthermore, that all the provisions of the law shall be applied to them, including the regulations pertaining to participation; in particular, the election of Councils by teachers and students, and the election of the presidents and directors."[30]

The hostility of the grandes écoles and of their respective ministerial chiefs to this project was made abundantly clear even before Faure had circulated this version of the bill.[31] The ministers indicated to Faure, to the Prime Minister, and to the President of the Republic that they felt it would not be in the national interest to include the grandes écoles in the Loi d'Orientation. They argued that the Ministry of National Education's jurisdiction could be exercised only over the universities. Indeed, when Faure first proposed that the Loi d'Orientation be made applicable to all institutions of higher learning, he was told in no uncertain terms by his colleagues that he was Minister of Education and not of the Ecole Polytechnique, the Ecole des Mines, ENA, and other grandes écoles. He was even accused of wanting not to reform the universities, but to extend the jurisdiction of his ministry. In turning a

[30] Jacques de Chalendar, *Une Loi pour l'université* (Paris: Desclée de Brouwer, 1970), p. 85. The law also attempted to attack the privileged position of professors which led former rector Capelle to characterize the pre-1968 French university as "a mere juxtaposition of various subjects, each represented by one professor, isolated in his field." Cited in Jack Hayward, *The One and Indivisible French Republic* (London: Weidenfeld and Nicolson, 1973), p. 212.

[31] De Chalendar, *Une Loi pour l'université*, p. 85.

sensitive political issue into an administrative squabble over jurisdictions, the ministers and their various administrations were able
to mobilize and unite against Faure. The issue remained, of course,
highly political throughout, a point that few could deny, and the
jurisdictional arguments were used as simply another weapon.

It is evident, in retrospect, if it was not already clear at the
time, that Faure had very little chance of realizing his desire to
bring the grandes écoles under the control of the Loi d'Orientation.
This was due in part to the fact that there was a great deal of
general hostility to the law even without the inclusion of the
grandes écoles (as well as hostility, coming from different groups,
to *specific* provisions of the law) and in part to Faure's willingness
to sacrifice his desire in order to secure passage of the law. Given
Edgar Faure's reputation for dexterity in arranging skillful political
compromises that sometimes find little room for principles, it is not
difficult to see his attempt to include the grandes écoles in the Loi
d'Orientation as merely a carefully orchestrated use of an issue that
would certainly provoke a vigorous reaction from people more
ideological than himself. Their ire would subsequently be appeased
by Faure's agreement to drop the issue of the grandes écoles—a
gesture that would render the Loi d'Orientation more acceptable
to its ideological opponents. This may have been a calculation, and
it is possible that Faure played it out to its fullest. But to insist on
Faure's possible *mauvaise foi* would be to miss the intense ideological (and administrative) hostility that the integration of the
grandes écoles provoked. Even if Faure had been truly committed
to reducing the impact of the grandes écoles, it is doubtful whether
he could have overcome the opposition.

It was argued by many that the Loi d'Orientation would have a
detrimental impact on the state's power.[32] Michel Debré, then an
influential member of the government, argued that the Loi d'Orientation would lead to the dismantling of the state. The autonomy
granted the universities would reduce the role of the state and
would augment that of groups who could dispose of their power
in a manner that was not necessarily in the national interest. This
was not merely a warning that the communists could come to the
control the universities, it was a defense of Jacobin ideas which
many Gaullist deputies shared.

The Ministry of Finance, and more particularly the Inspection

[32] Much of the discussion that follows is based on documents of ministerial cabinets and various committees, as well as on personal interviews.

des Finances, was hostile to the Orientation Law because they felt that if the universities were given more autonomy, this would reduce their control over university expenditures, or rather, the control exercised over expenditures would become *a posteriori.* The Inspection des Finances argued that, since the budget of National Education represented 20 percent of the total national budget, *a posteriori* control of expenditures simply meant an acceptance of the fact that expenditures would go beyond the allocated budget. And since no one, for political reasons, would be willing to put an end to overspending, it would become impossible to foresee actual expenditures.

If the universities were to be given autonomy in the domain of expenditures, this would have a direct impact on the power of the Inspection des Finances since it alone controlled the state's expenditures. Autonomy would mean simply checking expenditure after the fact, which falls within the jurisdiction of the Cour des Comptes. The Cour des Comptes, fearing a jurisdictional squabble with the Inspection des Finances, was itself opposed to the Orientation Law. Moreover, if its grip on university expenditures were to be loosened, the Inspection could not be certain that this would not set in motion a trend, one that would result in claims by other institutions and universities for similar autonomy.

The Ministry of Interior, with the outbreaks of May-June fresh in its mind, was hostile to the Orientation Law because it feared that its ability to use police intervention to maintain order and to prevent subversion would be curtailed. It wanted the Orientation Law to state clearly that the police would be permitted to intervene to maintain order in the universities, should the need arise, without being called to do so by the presidents of the councils of universities. Prior to the Orientation Law, the police could enter the grounds of a university only after a formal request had been made by the rector.

With regard to the grandes écoles in particular, every minister who had jurisdiction over such a school that did not fall within the purview of the Ministry of National Education raised a most determined objection to the Orientation Law. These ministers were backed and pressured by the schools, which also marshaled all the power that their boards of directors and their graduates in the ministries, in the ministerial cabinets, and in parliament possessed. The then Minister of Defense, Pierre Messmer, under whose jurisdiction fell one of the more glorious of the grandes écoles—the

Ecole Polytechnique—became the chief spokesman for the grandes écoles within the government and led the opposition to integrating the grandes écoles into the universities. As Minister of Defense, he maintained not only that the Minister of Education could not infringe on the status of institutions that had always been considered, juridically, as falling outside the Ministry of Education, but that to do so would ultimately jeopardize national defense and security. Messmer and his advisers noted that if the grandes écoles, and particularly the Ecole Polytechnique, were to be presented with the possibility of having the Ministry of Defense's or the state's tutelage lifted, most of the researchers in the laboratories of the grandes écoles would choose to become part of the autonomous university. This, Messmer argued, would have a disastrous effect on national defense.

At every point, therefore, in the drafting of the various versions of the Loi d'Orientation, Faure was made aware that any attempt to include the grandes écoles within this law would be unacceptable, both educationally and politically. And since the Orientation Law had encountered strong resistance from the Gaullist ranks, it was necessary to make it more palatable to those who were suspicious of the reform. The view was widely shared that the grandes écoles had no hand in the uprisings, that they provided a solid education for their students, and that they furnished highly qualified recruits to the public and private sectors. Faure, in effect, was told that he could set about reforming the universities in a manner that he deemed feasible on the condition that he did not attempt to alter the status of the grandes écoles. This indicates not merely the power of these institutions, but the little importance that the elites in France attach to the universities. The Cultural Affairs Commission was to express later a view shared by the political and industrial milieu when it noted: "One must not destroy that which has given excellent results, that which exists, that which already works well."[33] This is an old but powerful argument, and it has had an impact on political leaders of the Left and Right.

The passage of the Orientation Law did not solve the problems posed by a parallel system of higher education, and the question continued to be raised as to whether the grandes écoles could continue to exist as a separate part of the system of higher education. In an interview that Faure granted *Le Monde* in March 1969, he was asked whether the grandes écoles were going to remain

[33] Cited in de Chalendar, *Une Loi pour l'université*, p. 85.

totally outside the new universities. His reply, in addition to demonstrating a concern for the pedagogical issues, also showed an awareness of the political problems that he had confronted a few months earlier:

> It would seem to me personally very regrettable if the grandes écoles remained outside of the universities which are in the process of being created. Most of the grandes écoles are, in fact, very useful institutions, due as much to the quality of their students as to that of their professors.
>
> Even while maintaining their own particular character, they could still, through their ties to the other institutions composing each university, play a role of pedagogical leadership that seems to me essential.[34]

So much for the pedagogic advantages to be derived from a link between the grandes écoles and the universities. Faure went on to observe, however, that this posed problems: "I am aware that this is an important and complex problem: a certain number of these grandes écoles fall outside of the jurisdiction of my ministry, while others by their status, as well as by the content and the ultimate aim of their teaching, are very diverse."[35] Faure also noted in this same interview that in the long run it would be to the advantage of industry to have technicians trained by universities, for industry would come more and more to need research and development engineers in addition to the technicians that the grandes écoles habitually trained. It was evident that Faure had not totally abandoned the struggle to have the Orientation Law apply to the grandes écoles.

The government, for its part, had decided that the Orientation Law must under no circumstances cover the grandes écoles. A few days after Faure had expressed his views on the subject in the interview he granted *Le Monde*, an interministerial committee met to discuss the specific problem of the extent to which the Orientation Law should apply to the grandes écoles. "The president and the prime minister do not wish to include them within the law. They believe that it is necessary to preserve this sector 'which works' from the contagion of agitation which troubles the universities."[36] At the conclusion of this interministerial meeting, the government issued the following statement: "The essential object

[34] *Le Monde*, 23-24 March 1969.   [35] *Ibid.*
[36] *Le Monde*, 27 March 1969.

is to allow at the national level for a homogeneous policy regarding the grandes écoles, one which is likely to preserve and to augment the high level of training dispensed by these institutions of higher learning."[37]

This, of course, constituted no more than a reiteration of the policy the government had adopted the previous year. Both de Gaulle and his prime minister Couve de Murville were adamant about preserving the grandes écoles. When Pompidou succeeded de Gaulle to the presidency, he too held steadfast insofar as the grandes écoles were concerned. He was perhaps even more reluctant than de Gaulle to entertain any major changes in the status of the grandes écoles. Faure, attempting to explain Pompidou's attitude, put particular emphasis on Pompidou's academic origins which were firmly grounded in one of the major grandes écoles, the Ecole Normal Supérieure. "An *agrégé*," wrote Faure in a book published after he left the government, "who is also a normalien, does not free himself easily from a corporatist reflex. The most progressive minds often react conservatively, at least at first, when it concerns something that touches their milieu."[38] But the real explanation may have had more to do with Pompidou's ideology and view of French society than with his own normalien background, for he shared the belief that the grandes écoles formed the nation's leaders and in so doing formed people who accepted the existing social order. This was not the case with the universities, institutions that Pompidou, like many others across the political spectrum, saw as continually posing a challenge to political order and stability.

There were thus many factors—pedagogic, social, and political —that coalesced to prevent a serious reform of higher education in 1968. The last was probably the most important: the grandes écoles became in 1968 sacred institutions not only because they were important and necessary for providing the upper cadre of both the public and private sectors, but also because in the turmoil of May 1968 they were seen as crucial ingredients in maintaining the stability of the social system, or at least in cushioning the forces of instability. The outbreaks of May 1968 put into question all the traditionally accepted institutions, and it is not surprising that it appeared all the more important to those in power to maintain intact the institutions that supported, benefited from, and were

[37] *Ibid.*

[38] Edgar Faure, *Ce que je crois* (Paris: Grasset, 1971), p. 194.

part of the social system that prevailed prior to 1968. This is what is meant by "not destroying the institutions that work," a theme that runs throughout the discussions, speeches, and symposia published by the grandes écoles and the grands corps. This argument was also used against Edgar Faure's project of bringing the grandes écoles under the Loi d'Orientation. When the crisis of 1968 had subsided, Pompidou, as president of the Republic, took to their defense in categorical terms. In October 1969, while inaugurating the new buildings of the Ecole Centrale at Chatenay-Malabry, he noted: "At a moment when our old university is profoundly shaken and seeks feverishly to find its equilibrium, our grandes écoles remain the most solid bastions for the preparation of the nation's leaders."[39]

The crisis into which the universities were thrust had been simmering for many years, and no one supposed that the Loi d'Orientation would reform all that needed reforming in the universities, nor that the universities, traditional as they are as institutions in terms of hierarchy, defending their *situations acquises*, being closed to the outside world, would cease to question the society in which they existed. "Ce n'est qu'un début," was what the demonstrators proclaimed in May 1968. Given the magnitude of the 1968 crisis, as well as the possibility of the universities remaining a tinderbox ready to ignite in the future, the preservation of the grandes écoles became of critical importance. They came to be regarded as a kind of safety valve against future social upheavals, which they might be powerless to prevent but whose magnitude they could surely temper. Consequently, the parallel system of higher education may be undemocratic and wasteful of resources, but from the standpoint of order and stability, the system performs the function of at least making certain that not all those destined for a higher education are going to question the foundations of the society. This is the main reason for the timidity of the Left in the face of the grandes écoles and for its reluctance to advocate a far-reaching reform of higher education.

The graduates of the grandes écoles have had to expend a great deal of time and energy to enter these schools and to graduate from them. They receive an allowance while undertaking their studies and they are assured of employment upon graduation. Consequently, the perception they have of society and of the social

[39] Cited in Guy Herzlich, "Protéger les forts contre les faibles," *Le Monde*, 20 April 1971.

order is very different from those who enter the university (always without a *concours*), where there is no guidance, and often little hope of securing employment at the end.

It is important not to lose sight of the fact that most of the grandes écoles, with certain exceptions like the Ecole Normale Supérieure and ENA, train engineers and scientists.[40] These graduates form the upper and middle-level cadre of industry and the public sector, and their positions are assured them pretty much from the outset. The university graduate has no such grandiose expectations, either at the beginning or at the end of his studies. Boudon, then, is perfectly correct in arguing that the problem of employment was to a large extent responsible for the attacks on the university in 1968. In dividing the higher education system into two separate parts, the state assures itself that a small but important segment of each generation will have an interest in defending the existing social order.

When I use the term "state" in this context, I do not have in mind some abstract entity. Rather I am referring to a policy, consciously pursued, by those in power. And I have suggested that a left-wing government would, when confronted with the problem of the need for order and stability, find itself an ally of the grandes écoles. Not only did the now defunct Common Program of the Left indicate this, but the public and private elites in power today do not see themselves seriously threatened by a left-wing government, nor do they believe that such a government would move to abolish such institutions as the grandes écoles and the grands corps. The reason for this, according to our respondents, over two-thirds of whom took this view, is that a left-wing government could not sweep away such institutions without also sweeping the rug from under its feet. It would probably undertake to open up recruitment into these institutions, but that is a far cry from doing away with them. If even the Left would find a strong need to rely on these institutions—because a left-wing government needs trained and reliable engineers, scientists, and managers as much as a conservative government—how much more must the present regime depend on these institutions?

To be sure, the tendency of the present elite to see itself as indispensable even to a left-wing government is by itself no indication that the Left will see things in the same way, and one would not wish to conclude that because the graduates of the grandes

[40] The Ecole Normale also has a very important science section.

écoles and the members of the grands corps view themselves as indispensable to any government, the institutions on which their power depends will be kept intact when a left-wing government takes power. However, this view is not seriously at variance with what has occurred in the past. Indeed, major crises in France have often led to the reinforcement rather than to the reform or abolition of institutions that have been seen as outdated or that may have even precipitated the crisis. Three such examples can be cited.

The first illustrates what happened to the reform movement that preceded the outbreak of the First World War. During the entire period between 1880 and 1914, the Radicals and Socialists undertook a relentless attack on the grandes écoles and the grands corps. We have seen that these institutions resisted rather well the attempts to reform them. However, it was clear by 1914 that the government was preparing for a major onslaught against these institutions. The outbreak of the war brought to an end the great struggle between the grandes écoles and the government.[41] More than that, they now came to be seen as indispensable to the national war effort. As Shinn points out, "the need for national unity was not the sole element responsible for the closure of the great debate: the country, insecure after the shock of August 1914, turned again to the institutions and classes which had been dominant before the *Belle Epoque*. This meant that the *haute bourgeoisie, Grandes Ecoles*, and their monopoly were rejuvenated and, conversely, the semi-democratic aspirations of the *moyenne bourgeoisie*—evinced in the growth of faculties and the liberalization of recruitment in the privileged careers—could find no broad public support. Hence, the emancipatory element present within the reform movement of the early Third Republic was blocked by popular insecurity, patriotic fervor and a dread of untried organization and methods."[42]

A second example which illustrates how criticism of certain institutions can, following a crisis, turn into acceptance and defense of these institutions, is that of the Ecole Libre. Prior to World War II, this school was severely attacked by the Popular Front, which even envisaged its abolition. In 1945, this school, which was still heavily under attack, was rescued by its nationalization, a measure that in no way affected its preeminent role. Indeed, the

---

[41] Terry Shinn, "The Dawning of an Elite: The Ecole Polytechnique and the Polytechnician Circles" (unpublished manuscript, 1973), pp. 425-427.

[42] *Ibid.*, p. 589.

reform went even further in its past reliance on this school and on the grandes écoles by creating the Ecole Nationale d'Administration, which itself was modeled on the Ecole Polytechnique. As I concluded in an earlier analysis of the founding of ENA, the reformers of 1945, like the critics preceding the First World War, "were guided by an attachment to the past and an unmistakable fear of the novel and the untried. They fell back on the traditional system for their model [and] they relied solely on the traditional methods by which other elites were recruited."[43] The post-1945 governments made a point of restricting the purges of the members of the prewar elite who had collaborated with the Vichy government;[44] the people and institutions who had been seen as blocking change were now regarded as indispensable.

Both these episodes bear a remarkable similarity to the third case—the 1968 crisis and its consequences for the system of higher education—which I have analyzed at length. Rather than seeking to reform the institutions that had precipitated the 1968 outbreaks, the elite sought to preserve the preexisting structure and to reinforce the institutions whose impact on French society had been so vigorously under attack. In effect, crises rarely bring in their wake far-reaching reforms because the atmosphere of uncertainty that they generate—1918, 1945, and 1968 all point to this—creates timidity, and fear of further dislocation of existing order. The result is that a falling back on the "known quantities," however undesirable they may be, takes place.

CONCLUSION

The consequences of the events of May 1968 have, paradoxically, strengthened the position of the grandes écoles in French society. The state now has a more certain and determining hand in creating its own elite and that of the private sector. As Guy Herzlich has observed:

> Over the past three years, the "image de marque" of the engineering grandes écoles has gotten stronger. Compared to the university, they appear, more than ever, to incarnate the recognized values of the majority of the leaders and execu-

[43] Ezra N. Suleiman, *Politics, Power, and Bureaucracy in France* (Princeton: Princeton University Press, 1974), p. 98.

[44] Robert O. Paxton, *Vichy France* (New York: Alfred A. Knopf, 1973), pp. 333-343.

tives of French industry: discipline, order, a sense of reality, efficiency, and an ability to adapt to changes in the economy.[45]

The imbalance in the parallel system of higher education, an imbalance that manifests itself in the areas of pedagogy, number of students, allocation of funds, and, finally, employment opportunities, has in no way been modified by the post-1968 reforms. It must be strongly emphasized that the reasons for this can, and should be, kept distinct from the whole question of centralization. The present Ministry of Education, which until the formation of the Chirac government in June 1974 was called the Ministry of National Education and was responsible for the entire educational system, from primary schooling through university, is now responsible only for primary and secondary education. A separate Ministry of Universities has been created. This administrative reform has had little effect on centralization or decentralization, and even if it entailed the latter, it is difficult to see in what way it attacks the *real* problems posed by the parallel system of higher education. In effect, it is possible to interpret the limited degree of decentralization that the universities have been granted as a simple means of rendering them irrelevant, while the grandes écoles continue to enjoy their preeminent position. The latter supply the ruling elite of the society as well as its managers. They help preserve the social and political system, and they do not perpetually contest the nature of the educational system.

It follows that, as I have indicated, the higher educational system that now exists is not without its rationale. This is not to suggest that it is democratic or that it is egalitarian. It clearly is not. Nor is it to suggest that its rationale is not confined to the short term. The policy that underlies the system is, in effect, not without contradictions. The governments of the Fourth and Fifth republics sought a policy that would allow both a "democratization" of higher education and the preservation of its elitist elements. They found that policy in an unprecedented expansion of the universities, entry into which was facilitated by the absence of an entrance examination[46] (that is, an "open-enrollment" system), and in the maintenance of the small size of the grandes écoles, entry into which requires passing a highly competitive concours. Until 1968, it was possible to point to the expansion of the universities as the

---

[45] *Le Monde,* 20 April 1971.
[46] See Bourricaud, "La Réforme universitaire en France," pp. 17-24.

proof of the "democratization of French higher education." The events of 1968 were the heavy price paid for this policy, which devalued the university diploma and made no provisions for the employment of those who possessed it. The result has been to devalue the university itself. "When I ask the parents of my pupils toward what higher education institution they would like to orient their children," said the principal of a lycée, "I get a unanimous response: above all, not the university!"[47] Clearly, few of those who desert the university will find room in the grandes écoles, so that the universities will continue to produce unemployable "*diplomés*," while the grandes écoles will only produce employable ones who go on to constitute the elite and the subelite of the society. This is not a novel problem, though it has certainly been aggravated in recent years. We turn now, therefore, to an examination of the ways in which the elite institutions have sought to maintain their privileged positions in the society.

[47] *L'Express*, 14-20 July 1975, p. 54.

Part Two

❆ ❆

SURVIVAL

Chapter Four

POSITIONS

THE previous chapters have pointed to the importance as well as the endurance of the parallel system of higher education in France. We have confined our discussion to the significance of this system for the formation of elites. It becomes important now to examine the positions that the state-created elites occupy in French society. This is the task of the present chapter. The chapters that follow will attempt to explain why these elites have not only been able to hold on to their positions but have actually succeeded, over the past century and a half, in extending their influence over the major sectors of the society. This chapter, then, may be considered as a prelude to an analysis of elite transformation and stability in France.

The story of the French aristocracy's power and influence has been told many times. That of the endurance of the post-aristocratic elite has more often been condemned than analyzed. Our task is to understand why the elites and the institutions that succeeded the aristocracy in the nineteenth century have been more adept at holding on to their positions. It may be objected that, despite its century and a half of existence, the post-aristocratic elite is relatively young, so that one cannot really speak of stability and endurance. This may well be so. However, our task is not to predict the future, and no attempt is made to suggest that this will always be so, or that the life span of this elite and these institutions will equal or surpass that of, say, the defunct aristocracy. Rather, we maintain that institutions that have endured for so long in the face of at times severe criticisms exhibit certain characteristics that are of interest and bear examination. Before undertaking this analysis, it is first necessary to establish the importance of the elite and its connection with the formative mechanisms that we examined in the previous part of the study.

GRANDES ECOLES AND GRANDS CORPS

The main aim of the *écoles spéciales,* or grandes écoles, was to provide a number of highly trained and specialized elites to serve the state in various activities over which it had control. These elites were to be selected by a rigorous process that entailed long preparation for an entrance examination to determine if one would be admitted to the grandes écoles. The competitive element did not let up once entry had been gained into a grande école; on the contrary, it was particularly emphasized during the training at the schools, since careers would depend on one's rank in the graduating class. In effect, the creation of the grandes écoles constituted at once a pedagogical innovation and a conscious attempt to create an elite. The elites, as Napoleon put it, "have to conform to the state of the nation and to the society."[1]

The competitive spirit, which was to be encouraged in the formation of the state's elites, has always distinguished the grandes écoles from the universities. The characteristics that mark the former are: "(1) the selection of candidates after the baccalauréat; (2) the preparation for entrance examinations to the schools; (3) the entrance examinations; (4) the distribution of candidates among the schools; (5) the more or less specialized training of the students in these schools; and (6) the granting of diplomas and ranking of students at graduation."[2] All these characteristics are absent from the universities, entry into which is automatically secured by a baccalauréat diploma. The characteristics of the grandes écoles are fiercely defended as fundamental virtues, for without them, it is argued, there would be nothing to distinguish the grandes écoles from the mass institutions that are the universities. Writing in the Ecole Polytechnique's alumni journal, a former graduate of this school noted: "One need not have scruples about extolling the enthusiasm for and the habit of work which characterize the preparatory classes and which are shared by students and professors alike. One must not, by the same token, hesitate to reproach the Faculties for leaving too much freedom to the professors and too much leisure to the students."[3]

Since a grande école education was geared to fulfilling a specialized function, those having undergone the same training for the same *métier* would share a great deal in common. Indeed, the schools had as one of their objectives the fostering of a certain

[1] Pelet de Lozère, *Opinions de Napoléon* (Paris: Firmin Didot Frères, 1833), p. 168.

[2] Raymond Painé, "Classes préparatoires et grandes écoles dans une réforme de l'enseignement supérieur," *La Jaune et la rouge*, No. 194 (June 1965), p. 10.

[3] *Ibid.*, pp. 10-11.

camaraderie. It was with this purpose in mind that Napoleon sought to institute the hierarchy of the military in all those institutions to which he attached great importance. "We must imitate in the teaching corps the classification of the military hierarchy," he said.[4] The organizational principles of the military and the church, for which, as we noted earlier, Napoleon was to express his admiration time and again, symbolized what was most needed by a society such as that conceived by Napoleon: hierarchy, uniformity, order, functionality, and loyalty. The grandes écoles could go a long way toward fostering a feeling of pride in serving the state, a feeling that would be strengthened in the individual who had sustained the same hardships in gaining entry into such a school and who had experienced the same privileges upon leaving it as his comrades. As Ariès, citing Prony, observed, the *école spéciale* was ideally suited for the purpose of emulation and camaraderie: it would provide "common feelings and habits, bonds of mutual affection between individuals who enter the same career and who graduate from the same school."[5]

The grandes écoles could not alone inculcate once and for all the virtues associated with an "esprit de corps." The main mechanism for creating such an "esprit" was in fact to establish institutions that became known as "corps." One often speaks of the English "old-boy network" based on the "school tie," but important as the tie may be in binding people later on in life, it can scarcely compare with a system that institutionalizes the camaraderie of school days by ensuring that it continues during one's active life. School life itself becomes the beginning of one's career, for there is no sharp break between school life and working life in terms of colleagues. There is no other country where the term "esprit de corps" has such a literal meaning. Thus, upon completing their training in the specialized schools, the best graduates normally enter one of the grands corps. The choice of corps depends entirely on one's rank in the graduating class, for just as there is a hierarchy among the schools, so there is a hierarchy among the corps. Table 4.1 shows the corps that are most often chosen by graduates of the ENA and the Ecole Polytechnique. Table 4.1 lists only the two most important grandes écoles because it is their graduates and the corps to which they belong that exer-

[4] De Lozère, *Opinions de Napoléon*, p. 166.

[5] Philippe Ariès, "Problèmes de l'éducation," in *La France et les français* (Paris: Bibliothèque de la Pléiade, Gallimard, 1972), p. 932.

TABLE 4.1

Grand Corps Most Often Chosen
by Graduates of the ENA and the Ecole Polytechnique

ENA	*Polytechnique*
Inspection des Finances	Corps des Mines
Conseil d'Etat	Ponts et Chaussées
Cour des Comptes	Telecommunications
Administrateurs civils	Armaments
Diplomatic corps	
Prefectoral corps	

cise the dominant influence in French society today. We do not wish to suggest that other schools or other corps are of little importance. This would be contrary to established fact. However, the importance of other corps (Forestry, Telecommunication, Public Works) is generally very great in the limited area over which they have a monopoly. The schools that we are concentrating on are among the most prestigious and they serve as models for other schools. Moreover, they produce the graduates of the most powerful corps (Mines, Ponts et Chaussées, Inspection des Finances). What distinguishes the graduates of these schools and the members of these corps is their *generalized* power. Their corps constitute no more than a base from which to launch a number of careers that are in no way connected with the training the graduates receive.

The top graduates of the leading grandes écoles all go into certain corps. This serves not only to link the graduates in an intimate way, but also establishes an institutional link between the schools and the elite institutions (the corps). One writer has suggested that the technical corps no longer depend as in the past on the Ecole Polytechnique. He argues that although almost all the members of Corps des Mines and the Corps des Ponts et Chaussées are obliged to pass through the Ecole Polytechnique before going on to the Ecole des Mines and the Ecole Nationale des Ponts et Chaussées, these corps could and might even prefer to be totally independent of the Ecole Polytechnique.[6] This is actually a theoretical point, for in practice there has come to exist a symbiotic

[6] Gérard Grunberg, "L'Ecole Polytechnique et 'ses' grands corps," *Annuaire international de la fonction publique, 1973-1974*, p. 401.

relationship between the grandes écoles and the grands co.
top graduates of the Ecole Polytechnique choose to enter the
des Mines and the Corps des Ponts et Chaussées. These are
most prestigious technical corps in large part because they are
chosen by the most successful graduates of the leading grande
école. By the same token, the Ecole Polytechnique maintains its
preeminent position among the grandes écoles in part because it
supplies the key corps with its ablest graduates. This type of relationship serves to legitimize both the corps and the school, a function that cannot be underestimated and one that we will explore
more fully in Chapter Five. Nor are the grandes écoles and the corps
unaware of their dependence upon each other. When, for example,
the 1970 graduating class at ENA revolted against the tradition
that led the top graduates to choose entry into the *grands corps*
(Inspection des Finances, Cour des Comptes, Conseil d'Etat), the
corps were severely shaken. They even threatened to demand the
reinstitution of the pre-1945 system of recruitment, a system that
left the corps entirely free to recruit (and coopt) their members.[7]
The corps had come to depend on a system of recruitment in which
a leading grande école supplied them with its top graduates. The
school itself became almost instantly a leading grande école because its top graduates had access to the prestigious corps. Given
that this relationship was put into question, it was understandable
that the corps should react the way they did. For the corps, as for
the school, the entire system from which both derive great benefit
is upset when the graduates do not choose the prestigious corps.
Similarly, Thoenig observes that some of the important personali-
ties of the Corps des Ponts et Chaussées would like to eliminate
nonpolytechnicians from the corps altogether, because the corps'
prestige would be augmented if it included only polytechnicians.[8]

[7] The incident that took place in 1970, and its consequences are discussed
in Ezra N. Suleiman, *Politics, Power, and Bureaucracy in France* (Princeton: Princeton University Press, 1974), pp. 88-94.

[8] Most corps accept certain members who have not traveled the normal
route. In some corps the number is totally insignificant (for the Inspection
des Finances, which began admitting non-ENA graduates in 1974 it amounts
to three persons), while for others it is considerably larger (for the Ponts
et Chaussées and for the Conseil d'Etat it represents one-third of their membership). There is always something of a stigma attached to those who enter
the Corps des Mines and the Corps des Ponts et Chaussées by the nonpoly-
technique route—by passing an exam that allows entry into the Ecole des
Mines and the Ecole des Ponts et Chaussées. They are second-class citizens

grand corps should include only individuals who have gone through a grand école. The presence of a third of former T.P.E. engineers [nonpolytechnicians] is a serious handicap for the homogeneity and for the name of the corps."[9]

The link between the grandes écoles and the grand corps in which the prestige of each is reinforced depends on yet another crucial factor: that the members of these corps enjoy greater career mobility and success than do graduates of other schools and members of other corps. This implies, above all, that the top graduates choose entry into the grands corps and that the latter offer their members interesting careers outside of the narrow functions of the corps, relatively high salaries, and rapid occupational mobility. There is thus created a situation in which the grandes écoles come to have strong ties throughout the society as a result of the organizational structures which their graduates enter. Their graduates gain legitimacy because they are graduates of the grandes écoles, and the grandes écoles reinforce their position because of the success of their graduates.

Since the grandes écoles generally had the aim of training people for the public sector, "success" was conceived of as holding an important position in the regional or central administrations. This is no longer the case, a fact that implies a major metamorphosis in the role of these schools. This transmutation of the schools' *raison d'être* implies a willingness to reappraise and redefine their role. This, as we shall see, has entailed profound consequences for the endurance of the grandes écoles and the grands corps. Before turning to this analysis, however, it is first necessary to situate this elite in the society. In this way, we shall gain a glimpse of the positions occupied by the graduates of the grandes écoles and the members of the grands corps, and this in turn will facilitate our understanding of what a state-created elite implies.

---

for they are not "X" (that is, graduates of the Ecole Polytechnique). Entry into the nontechnical corps by a route other than ENA is known as the *tour extérieur* entry. The government names these people to the Conseil d'Etat and to the Cour des Comptes, usually as a reward for long service. These are often highly political appointments. On the "tour extérieur" of the Conseil d'Etat, see Marie-Christine Kessler, *Le Conseil d'Etat* (Paris: Armand Colin, 1968), pp. 155-165.

[9] Jean-Claude Thoenig, *L'Ere des technocrates: le cas des ponts et chaussées* (Paris: Les Editions d'Organisations, 1973), p. 235.

Equally important, this may be construed as a portrait of those who occupy the key positions in French society.[10]

POLITICS

The graduates of grandes écoles, particularly Polytechnique and ENA, play a rather active role in the political arena. It would be a mistake to assume that, because the grandes écoles trained their students mostly for administrative careers throughout the nineteenth century, their graduates did not find their way into the political arena. Normaliens, for example, played an important part in the politics of the Third Republic, not only because they were well represented in parliament, but also because almost half of those who did become deputies also became ministers.[11] While it was normaliens like Jaurès, Blum, Painlevé, and Lebrun who directed attention to the intense political interest of the Ecole Normale, we need to bear in mind that the scientists—that is, polytechnicians—were not repelled by a political career.[12] Consequently, we may observe that despite the emphasis placed on the formation of elites by and for the state, civil service graduates of the grandes écoles have in the past played an important role, though by no means as a unified group.

Nevertheless, we cannot fail to note that some important changes have taken place since World War II. The establishment of the ENA, which centralized recruitment into the grands corps and rendered it akin to that of Polytechnique, meant in effect that the nontechnical corps would have a greater cohesion and would therefore be likely to pose a greater threat, particularly on the administrative front, to the technical corps. In other words, the danger now became greater that graduates of ENA belonging to the grands corps would encroach on the territory of the Corps des Mines or the Corps des Ponts et Chaussées. Consequently, the move

[10] It is a portrait only in a limited sense, for I have not sought to give all the details about those who occupy the "command posts." I wish only to show how the educational system is intimately tied to the organizational sructures of elites, a fact that has a definite bearing on problems of equality and social and occupational mobility.

[11] See Robert Smith, "The Ecole Normale," unpublished manuscript, Chapter VIII.

[12] See Terry Shinn, "The Dawning of an Elite: The Ecole Polytechnique and the Polytechnician Circles" (unpublished manuscript, 1973).

into the political sector was in part dictated by this new struggle between the technical and nontechnical corps, for it became the surest way of preserving one's position. Second, the rapid success which the graduates of ENA experienced in their careers suggested to many that the school offered a shortcut to a political career. Figure 4.1 shows that participation in ministerial cabinets by ENA graduates had already begun in the early 1950s. Third, De Gaulle's practice of appointing civil servants as ministers set an important example, for it showed that graduation from ENA could lead not just to high positions within the administration and in ministerial cabinets, but to the highest and most coveted political posts. De Gaulle's practice has been followed by his two successors, Georges Pompidou and Giscard d'Estaing.

We noted earlier the relationship between the grandes écoles and the organizational structure of elites, and we suggested that this had a direct impact on occupational mobility. How can this be shown? We need to demonstrate not just that graduates of the grandes écoles occupy key positions, but that it is those graduates who enter the organized elite structure—the prestigious corps—who experience the most rapid mobility in their careers. Hence, we find that not all ENA graduates, just as not all polytechnicians, experience the same rate of occupational mobility. Table 4.2 shows the high representation in ministerial cabinets of those who enter the grands corps. As Bodiguel notes:

> We can derive a rather clear conclusion: the members of cabinets graduating from ENA are, to a greater proportion than is the case for their colleagues who have not gone through this school, recruited through the *concours étudiant,* come from the Paris region, graduated from the Institut d'Etudes Politiques of Paris and belong to the highest social categories. This portrait is, in fact, that of the members of the grands corps whose characteristics are always superior to that of other civil servants.[13]

Ministerial cabinets are important not only as institutions where politico-administrative powers lie; they are of extreme importance insofar as career mobility and career alternatives are concerned, since promotions within the politico-administrative sector come to

[13] Jean-Luc Bodiguel, "Les Anciens élèves de l'E.N.A. et les cabinets ministériels," *Annuaire international de la fonction publique, 1973-1974,* p. 369. See also the table given on p. 363 of this article.

Figure 4.1 First Entry into Ministerial Cabinets by ENA Graduates

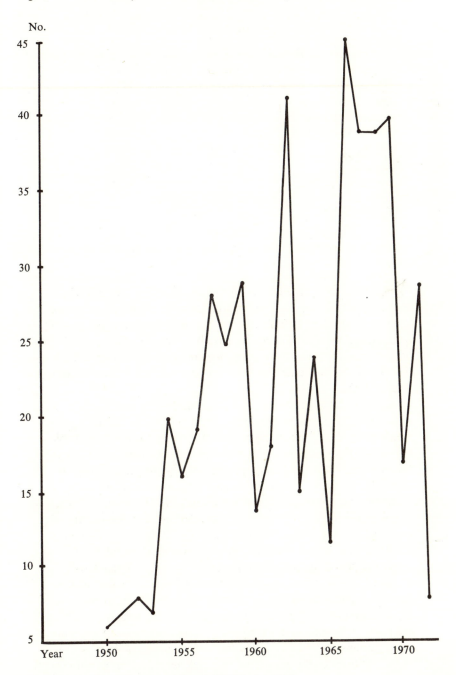

(Source: Bodiguel, "Les Anciens élèves de l'E.N.A.," p. 361.)

TABLE 4.2

Professional Background of ENA Cabinet Members

Corps	Percent
Inspection des Finances	19.4
Administrateurs civils	
(Ministry of Finance)	17.2
Prefectoral corps	12.0
Cours des Comptes	11.6
Conseil d'Etat	11.2
Administrateurs civils	10.7
Foreign affairs	
(Diplomatic corps)	9.5
Other corps	8.5

Source: J.-L. Bodiguel, "Les Anciens élèves de l'E.N.A.," *Annuaire international de la fonction publique, 1973-1974*, p. 362.

depend to a very large extent on the contacts that one has established while serving in a ministerial cabinet. Now, one is more likely to be chosen by a minister for a ministerial cabinet post if one belongs to a grand corps because it is assumed that a member of such a corps will already have wide contacts. This is very clearly recognized by the elite, in both the public and private sectors (Table 4.3).

Although ENA graduates, and particularly members of the non-technical grands corps, predominate in ministerial cabinets, the members of the technical corps also play an important role. Table 4.4 shows the composition of all ministerial cabinets, and it can be seen that the technical corps are not without importance. Indeed, the competition among corps, and particularly between the technical and nontechnical corps, for places in ministerial cabinets is rather fierce. This competition is important for the individual corps because it reflects in a direct way on their organizational strength; and it is important for the individual member of the corps because of its impact on his career mobility. Indeed, as will be seen in subsequent chapters, it is at the level of competition for posts that conflicts within the elite occur rather than at the level of choices implying profound changes for the society. For the moment, it is sufficient simply to indicate the hold of the elite organizations on one of the key institutions in the political sector.

In addition to the important role that members of the grands

TABLE 4.3

Why Members of the Grands Corps are Chosen for Ministerial Cabinets[1]

Reasons	Public Sector		Private Sector	
	1st choice	2nd choice	1st choice	2nd choice
1. The members of the grands corps add to the prestige of ministerial cabinets	10.7 (6)	8.7 (5)	7.1 (4)	14.3 (8)
2. They possess a unique kind of general competence	32.8 (19)	36.2 (21)	35.7 (20)	35.7 (20)
3. They possess technical competence	3.4 (2)	5.2 (3)	3.6 (2)	5.4 (3)
4. They have a sense of reality	5.2 (3)	6.9 (4)	5.4 (3)	7.1 (4)
5. They dispose of a large network throughout the various sectors of society	43.1 (25)	39.7 (23)	44.6 (25)	33.9 (19)
6. Don't know	5.2 (3)	3.4 (2)	3.6 (2)	3.6 (2)
TOTAL	100.0 (58)	100.0 (58)	100.0 (56)	100.0 (56)

[1] Question: It has been observed that the staff of ministerial cabinets tends to be largely recruited from among members of the grands corps. Which two of the following reasons appear to you to be the most important for explaining this?

Note: The pairing of cells indicates 1st choice (top) and 2nd choice (bottom).

Table 4.4

Grands Corps in Ministerial Cabinets

Ministry	Total No. in Cabinet	Corps of Directeur de Cabinet	I.F.[1]	C.C.[2]	C.E.[3]	Prefectoral	Mines	Ponts et Chaussées	Total Corps Members
Presidency of Republic	25	I.F.	1	1	2	2	1	1	8
Prime Minister	23	Prefect	2	1	—	3	1	—	7
Defense	13	C.E.	—	1	2	1	1	—	5
Relations—parliament	4	—	—	—	—	1	—	—	1
Justice	9	—	—	—	1	1	—	—	2
Foreign affairs	9	—	1	—	—	—	—	—	1
Interior	12	C.E.	—	—	1	1	—	1	3
Economy & finance	12	I.F.	3	1	1	—	—	—	5
Education	9	Prefect	—	—	—	1	1	—	2
Industry & research	9	I.F.	1	—	—	—	2	1	4
Agriculture	9	C.E.	—	—	1	1	—	—	2
Transport	7	Ponts et Chaussées	—	—	—	—	1	1	2
Labor	9	—	—	—	1	—	1	1	2
Health	9	C.E.	—	—	2	1	—	—	3

[1] I.F.—Inspection des Finances.
[2] C.C.—Cour des Comptes.
[3] C.E.—Conseil d'Etat.

corps play in ministerial cabinets, they have also come to occupy under the Fifth Republic key political posts as ministers.[14] Few people, of course, have failed to be struck by the fact that the President of France is a graduate of the Ecole Polytechnique and of ENA, as well as being an Inspecteur des Finances, and that his first prime minister (Jacques Chirac) was a graduate of ENA and a member of the Cour des Comptes. Surely one cannot any longer be surprised by the fact that ENA, originally conceived as a school for the training of the *grands commis de l'Etat*, is now more and more seen by those who enter it as a school that leads only incidentally to an administrative career and that it is most likely to facilitate a political career. The graduates of this school are to be found not only in official posts; they serve in numerous other capacities that are highly political. For example, François Mitterrand has established a veritable opposition brain trust whose task is to analyze and make recommendations on all the various spheres of French society. The graduates of ENA, and members of the grands corps figure prominently on this team.[15]

That the holders of the key decision-making posts in the political sector have a loyalty to an institution which nurtured and promoted them is undeniable. The question is raised, however, as to the exact nature of the relationship between a minister, or a member of a ministerial cabinet, and his corps. This is a complex question, for it deals with the whole problem of elite integration and differentiation, as well as with the problem of roles. Although we will return to discuss this question in greater detail in Chapter Six, we need to note that the fact that ministers may belong to the grands corps does not necessarily mean that they will undertake to defend or promote their corps of origin. They may do so more tacitly than openly, and it is more likely to be the case that their corps will not be at the center of their preoccupations. It is undeniable, however, that they will choose as their colleagues or direct subordinates men (and this is almost exclusively a man's world) whose professional backgrounds are similar to theirs. This is because either they will know these men personally or they will know their

---

[14] See Pascal Antoni and Jean-Dominique Antoni, *Les Ministres de la Ve République* (Paris: Presses Universitaires de France, 1976). See also Mattei Dogan, "Comment on devient ministre en France, 1870-1976," a paper presented at the 10th World Congress of the International Political Science Association, Edinburgh, Scotland, August 1976.

[15] See "Les 'grosses têtes' de Mitterrand," in *Le Nouvel observateur*, 21-27 July 1975, pp. 22-23.

characteristics. Membership in a corps denotes a profile that carries with it certain qualities that are highly appreciated. This explains why members of this elite are simply defined as "X," "Mines," "Inspection," for the moment one's professional origins are established, one's essential characteristics are then defined. This clearly simplifies the formation of networks because the networks have an organizational structure. But these are highly complex networks and their bases are not merely, or even primarily, social. Rather, the networks are based on a highly successful educational background, membership in a corps, a rigorous working method, and an absence of expertise. This last factor may appear to be in contradiction with the training that the members of the elite undergo in specialized schools. But the contradiction disappears as soon as we understand that since the graduates of the grandes écoles are well represented in what may be termed the "command posts" in French society, the qualities they seek in a colleague or immediate subordinate need not be linked to a particular specialty. They are, in effect, recruiting leaders who, like themselves, need not—indeed, it is highly desirable that they should not—be specialists. This rationale enables the elite to recruit its own members with total justification, a fact that touches very closely the problem of the elite's legitimacy, which we will examine in the next chapter.

Public and Semipublic Sectors

In light of the fact that the grandes écoles ostensibly train people for the public sector, it should not be surprising to find that the graduates of these schools do in fact occupy the key posts in this sector. In a study that examined the nomination procedure to the directorial posts it was found that even when a minister appeared to have a wide latitude for naming directors in his ministry, he was in fact constrained by a number of factors, chief among which was the power of particular corps to monopolize particular posts.[16]

The importance of the grands corps in the ministries is not limited to the directorial posts. It can be found lower in the hierarchy, a fact that strengthens the hold of the corps on the ministries. It is a hold that is well-nigh unbreakable because each corps has what amounts to a monopoly over a given sector, which enables it in turn to exercise a monopoly over a ministry. The recog-

[16] Suleiman, *Politics, Power, and Bureaucracy in France*, pp. 137-151.

nition of mutual spheres of influence reduces .the possibilities of fierce competition among the corps. Thus, just as the Corps des Mines has an undisputed claim over the Ministry of Industrial Development and Scientific Research, so the Corps des Ponts et Chaussées has a similar claim over the Ministry of Equipment. This does not mean that a sphere of influence is immune from challenge, for it often happens that a corps is able to transcend its own ministry, thus succeeding in making inroads into the sphere of another corps. Alternatively, a new sphere is created and the competition for controlling it becomes very severe among the corps. This type of intra-elite competition is of paramount importance not, as we shall have occasion to see, because of the nature of the policies that are ultimately adopted but for the elite's adaptability which determines whether it will endure.

In addition to the administrative sector, there is also the semi-public, or nationalized, sector of the economy, which is relatively vast. This sector operates under different juridical statutes from the public sector proper and is, in some ways, more akin to the private sector. For example, appointments to directorial posts are at the discretion of the government and the salaries paid to directors are not covered by the limitations imposed by *statut de la fonction publique*, which makes remuneration much greater than for similar posts in the public sector. These posts have always been highly desirable, not only because of the high salaries, but because the semipublic sector, which has been protected by the state, was not expected to be very competitive. Thus, its directorial posts were more often than not regarded as rewards for public service. The Nora Report, in fact, proposed making the nationalized industries an integral part of the dynamic economy and suggested that they be given greater autonomy and made more competitive.[17]

That the members of the grands corps are well represented in the key posts in this sector can be seen from Table 4.5. Again, nominations are based partly on a recognition of spheres of influence among the various corps, and partly on political contacts. The nomination to the post of president or director-general of a nationalized industry constitutes, in effect, a reward for public service and a recognition that one is willing to move outside the mainstream of administrative power. Although this is not the case with, say, the president of Renault, it is very nearly the general case.

[17] Simon Nora, *Rapport sur les entreprises publiques* (Paris: La Documentation Française, 1967).

TABLE 4.5

Members of Grands Corps Holding Directorial Posts in Nationalized Sector

	Inspection des Finances	Conseil d'Etat	Cour des Comptes	Cour des Mines	Ponts et Chaussées	Prefectoral Corps	Admin. Civils	Total for Grands Corps	Grands Corps as % of Total No. of Directors
Establishments d'état	19	7	3	21	8	6	9	73	60.8
Société d'Economic Mixtes	1	5	2	5	8	5	2	28	46.5

Source: Calculated from *Nomenclature des entreprises nationales* (Paris: Imprimerie Nationale, 1973).

One does not move from being director-general of taxation at the Ministry of Finance to being president of the Compagnie Générale Transatlantique (which was to lose its chief asset, the luxury liner *The France*) without losing power.[18] Few within the elite deny the political nature of appointments to executive posts, as Table 4.6 shows. They recognize that nominations to such posts have always been a means for ministers to compensate their loyal collaborators with highly remunerative posts. Alternatively, the ouster from such posts can often be seen as a political punishment. As a result, these posts have been offered not to the most capable, but to those who have given the maximum service—political or otherwise—in ostensibly administrative posts; in a word, to the members of the grands corps.

INDUSTRY

Public service has always been regarded as the most illustrious of careers in France. This is still the case today, though it tends more and more to be seen as the main avenue to other careers. Just as entry into politics and the rise to ministerial posts is considerably facilitated by the stamp of distinction—a grande école education and membership in one of the grands corps—so it has become the case for entry into high executive posts in the private sector. The traditional disdain that characterized the attitudes of the state's servants to business and private affairs has now considerably abated. No longer do the state's agents regard with contempt those who are in positions to direct large industrial enterprises. There are many reasons for this change in attitude, a change which carries with it important ramifications for the formulation of public policy. We will examine both the reasons for this change and its consequences when we come to discuss how the notion of "serving the nation" has itself undergone a profound change. It is important to bear in mind that the economic transformations that France

---

[18] Dominique de la Martinière, an Inspecteur des Finances, who actually made this move, was a key supporter of Chaban-Delmas' candidacy for the presidency in May 1974. Shortly after Giscard d'Estaing was elected president, he ousted de la Martinière, who had been a former colleague at the Ministry of Finance, from the presidency of the C.G.T. Giscard also ousted François Bloch-Lainé, another Chaban supporter, from the presidency of the Credit Lyonnais, the largest public bank in France. For an explanation of Bloch-Lainé's removal, see his comments in *Profession: fonctionnaire* (Paris: Editions du Seuil, 1976), pp. 227-228.

TABLE 4.6

Why Members of the Grands Corps Are Chosen to Head Nationalized Industries[1]

Reasons	Public Sector		Private Sector	
1. The members of the grands corps add to the prestige of the nationalized sector	11.7 (7)	11.7 (7)	10.3 (6)	12.1 (7)
2. They possess a unique kind of general competence	13.3 (8)	13.3 (8)	15.5 (9)	13.8 (8)
3. They possess technical competence	3.3 (2)	1.7 (1)	3.4 (2)	1.7 (1)
4. They have a sense of reality	5.0 (3)	1.7 (1)	6.9 (4)	1.7 (1)
5. They dispose of a large network throughout the various sectors of society	25.1 (15)	23.3 (14)	31.0 (18)	24.1 (14)
6. They are chosen by the ministers and the government for political reasons	39.1 (24)	46.6 (28)	29.3 (17)	43.1 (25)
7. Don't know	1.7 (1)	1.7 (1)	3.4 (2)	3.4 (2)
TOTAL	100.0 (60)	100.0 (60)	100.0 (58)	100.0 (58)

[1] Question: It has been observed that the directors of the nationalized enterprises tend more and more frequently to be chosen from among members of the grands corps. Which two of the following reasons appear to you to be the most important for explaining this?

Note: The pairing of cells indicates 1st choice (top) and 2nd choice (bottom).

has undergone since World War II have not been without their impact on the administrative sector and on those seeking to enter it. The grandes écoles themselves have felt the impact of industrialization and have felt the need to adjust to the changing demands not only of the state but of the economy and the society as a whole.

The phenomenon of *pantouflage* has received considerable attention in recent years in large part because it is regarded as the clearest manifestation of the "technocratic state."[19] If one concentrates, however, on the shift in careers from the public to the private sectors, one misses the direct links that are established between the grandes écoles and the private sector. These schools now train people with a view toward providing the executives of the private sector. That the grandes écoles now have the major responsibility for training the presidents of the largest industrial enterprises has been clearly established. Their role in this regard vis-à-vis that of the universities is shown in Figure 4.2, which is derived from a comparative study of the presidents of the largest industrial enterprises in five countries. The results of the French part of the study are based on 159 responses, which represent about one-third of the 500 largest companies that questionnaires were sent to. For our purposes, what is important in this study—which offers no startling information about the presidents' social backgrounds, regional origins, and the like—is the importance of the grandes écoles in general, and of the Ecole Polytechnique in particular. The authors of the study make the following observation about the sample of company presidents:

> At least one-third of the P.D.G.'s have two or several diplomas and more than one-third of them belonged to a grand corps. The latter received a second diploma from another grande école, such as the Ecole des Mines or the Ecole des Ponts et Chaussées, after having graduated at the top of their class at Polytechnique. The other executives having more than one diploma are either graduates of a grande école who also have a licence from a university, or men with two licences. Only one P.D.G. out of ten did not have a higher education.[20]

[19] See David Granick, *The European Executive* (New York: Doubleday Anchor, 1962).

[20] D. Hall and M. de Bettignies, "L'Elite française des dirigeants de l'entreprise," *Hommes et techniques*, No. 291 (January 1968), p. 24.

Figure 4.2   Training of Presidents of Industrial Corporations

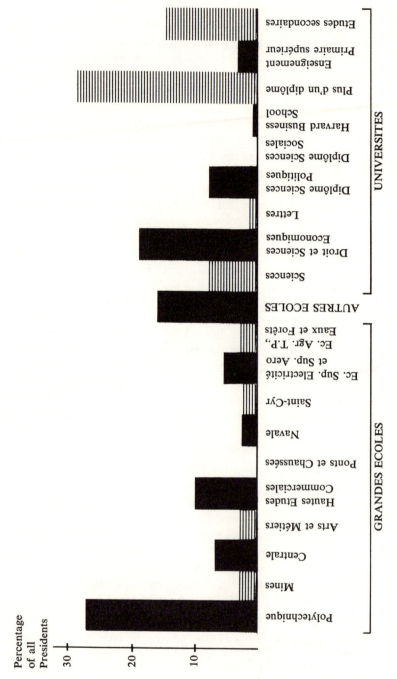

(Source: D. Hall and M. de Bettignies, "L'Elite française des dirigeants de l'entreprise," *Hommes et Techniques*, No. 291 [January 1968], p. 23.)

In a separate study that we have undertaken of the directors of the 500 largest industrial corporations in France where more complete data were obtained, the results were substantially similar. The data for the recent past suggest that the Ecole Polytechnique and the grandes écoles have become in recent years more important for the training of the highest executives. In a study of directors of industrial enterprises undertaken more than fifteen years ago, it was already possible to see that the importance of the grandes écoles had become an established fact. What the data from this study show (Table 4.7), when compared to the contemporary situation, is that the universities even then provided only a small proportion of the directors of industrial enterprises. A uni-

TABLE 4.7

Directors of Industrial Firms, According to Their Diplomas

	No. of Directors	Percent of Directors with Diplomas	Percent of Total No. of Directors
Ecole Polytechnique	456	21.4	15.5
Other engineering schools	640	30.1	21.7
Ecoles Supérieures professionelles	86	4.1	2.9
Ecole Militaire	56	2.6	1.9
Sciences	81	3.8	2.7
Letters	81	3.8	2.7
Law	188	8.8	6.4
Ecole des Sciences Politiques	190	8.9	6.4
Various studies (medicine, architecture, etc.)	23	1.2	0.8
No information	76	3.6	2.6
Total number with diplomas	2,126	100.0	72.1

Source: Delefortrie-Soubeyroux, *Les Dirigeants de l'industrie française* (Paris: Armand Colin, 1961), p. 58.

versity education, however, was a training that was no longer acceptable to industry. As the author of this study concluded at the time: "Those possessing diplomas are clearly becoming more frequent among the directors of enterprises. Promotion is certainly quicker for the most qualified executives, but there exists a transformation in the distribution of those possessing degrees: the scientists are proportionally more numerous among the youngest directors."[21]

That industry should be attracting the elite that was originally destined for the public sector can be explained in part by the development of large industrial enterprises that compete on an international scale. Because this is a relatively recent phenomenon, it follows that those belonging to the administrative elite would not have found the private sector nearly as attractive in the nineteenth century as they do today. This sector was dominated by family businesses which never attracted the *grands commis*. But this begs rather than answers a central question: when industrial development did begin to get under way and the need for industrial managers became evident, why was it the grandes écoles, and particularly the Ecole Polytechnique, that began to supply these managers? Why did the universities or other institutions not respond to this need? Of course, even in the United States, business schools are specialized schools outside of, or only marginally integrated into, the universities. Nevertheless, institutions might have been created in France to provide specialized training in the industrial and managerial techniques that were sorely needed in the private sector. Although a few such institutions were created—the Ecole Centrale and the Ecole des Hautes Etudes Commerciales (HEC) —and were quite successful, what occurred for the most part was that existing institutions with no particular bent for industry began to transform themselves and adjust to a new need.

In saying that the grandes écoles were the only institutions to respond to the needs of the private sector, we are not implying that the private sector did not have its own reasons for preferring the graduates of the grandes écoles irrespective of whether these graduates possessed the particular qualifications needed. This preference was shown particularly for those who had already passed through the administrative sector. Administrative experience was, to be sure, valued by industry, but so were the contacts that came with an administrative career. As large industrial enterprises succeeded, or took over the "capitalist dynasties," the directorates of these enterprises changed. Much has been written about the change

[21] Nicole Delefortrie-Soubeyroux, *Les Dirigeants de l'industrie française* (Paris: Armand Colin, 1961), p. 267. See also, Pierre Bize, "Nouvelles orientations intellectuelles des dirigeants des entreprises," *Sociologie du travail* (April-June 1960).

from family to managerial control of enterprises in all capitalist economies. What is important in the case of France is that "the posts went repeatedly, for the most part, to members of restricted elites whose members had access to the *grands corps de l'Etat*."[22] This phenomenon is clearly supported by the data that we have presented. The following chapters will seek to answer the question why this was the case. In so doing we shall also try to explain why industry is but one example of the manifestation of the growing importance of this elite which, as this chapter shows, has made similar inroads into other spheres of national life. This is a phenomenon that cannot really be explained by simple reference to the need for managers and the "rise of technocrats," for what allows such an elite to extend its position is precisely the *lack* of technical expertise. Expertise is, in fact, regarded as a handicap by this elite because of its confining aspect. Moreover, the question of why this particular elite should have stepped in everywhere would still need to be answered.

BANKING

Just as the nationalization of various sectors of the economy after the Second World War enabled the grands corps to extend its position, so the nationalization of the banks enabled them to occupy the major posts in all the banking and credit institutions. In effect, one corps—the Inspection des Finances—controls this sector to such an extent that it has now become difficult to conceive of a non-Inspecteur des Finances—let alone of someone not belonging to a grands corps—as a director of one of the major banks. Table 4.8 shows that the majority of Inspecteurs des Finances who are on leave from their corps or who have left it occupy posts in banking. Indeed, over 60 percent of the directors of the largest (public) banks in France are former Inspecteurs des Finances.[23]

[22] André Vène, *La Lutte du pouvoir dans les sociétés par actions* (Paris: Les Editions d'Organisations, 1972), p. 43. For additional data on the role of the grands corps in industry, see Pierre Birnbaum, *Les Sommets de l'état: essai sur l'élite du pouvoir en France* (Paris: Editions du Seuil, 1977), pp. 142-144.

[23] Jeffrey L. Malek, "An Empirical Study of the Composition of French Bank Directors," unpublished paper, 1975. For further data on bank directors, see François Morin, *La Structure financière du capitalisme français* (Paris: Calmann-Levy, 1974).

TABLE 4.8

Distribution of Members of Inspection des
Finances, by Sector

Inspection des Finances	*Commissions*	*Adminis- tration*	*Minis- terial Cabinets*	*Ministers, Deputies, or Mayors*	*Banking & Credit*
51	20	54	18	7	87

Insur- ance	*Industry*	*Public*	*Other*	*Total*
6	47	12	10	292

Source: Calculated from Yearbook, Inspection des Finances, 1972.

The hold the Inspection des Finances has over the banking sector is by no means a novel phenomenon. As Lalumière notes in his study of the Inspection des Finances, the nationalized banks "constitute the preferred sector of the Inspecteurs des Finances who in this domain face no competition from another specialized corps."[24] He notes, too, that only part of the banking sector is nationalized, but that "nationalized or not, it's according to the same processes that the directorial posts continue to be allocated. Tradition has won out."[25]

Nothing has occurred in the past century to displace the Inspecteurs des Finances from the banking sector. On the contrary, they have steadily increased their hold on the directorial posts in newly created banks and credit institutions. Although the Inspecteurs des Finances have had experience in some aspect that touches the economy, it cannot be said that they have any particular expertise in the area of banking. They generally enter banking at the highest levels and thus do not even give themselves the opportunity of learning the métier before becoming directors. It's not surprising that any discussion of banks in France, particularly when this in-

[24] Pierre Lalumière, *L'Inspection des Finances* (Paris: Presses Universitaires de France, 1959), p. 154.
[25] *Ibid.*, p. 155.

volves a critical examination, should point to the preponderant position of the Inspecteurs des Finances. "The Minister of Finance assures comfortable resting places for his higher civil servants. MM. Maurice Lauré, Jacques Chaine, and Pierre Ledoux, respectively presidents of the Société Générale, the Credit Lyonnais and the B.N.P., are, like most of their collaborators or younger colleagues, all Inspecteurs des Finances. And the general view is that the proportion of Inspecteurs des Finances in banks has reached a critical level."[26] However, since banking is a sector that provides prestigious, secure, and well-paying jobs for those fortunate enough to have entered the Inspection, there is no doubt that the hold on this sector will remain in the hands of this corps whether they are qualified for the job or not. As Michel Drancourt put it: "Examples of glorious careers can be found in all the corps of the state, but the most spectacular are those of certain Inspecteurs des Finances."[27]

EDUCATION

There is one sector where we might not expect to find graduates of the grandes écoles and members of the grands corps present in significant numbers—the educational sector. Yet, they play a very important role that has both positive and negative aspects. The members of this elite teach only in the grandes écoles, where, as the following tables show, they constitute in some cases up to 90 percent of the teaching staff. Their teaching responsibilities reflect their professional preoccupations; consequently, they seek to transmit practical knowledge and to serve as models for the next generation of the elite. Second, because they themselves have been trained in the grandes écoles and because they now teach in these schools, they help to contribute in important ways to the separation between the universities and the grandes écoles. Higher education means for them an education that is practical, concrete, useful, and not abstract, theoretical, and of little immediate use to the society. In short, the type of education that needs hardly any justification is that dispensed by the grandes écoles. This view of the purpose of education has a further consequence: it di-

[26] "A Quoi servent les banques nationales?" *L'Express*, 6-12 January 1975, p. 27. Jacques Chaine was assassinated in 1976.
[27] Michel Drancourt, *Les Clés du pouvoir* (Paris: Fayard, 1964), p. 115.

TABLE 4.9

Professional Background of Teaching Staff:
Ecole Nationale des Ponts et Chaussées

Ponts et Chaussées	Conseil d'Etat	Architects[a]	Academic	Total
231	13	10	6	260

[a] Some of these are graduates of the school.

TABLE 4.10

Professional Background of Teaching Staff:
Ecole Nationale des Mines de Paris

Mines	CNRS	Academic[a]	Other	Total
104	20	30	46	210

[a] Many in this category are graduates of the school, but they have full-time appointments as professors.

TABLE 4.11

Professional Background of Teaching Staff:
Institut d'Etudes Politiques de Paris

	Inspection des Finances	Conseil d'Etat	Cour des Comptes	Total Grands Corps	Academic[a]	Other	Total
Corps enseignant	11	10	9	36	54	27	117
Seminars: Politics and economics	6	8	20	35	1	25	61
Seminars: Political and administrative institutions	—	21	9	30	2	13	45
Seminars: economics	15	—	11	26	9	88[b]	128

[a] Includes all ranks from *assistant* to *professeur*, as well as full-time research appointments.

[b] Includes 41 who are civil servants but not members of the grands corps (15 of whom are *administrateurs civils* from the Ministry of Finance), and 47 who are employed in the private sector (banking, industry, and commerce).

minishes respect for research.[28] This may account in part for
the unfortunate and detrimental separation between teaching and
research in France. This situation is not peculiar to the grandes
écoles, but it is possible to understand why this should be the case
in these schools where education is conceived of as "instruction,"
to use Renan's term—where, in other words, the purpose is merely
to transmit a certain amount of knowledge that is likely to have
practical applications and to surround the younger generation of
the elite with models. As Shinn noted in his historical study of the
Ecole Polytechnique:

> The presence of Polytechnicians as administrators, profes-
> sors, and disciplinary personnel made it easy to develop a
> Polytechnician spirit. This spirit was based on the principles
> of hierarchy, discipline and patriotism. Students were taught
> to give their first allegiance to the State and to their fellows.
> The development of this spirit was readily achieved by oblig-
> ing students to live as well as to study at the institution. Stu-
> dents spent their time in a closed universe where the con-
> stant surveillance of their officers and fellows assured the im-
> possibility of the diversification of behavior or attitude.
> Hence, the circle was formed loyal to itself, to the institution
> which formed it, and to the philosophy and prerogatives of
> the *haute bourgeoisie*.[29]

Nor is this peculiar to France, for the transmission of knowledge
is, in effect, secondary when compared with the importance that
an elite attaches to the transmission of values. The headmasters of
English public schools have been described in much the same way,
for their task consisted, like the teachers in the grandes écoles,
of serving as models:

> From a statistical analysis the most striking fact about these
> headmasters is that they are predominantly drawn from the
> public schools themselves. The majority have moved from
> public schools to the cloistered worlds of Oxford and Cam-
> bridge, and then back again to public schools, with perhaps
> an intermission in the form of military service. They have
> tended to spend the greater part of their lives among people

[28] A few of the grandes écoles (Polytechnique, the Ecole Normale, the
Ecole des Mines) have important research laboratories.
[29] Shinn, "The Dawning of an Elite," p. 603.

and in places where the characteristics of the public school are accepted.[30]

Those who teach in the grandes écoles, being to a large extent members of the grands corps, were themselves the most successful students at these schools. The model for the students is therefore a very particular one: it represents the strongest commitment to the school, and, being the epitome of success, it is the one that will most likely inspire emulation. As one of the respondents—a student at ENA—in Schonfeld's study put it so well:

> The role of the maître de conférence [teacher] is very directive, because he is not simply the dispenser of knowledge, but more importantly, he is a social model on which the students must pattern themselves. The maître de conférence is, generally, an alumnus (of the school) who has succeeded; the alumnus of ENA who is Inspector of Finances or subdirector of a ministry. He is the social model on which everyone models himself. This mimicry is unbelievable; it goes far beyond the intellectual domain, almost to the affective domain—it includes questions as to how to dress and the structure of the language—in the sense that the vocabulary, sentences, and patterns of thought closely imitate those of the maître de conférence.[31]

Equally important is the fact that the members of the grands corps who teach in the grandes écoles have had different professional experiences. The members of the same corps who graduated from the same grande école will return to teach as civil servants, industrialists, politicians, financiers. Despite their specialized training, they do not represent an elite confined to a narrow sector. Therefore, entrusting pedagogical responsibilities in the grandes écoles to the most successful graduates of these schools has decisive advantages. This is especially evident in view of the fact that the *cours magistraux* (large lectures) are generally given by full-time academicians, whereas the seminars, the *travaux pratiques*—the very kind of teaching that allows for a personal rapport between teacher and student—are entrusted to nonacademi-

---

[30] Ian Weinberg, *The English Public Schools: The Sociology of Elite Education* (New York: Atherton Press, 1967), p. 86.

[31] William R. Schonfeld, *Obedience and Revolt: French Behavior Toward Authority* (Beverly Hills: Sage Publications, 1976), p. 76.

cians, the successful members of the elite whose principal activity is wholly unrelated to an academic or research career.[32] Teaching, for these teachers, is an incidental activity, but one that is important both for the elite and for the schools. As John Armstrong has said of ENA's teachers: "These men are carefully selected by the school's council not only for their expert knowledge of administration but for their ability to inspire—i.e., to socialize—students to the values of the elite administration. Increasingly instructors have been alumni of ENA itself, only a decade removed in age and experience from the students they guide. The ambitious student is set a model sufficiently close in age to make the rewards of emulation seem proximate and calculable."[33] In its earlier years, the Corps des Mines used only members of the corps as teachers in all its schools, not only in the Ecole des Mines de Paris but in its schools in Saint-Etienne, Alais, and Douai.[34] In fact, as André Thépot notes, no corps matches the Corps des Mines in the importance it accords teaching, which is why it prefers to leave the training of its future members exclusively in the hands of its current members.[35]

To have the members of the elite act as *maîtres* undoubtedly increases the desire for emulation; it also indicates to the students that "success" can be achieved in any number of areas and that it need not be confined to a specialized area. In addition, it has certain advantages for the training of the future generation of this elite who, while not being exposed to widely differing viewpoints, are at least provided with a certain amount of diversity. However, the most important aspect of this system is its ability to renew or replenish the elite's ranks in a carefully controlled manner, practically in accordance with Pareto's theory of the circulation of elites. For the elite has devised a system that allows for the careful selection of those desiring to enter its ranks and for the painstaking

[32] At the Institut d'Etudes Politiques in Paris, even large lecture courses are very often given by nonacademic members of the elite. At ENA, all teaching is done within the framework of seminars. For a succinct statement of the advantages that the elite sees in having "professionals" teach, see Bloch-Lainé, *Profession: fonctionnaire*, pp. 151-154. Bloch-Lainé regrets that the example of the Institut d'Etudes Politiques did not become more widespread (p. 150).

[33] John A. Armstrong, *The European Administrative Elite* (Princeton: Princeton University Press, 1973), pp. 196-197.

[34] See André Thépot, *Le Corps des Mines*, Thèse de Doctorat d'Etat, forthcoming, p. 222.

[35] *Ibid.*

transference of knowledge and of values.[36] The contact between present and future generations of the elite continues uninterruptedly from the moment one has passed the first selection hurdle. It is hardly surprising that those who come to the defense of the grandes écoles almost always insist on the selection process as the feature that distinguishes these schools most from the universities.

If the use of the elite in teaching future generations of the elite has undeniable advantages for the circulation of elites in France, it also has certain disadvantages for the society. In the first place, higher education comes to mean for the elite no more and no less than the education that is dispensed by the grandes écoles. The elite has no contact with and no appreciation of the universities, which have come to be regarded as one of the prices that society has to pay for democracy. It follows that the distinction between the two types of institutions is accentuated. Second, the distinction between theory and practice comes to assume a real importance in pedagogy. That which is "concrete" and "useful" is regarded as the ultimate virtue of an educational system, whereas theory, ideas, and the accumulation of knowledge are seen as having a marginal value to the society. Third, and this is a corollary of the preceding factor, there comes to exist a disjunction between the students in the grandes écoles and the educational process outside of the grandes écoles. As Armstrong observes: "By limiting academic instructors to about one-tenth, ENA effectively interrupts the relation of its students to educational elites. Politically this removes a leftist influence from an administrative body which has been consistently, though slightly, right of center, and facilitates rapprochement with private sector managerial elites."[37] Finally, this system undoubtedly helps foster what amounts to anti-intellectual attitudes on the part of the elite. The disdain for theory that is so characteristic of this elite helps to explain the attitude of the governments of the Fourth and Fifth republics toward the universities and the grandes écoles. For theory implies more than the quest for knowledge; it is often a euphemism for *contestation*. Because it involves constant questioning, it is inherently dangerous. It precludes unconditional service and loyalty. By contrast, a utilitarian, practical education involves, not just the acquisition of a given body of knowledge, but by assuring its recipient a privileged

[36] See Vilfredo Pareto, *The Mind and Society: A Treatise on General Sociology*, Vol. 2 (New York: Dover Publications, 1963), pp. 1,421-27.
[37] Armstrong, *The European Administrative Elite*, p. 197.

place in the social as well as in the professional hierarchy, it leads to the acceptance of the existing order. Hence the contribution of the grandes écoles to political stability which governments of all shades have recognized.

In attempting to show the place of the state-created elite in French society, I have tried to show the consequences of the educational system that I described in Part One. To the extent that the members of this elite are trained by the state, have experience in public service, and are linked to organizational structures that form part of the state apparatus—the corps—we are justified in speaking of a state-created elite. It may be argued that not all members of this elite rise to the top, or that a majority who pass through the grandes écoles and even enter a grands corps do not attain the summits of power. This is undoubtedly so, but it does not alter the fact that, as the data in this chapter show, membership in the grands corps gives one extraordinary advantages for reaching the top in a variety of sectors. Surely one cannot quarrel with the observation that all Inspecteurs des Finances cannot become bank presidents. But one can raise questions about the fact that membership in the Inspection is a crucial requirement for becoming a bank president.

The concern of the following chapters is not with the theme of privilege and inequality in French society, about which much has already been said and to which we will return again. Instead, we shall look at the existence and growing importance of the elites and their institutions as a given, and we shall attempt to analyze the factors that account for their endurance.

❊ Chapter Five ❊

SELF-IMAGE AND LEGITIMACY

IN order properly to understand the role of the dominant elite in French society it is not sufficient merely to describe its position in the society. Nor, as we indicated at the outset of the study, can one understand the bases of its power by merely examining its social composition. What is essential, and what has been lacking in studies of governing elites, is an understanding of the elements on which the elite bases and in turn justifies its dominant position. All the more does this need explaining in view of the fact that elitist ideas and organizations have maintained their hold in societies that proclaim their unequivocal commitment to democracy. The coexistence of powerful democratic norms and forces on the one hand, and of elitist reality on the other, requires explanation. While democracy may not be the sham that its numerous enemies of the Left and the Right have claimed it is, neither is the existence of elitism a mere illusion. The question whether a particular society is "democratic" or "elitist" is not one that concerns us here, because it is clear that few societies can be characterized as being exclusively one or the other—hence the attempts of men like Schumpeter to reconcile them in terms of what has been referred to as "democratic elitism."[1] Our approach to this problem is more modest for it seeks to deal with the question of the perseverance of certain forms of elitist rule in democratic societies.

Elites that rule for considerable periods in ostensibly democratic societies achieve a certain degree of acceptance. Their dominance is anchored in something that is fundamental to the society, something that allows for their endurance. It does not matter that the legitimizing base of the elite's power is not universally accepted, for no leadership group, whether in an organization or in a regime, has the luck of enjoying universal acceptance. It matters only that, by its actions, the elite comes not to elicit the opprobrium of the

[1] Peter Bacharach, *The Theory of Democratic Elitism* (Boston: Little, Brown & Co., 1967).

society as a whole. This means, at the very least, that the elite is aware of itself and that it seeks, consciously, to attain a certain degree of legitimacy. Self-image and legitimacy are, then, crucial elements in the survival of elites. Before we turn to an examination of these two dimensions as they pertain to the French elite, we need to look briefly at their theoretical significance.

THEORETICAL PERSPECTIVE

The manner in which an elite views itself on the one hand, and the degree of acceptance it enjoys in the society on the other, raise two different sets of problems that are by no means unrelated. The self-image of the elite is partly a psychological state that affects the members of the elite as individuals; the elite's acceptance by the society concerns its actions, its behavior, its role, which are judged by those who do not belong to it. The task of the elite is therefore a difficult one, for it needs to reconcile two goals that are seemingly irreconcilable: to believe in itself—to have, in other words, the kind of self-image that is required of a leadership group —it must embrace norms that run counter to those that govern the society; to fulfill, at least minimally, what the society expects of it, it must act in accordance not with the norms that govern its image but with those that govern the society. The more successful the elite is in transferring the key elements of its self-image to the society, the greater will be its chance for endurance. Frank Bonilla touched on this problem in his study of Venezuelan elites when he noted that the preservation of an elite's self-image requires that the elite not be constantly subject to pressures from those over whom it exercises authority:

> At issue here is a fundamental feature of self-image among elites and a keystone of any ideology or theory of political development. As a result of the consolidation of elite power in countries where democracy has survived longest, such groups have come to be widely regarded as the most genuinely dynamic and innovative force and as the guarantors of continuity in national systems. In this view the vital functions of the gifted, the expert, and the entrepreneurially able require that they be shielded from mass pressures.[2]

[2] Frank Bonilla, *The Failure of Elites* (Cambridge, Mass.: The M.I.T. Press, 1970), p. 256.

This reference to Venezuelan elites emphasizes the two most important points concerning the acceptance of elites: the self-image of the elite and the acquiescence of the outside world to this image. Now, before an elite can even acquire legitimacy in the society, it must recognize itself as an elite; its members must share, in Shils' words, "some sense of affinity which, more or less, unites the different sectors of the elite." He goes on to say:

> This sense of affinity rests ultimately on the high degree of proximity to the center which is shared by all these different sectors of the ruling class. They have, it is true, a common vested interest in their position. It is not, however, simply the product of a perception of a coalescent interest; it contains a substantial component of mutual regard arising from a feeling of a common relationship to the central value system.[3]

The "central value system" serves to link the members of the elite by making them share what they define as the ultimate goals of the society. "This consensus has its ultimate root in their common feeling for the transcendent order which they believe they embody or for which they think themselves responsible."[4] However, regardless of the affinity that members of the elite share and regardless of how much they believe that they are "fit to rule," they cannot long endure if the society does not in some measure accept the elite and its view of itself. Shils suggests that the possession of power by the elite allows the elite to profit from what he calls "the charisma which informs the center."[5] He maintains, in a rather general fashion, that "the qualities which account for the expansiveness of authority have come to be shared more widely by the population, far from the center in which the incumbents of the positions of authority reside. In the eyes of the elites of the modern states of the West, the mass of the population have somehow come to share in the vital connection with the 'order' which inheres in the central value system and which was once thought to be in the special custody of the ruling classes."[6] In other words, it is imperative that an elite possess self-confidence and willingly accept being regarded as the elite. Unless this is the case, there can be no harmony between the elite and the nonelite. Ralf Dahrendorf has argued at length, for example, that the elite in Germany lacks

[3] Edward Shils, *Center and Periphery: Essays in Macro-sociology* (Chicago: University of Chicago Press, 1975), p. 12.
[4] *Ibid.*   [5] *Ibid.*, p. 15.   [6] *Ibid.*, pp. 15-16.

the cohesion, unity, and self-confidence that are indispensable for a democratic elite. "Germany's political class," he writes, "governs its society against its own will."[7] This has serious consequences for the ability of the elite to govern. As he noted, one of the consequences is that:

> Nobody wants to consider himself a member of the elite or the powerful. Another is that nobody is in fact regarded as belonging to this elite. Thus the public image of those politically at the top corresponds to their own self-image. This does not alter the position of the powerful, of course, but it underlines the suspicion that actually there is no elite, because the elites lack self-confidence and a sense of social cohesion.[8]

Thus, two inseparable requirements of effective rule are postulated by Dahrendorf: the willingness of the elite to see itself as the elite—that is, to have a measure of self-consciousness—and the willingness of the nonelite to accept the leadership of the elite. He maintains that both are necessary and that both are lacking in Germany. The German elite, according to Dahrendorf, not only lacks ties, what Shils calls the "sense of affinity," but it carries with it a "defensive attitude,"[9] all of which severely reduces its ability to govern. One need not advocate the opposite extreme of a totally unified elite that is separated from the rest of society by class background, culture, and interests, for the result would be oligarchy, at best. To say, however, that an elite needs self-confidence in its ability to govern is to postulate a key element in its ability to survive. To say, moreover, that its members need to share a mutual regard is to suggest but another factor that contributes to its self-confidence. As Schumpeter, one of the most perceptive analysts of social classes, observed:

> Yet one essential peculiarity—possibly a consequence, possibly an intermediate cause—of the class phenomenon lies in the fact that class members behave toward one another in a fashion characteristically different from their conduct toward members of other classes. They are in closer association with one another; they understand one another better; they work more readily in concert; they close ranks and erect

[7] Ralf Dahrendorf, *Society and Democracy in Germany* (New York: Doubleday & Co., 1967), p. 278.
[8] *Ibid.*   [9] *Ibid.*, p. 269.

barriers against the outside; they look out into the same segment of the world, with the same eyes, from the same viewpoint, in the same direction.[10]

If elites, or classes, lack "a sense of affinity," if "they are not a real group, stratum, or class, but a mere category," they become only, what Dahrendorf calls, an "abstract elite."[11] Hence, their ability to endure becomes highly problematical, for they cannot acquire a sufficient degree of legitimacy. Elite survival depends on the willingness to exercise power and on the elite's ability to fashion an ideology that it uses to legitimize itself. As Dahrendorf put it: "There is no political class in history that has willingly and happily abdicated its possession of authority. For those who have, or once had it, power holds a strange fascination. For that very reason power waxes men inventive. It is almost invariably surrounded by ideologies of legitimacy, which adduce tradition, divine grace, or the law in order to support the establishment of those at the top. These ideologies are, strictly speaking, instruments of mystification; yet they are permissible weapons as long as they do not prevent the other side from returning them in kind."[12] But the legitimacy of an elite, or its ability to effect successful "mystification," is not acquired once and for all. Like the charismatic leader who needs to renew his "magical powers" continually,[13] legitimacy needs to be sustained. That it often is not renewed is one of the chief factors leading to the decline of elites. For just as spectacular successes and actions are the bases of the charismatic leader's power, so the acceptance of the elite by the society must be continually maintained. This means that an elite that wishes to endure cannot long remain oblivious to the need to maintain ties with the society. One could see, Dahrendorf argues, that the rule of the elite of Imperial Germany was coming to an end "because this elite had no basis in civil society" so that "it had to try to sever the ties that connected society with government and . . . to force both into a synthetic rank order."[14]

Now, the ties that the elite maintains with society can be more

[10] Joseph Schumpeter, *Imperialism and Social Classes* (New York: The World Publishing Company, 1971), pp. 107-108.

[11] Dahrendorf, *Society and Democracy in Germany*, p. 277.

[12] *Ibid.*, pp. 218-219.

[13] Max Weber, *The Theory of Social and Economic Organization* (New York: The Free Press, 1965), p. 364.

[14] Dahrendorf, *Society and Democracy in Germany*, p. 221.

or less tenuous, and they can be based on certain myths which the elite embraces and which it tries to foist on the society. The more the elite itself believes in these myths, the easier it will be to have them accepted by the society. Hence, self-image and legitimacy are intimately related. An elite securely anchors itself in the society when the elements, mythical or not, that underlie its power become the generally accepted norms of the society. The deference which society has accorded the highborn, and which constituted Bagehot's explanation of the functioning of British democracy, manifests precisely the symmetry between the elite's belief in its capacity to rule and the society's acceptance of the elite's belief in itself. If the elite loses its self-confidence, if it loses the exalted image of itself, or if the society ceases to accept it—the two are often linked —then that signals the beginning of the end of the elite's rule. The loss of confidence, followed by the society's withdrawal of support, leads to internal conflicts within the elite and so accelerates its demise. "Except during short intervals of time, peoples are always governed by an elite," wrote Pareto. "I use the word elite in its etymological sense, meaning the strongest, the most energetic, and the most capable—for good as well as evil. However, due to an important physiological law, elites do not last. Hence, the history of men is the history of the continuous replacement of certain elites: as one ascends, another declines."[15]

Pareto suggested that elites come to lose their legitimacy because they take their power for granted and their arrogance eventually leads them to lose their sense of responsibility, after which their demise becomes inevitable. Once they are no longer in tune with their society, they will begin to perish. Pareto argues that two signs manifest themselves simultaneously when an elite declines: "The declining elite becomes softer, milder, more humane and less apt to defend its own power," and, at the same time, "it does not lose its rapacity and greed for the goods of others, but rather tends as much as possible to increase its unlawful appropriations and to indulge in major usurpation of the national patrimony." The consequence is that "on the one hand it makes the yoke heavier, and on the other it has less strength to maintain it. These two conditions cause the catastrophe in which the elite perishes, whereas it could prosper if one of them were absent."[16]

[15] Vilfredo Pareto, *The Rise and Fall of Elites* (New York: Bedminster Press, 1968), p. 36.
[16] *Ibid.*, p. 59.

Pareto's analysis of the decline of elites is not always easy to follow because one is tempted to see in it a rather severe critique of the "humanitarianism" of elites. He sees in such actions a sign of weakness and a manifestation of the "effete" nature of these elites. He maintains that an elite must always be prepared to defend itself and never hesitate to use force. Like Taine, he is remorseless in his critique of Louis XVI, whom he believes could have survived had he only been willing to fight. The humanitarian sentiments which elites often display are merely signs that they are not prepared to use the force necessary to defend themselves. But if Pareto insists on the willingness of the elite to fight to preserve itself, he is also saying that an elite that cannot do this is an elite that no longer believes in itself or in its capacity to rule. Without self-confidence (that needs to characterize the self-image of all elites) no elite can long remain in power. Moreover, the willingness of elites to use force and not to carry their humanitarian actions to great lengths is only one aspect of Pareto's analysis of the decline of elites, and undoubtedly the one that has led to his classification as a reactionary theorist. It would be a mistake, however, to ignore another side of Pareto's analysis, one that stresses the elite's need to remain constantly on guard to preserve its acceptance by the society.

> Our ruling class is insatiable; as its power wanes, its fraudulent practices increase. Every day in France, in Italy, in Germany, in America, it demands new tightenings of duties, new provisions to safeguard trade, new obstacles to commerce under the pretext of sanitary provisions, new subsidies of every kind. . . . Such is the method of despoiling the poor, applied by our foremost "humanitarians." Congresses against tuberculosis are fine, but it would be even better not to steal the bread from those who starve and it would also be preferable, either to be a little less "humanitarian," or to respect the property of others a little more.[17]

Mosca exhibits the same concerns as Pareto with the ability of the elite to defend itself and to preserve its legitimacy. The elite begins to decline, he notes, when there "is decline in energy in the upper class, which grows poorer and poorer in bold aggressive characters and richer in 'soft,' remissive individuals."[18] He empha-

[17] *Ibid.*, pp. 69-70.

[18] Gaetano Mosca, *The Ruling Class* (New York: McGraw-Hill, 1939), p. 117.

sizes, however, to a far greater extent than Pareto, the elite's need to be considered legitimate. For him, the maintenance of power always requires a justification that is more or less universally accepted. "In fairly populous societies that have attained a certain level of civilization, ruling classes do not justify their power exclusively by de facto possession of it, but try to find a moral and legal basis for it, representing it as the logical and necessary consequence of doctrines and beliefs that are generally recognized and accepted."[19]

The misfortunes that befall elites are, according to Pareto and Mosca, due ultimately to the inability of those elites to carry out their functions in a responsible manner. They eventually lose legitimacy both in their own eyes and in the eyes of those they govern. The first is as important as the second, for once they cease to regard themselves as being fit to rule, they become unable to rule. There is no contradiction, therefore, between a self-image of superiority and responsible behavior; the two may indeed belong together, for self-assurance on the part of the elite leads to actions whose purpose is to attain legitimacy. When the self-image of superiority and confidence falters, for whatever reason, the elite will no longer be able to act in a responsible manner, and it will be more and more inclined to lose touch with the society, to be greedy and defensive; at this point, its end is in sight. As Mosca put it: ". . . and so it may come about that considerable portions of the governing class, especially the circles that give the society its intellectual tone and direction, lose the habit of dealing with people of the lower classes and commanding them directly. This state of affairs generally enables frivolousness, and a sort of culture that is wholly abstract and conventional, to supplant a vivid sense of realities and a sound and accurate knowledge of human nature."[20]

The elitist theorists, particularly Mosca and Pareto, have often been criticized for the antidemocratic implications of their theories. That they did not believe in the basic equality of man is not open to question, neither is the fact that their theories have often been put to use by political movements that have sought to destroy democracy. Our purpose in referring to their theories is to salvage certain analytical insights that these theories contain and to apply them to an empirical situation. Both Pareto and Mosca remain relevant because their theories deal with the problem of leadership

[19] *Ibid.*, p. 70.　　　　　　　　[20] *Ibid.*, p. 118.

in modern democratic societies. We refer to their theories because we wish to understand the bases of the elite's power, as well as its capacity for survival. We have already suggested that the image which the elite has of itself is crucial to this discussion. We have also suggested that an elite's actions need to be such as to win for it legitimacy and acceptance. In addition, there are two other factors that are of primordial importance: the organizational structure of the elite and the capacity of the elite to adapt to changing conditions in the society. All these factors are intimately linked with one another, for the organizational structure of the elite determines the solidarity of the members of the elite, the "sense of affinity"; it also determines the flexibility of the elite, its capacity to adapt to new requirements, which ultimately affects both the self-image of the elite and its legitimacy. Consequently, in attempting to analyze the survival of elites in France, we are inevitably dealing with internal aspects of the elites—organization, solidarity, self-image— and with their external relations—policies, behavior, and adaptation. This, and the following two chapters, will be devoted to an analysis of these key elements in the stability of elites in France.[21]

SELECTION, SUPERIORITY, AND SECURITY

The elite that is produced by the grandes écoles is often criticized for being "self-assured" and for exhibiting an attitude of superiority. There is a good deal of truth in this characterization. What is also true, however, is that the elite is not defensive about its feelings of superiority. The specialized schools do not hide the fact that their task is essentially that of training leaders who are rigorously selected precisely because they are distinguished by their superior qualities. From the very outset, even before gaining entry into a grande école, a student who prepares for the concours comes to see himself as preparing for a privileged position in society. Once he succeeds in gaining entry into a grande école, that privileged position is secured. He is treated as a future member of the elite, and he is made aware that his education is highly distinct from that of the rest of the population. Is it any wonder that his ambitions should come to know few bounds? Perhaps no one has better described this than Balzac in his severe attack on the grandes écoles

---

[21] On the general problem of elite transformation, see the fine discussion in Robert D. Putnam, *The Comparative Study of Political Elites* (Englewood Cliffs, N. J.: Prentice-Hall, 1976), pp. 165-214.

in *Le Curé de village*. In the famous letter of Gérard to Grossetete, the young man writes: "At the age of twenty-one, I possessed a knowledge of the mathematical sciences as far as they had been developed by so many men of genius, and I was impatient to distinguish myself by continuing their work. This desire is so natural that almost all the students [of the Ecole Polytechnique] have, upon graduation, their eyes fixed upon that moral sun known as *la Gloire*! The first thought of all of us was to be Newtons, Laplaces or Vaubans. Such are the efforts that France demands of the young who graduate from this celebrated School!"[22] While Gérard's letter argues, in effect, that the nature of the education dispensed by the Ecole Polytechnique and the grandes écoles in general precludes the development of scientific genius, the fact remains that it instills the search for "Glory" because of the belief in one's superiority. There is no denying that the Ecole Polytechnique has always regarded as its central mission the training of France's elite. In resisting the reforms that the early governments of the Third Republic were trying to push through, the defenders of the Ecole Polytechnique argued that the reforms were simply aimed at destroying one of France's greatest accomplishments. In his study of the Ecole Polytechnique, Shinn summarizes the arguments put forward by one of the defenders of the school:

> The strict discipline, hierarchy, and emphasis on order found in the EP was essential to the development of "character." Polytechnicians [it was argued] were men of conviction and made outstanding leaders. They were not prone to caprice and anarchy as were the graduates of *facultés*. . . . [It was] gladly admitted that the EP trained an elite, but not an elite in the pre-1789 aristocratic sense. Instead the Polytechnician elite was a meritocracy. Polytechnicians were men of power and importance because they were more capable than others in society. It was unthinkable . . . that everyone in France must decline to the level of the lowest simply in order to escape being labeled an elite. An elite, the writer concluded, was necessary and desirable—and Polytechnicians were France's finest.[23]

[22] Honoré de Balzac, *Le Curé de village* (Paris: Garnier-Flammarion, 1967), p. 183. The novel was published in 1846.

[23] Terry Shinn, "The Dawning of an Elite: The Ecole Polytechnique and the Polytechnician Circles" (unpublished manuscript, 1973), pp. 407-408.

Because the members of the elite pass through a rigorous selection process before reaching their positions, they have a firm belief in their competence. Table 5.1 shows that they attach a great importance to the belief that they, together with their institutions, help ensure the effective and continuous functioning of state (broadly defined) services. They see themselves as being able to do this largely because of their qualifications.

Although those in the public sector are more inclined than their counterparts in the private sector to link the task of ensuring the continuity of state services with their unrivaled competence, there is nonetheless an equally firm belief on the part of the private sector elite in the competence of those who have been tested by the grandes écoles and molded by the grands corps. Life for those who have experienced the rigor and the pace of work within these institutions has consisted of a long series of hurdles. To arrive at their present position, they have always had to be among the most successful of their generation. Hence, they are scarcely inclined to question their competence.

Apart from showing the extent to which the elite believes itself to be highly qualified, Table 5.1 also shows that this elite views itself as being chiefly responsible for shouldering the burden of carrying out the day-to-day activities on behalf of the state. That this burden will pass on to a generation of similarly trained people ensures "continuity" and "regularity." Far less importance is attached to the "homogeneity" of the elite and to the need to select an elite with sufficient authority. This is probably because the term "homogeneity" may suggest an ascriptive pattern of recruitment which is in flat contradiction to the *merit* criterion which is responsible for their own selection and which is so strongly emphasized by the elite. It is not that homogeneity and authority are of no consequence; rather, they happen to be assured in any case as a result of the organization of the elite into corps. The point is that for the elite, competence is considered its hallmark. From the viewpoint of the self-image of the elite, what is important is that each individual member sees himself as belonging to the elite because of demonstrated and incontestable merit. As one member put it: "It is that the members of the grands corps are something of an aristocracy in French society. But why? Simply because they are superior to others. They are the most brilliant. They are the top graduates of their schools and they have been very carefully selected. Put in a nutshell: they are the ones who have performed

TABLE 5.1

Importance of Elite Institutions for the Society[1]

	Very Important		Quite Important		Hardly Important		Not At All Important		Don't Know		Total	
	%	No.	%	No.	%	No.	%	No.	%	No.	%	No.
1. Ensure a certain continuity and regularity in state functions												
Public sector	75.4	46	14.8	9	3.3	2	3.3	2	3.3	2	100.0	61
Private sector	51.7	31	33.3	20	11.7	7	0.0	0	3.3	2	100.0	60
2. Ensure the homogeneity of the elite												
Public sector	24.6	15	29.5	18	36.1	22	4.9	3	4.9	3	100.0	61
Private sector	25.0	15	20.0	12	46.7	28	3.3	2	5.0	3	100.0	60
3. Select the most qualified												
Public sector	58.3	35	23.3	14	13.3	8	5.0	3	0.0	0	100.0	60
Private sector	39.0	23	45.8	27	8.5	5	3.4	2	3.5	2	100.0	59
4. Select an elite that has the authority to direct the essential activities of the society												
Public sector	23.3	14	36.7	22	23.3	14	13.3	8	3.3	2	100.0	60
Private sector	5.2	3	43.1	25	43.1	25	3.4	2	5.2	3	100.0	58

[1] Question: It is said that institutions like the grandes écoles and the grands corps have certain advantages for the society. Here are the most cited advantages. What importance do you accord to each one?

the best." The mutual regard which the members of the elite hold for one another stems from the recognition that all of them belong in their places because they have "performed the best." Pierre Laroque, one of the most distinguished and enlightened members of the grands corps (he belongs to the Conseil d'Etat) also believes that the members of the grands corps are intellectually superior. He notes:

> The extensive reliance of ministers and of the government on members of the grands corps for staffing their ministerial cabinets and the directorial posts in the central administration has an additional basis which is crucial: it is that the members of the grands corps are intellectually the most outstanding members of the civil service. It is a fact that the methods of recruitment and selection lead to entry into the grands corps of people who are intellectually very superior to the average of other civil servants.[24]

Despite their firm conviction that they are the most qualified and best trained people in the society, the members of the elite are not, as Table 5.2 shows, unequivocally convinced that they constitute the main driving force behind innovations in the society.[25] Nevertheless, they do regard themselves, again by virtue of their qualifications, more likely to succeed in a particular post, within the administrative sector (Table 5.3) and within the private sector (Table 5.4), than others who do not happen to possess these particular qualifications. There are, to be sure, some differences among the public and private sector elites with regard to the probability that a corps member will be more efficient than a noncorps person. But the differences are not really significant because (and this is indicated in the data) it is generally maintained that one who has shown the qualities necessary for entry into the elite is likely to possess qualifications that will enable him to perform better than those who do not belong to the elite. These are the subjective views of the elite and they do not, of course, relate to any objective criteria by which competence is measured. The important point is

[24] Pierre Laroque, in a private letter to the author. M. Laroque kindly authorized me to quote from this letter.

[25] Michel Crozier has suggested that the grands corps are chiefly responsible for innovations in the administrative sector. See his *The Bureaucratic Phenomenon* (Chicago: The University of Chicago Press, 1964), p. 309, and his *La Société bloquée* (Paris: Editions du Seuil, 1970), p. 113.

TABLE 5.2

The Grands Corps as Chief Element of Innovation in the Society[1]

	Absolutely		Probably		Not Really		Not At All		Don't Know		Total	N
	%	No.	%	No.	%	No.	%	No.	%	No.		
Public sector	49.2	30	34.4	21	8.2	5	3.3	2	4.9	3	100.0	61
Private sector	35.0	21	33.3	20	11.7	7	18.3	11	1.7	1	100.0	60

[1] Question: It has been argued that the grands corps constitute the chief innovative force in an otherwise rigid society. Do you agree with this analysis?

TABLE 5.3

Efficiency of Corps Members vis-à-vis Noncorps Members:
in the Administration[1]

	Always % No.	Very Often % No.	Sometimes % No.	Never % No.	Total	N
Public sector	41.9 26	29.0 18	21.0 13	8.1 5	100.0	62
Private sector	8.5 5	62.7 37	23.7 14	5.1 3	100.0	59

[1] Question: Are the members of your corps employed in the administration more efficient than their colleagues who do not belong to a grand corps?

that judgments about self-image also carry with them criteria by which others are judged. The elite, having a monopoly on the key positions in society, comes to set standards by which it judges potential aspirants for a post. It ultimately succeeds, to a greater or lesser extent, in having its own criteria accepted by the society. It is in this respect that the self-image of the elite may not deviate to a noticeable extent from generally accepted notions of "competence," "quality," and "excellence." The smaller the gap between the criteria by which the elite judges itself and the criteria by which society generally measures its leaders, the greater the chances for survival. As one writer has noted in a different context:

> The public schools not only socialize and educate a significant proportion of the British elite. They also perform what may be described as a custodial function. They conserve within themselves and protect from corruption the norms and values of elite behavior which are to be passed on to successive generations. Because of this custodial function the norms of elite behavior, and the value system associated with them, have been retained to a remarkable degree within the social structure.[26]

Now, one needs always to try to separate the extent to which the elite's norms and criteria, which it successfully transfers onto the society, reflect an actual state of affairs and the extent to which they constitute a rationalization for what is otherwise an attempt at manipulation or mystification. For example, we noted earlier

[26] Ian Weinberg, *The English Public Schools: The Sociology of Elite Education* (New York: Atherton Press, 1967), p. 8.

TABLE 5.4

Efficiency of Corps Members vis-à-vis Noncorps Members:
in Private Sector[1]

| | Always | | Very Often | | Sometimes | | Never | | Don't Know | | Total | |
	%	No.	%	No.	%	No.	%	No.	%	No.		N
Public sector	30.5	18	27.1	16	28.8	17	10.2	6	3.4	2	100.0	59
Private sector	14.0	8	50.9	29	29.8	17	5.3	3	0.0	0	100.0	57

[1] Question: Are the members of your corps employed in the private sector more efficient than their colleagues who do not belong to a grands corps?

that in France the elite regards itself as more competent than others in both the public and private sectors. This, of course, raises a whole series of questions about technical as opposed to general competence, and about the definition of competence. As we shall see, the way in which the elite reconciles the need for specialized knowledge with its desire to occupy diverse posts in various sectors based on a particular type of education reflects a remarkably successful rationalization. I shall return to this particular problem in the next chapter.

The way in which an elite reacts under attack is one of the key tests of its self-confidence. As Tocqueville put it: ". . . experience teaches us that, generally speaking, the most perilous moment for a bad government is when it seeks to mend its ways."[27] Hence, if the elite reacts defensively, in the manner that Pareto suggests, one may have reason to suspect that it may not be on solid ground. If it makes no concessions, it may be doomed; if it makes too many, it may be equally doomed. Consequently, an elite's reaction to pressure requires changes that will stave off criticism but will not alter its basic character. Invariably, each concession on the part of the elite is thought to be the last. How the elite manages each succeeding demand for yet another concession has a great impact on its ultimate survival. After 1945, the grands corps were called upon to make important concessions—to give up the monopoly over their own recruitment, to accept the nationalization of the school that trained its members, to accept a greater move toward equality. They accepted these changes reluctantly at the time because they believed that no more would ever be demanded. Also, although these changes appeared to transform radically the nature of these elites, actually, they were no more than the minimum that would leave intact the essential character of the elite. The consequence of their acceptance was, in fact, to strengthen the self-confidence of the elite. Following the outbreaks of 1968, a similar reaction to the demands for change was manifested on the part of the elite. Its institutions accepted discussions of and proposals for reform. It even accepted reforms, but again, only to the degree that made it appear flexible so as to stave off further criticism and to remain intact. Prior to World War I, the elite institutions experienced, as we saw, unrelenting demands for change which they

[27] Alexis de Tocqueville, *The Old Regime and the French Revolution* (New York: Doubleday & Co., 1955), pp. 176-177.

long resisted but which they came gradually to accept in a manner that did not affect their basic structure.

The elite's reactions to demands for the reforms of its institutions have been such as to preserve their fundamental nature. It can be observed that, despite the criticism that the grandes écoles and the grands corps have come under in recent years, their self-image and self-confidence have in no way been shaken. The elite remains convinced that it is solidly anchored and that the bases of its power remain legitimate. Indeed, as Table 5.5 shows, the elite firmly believes that there are few prospects for its eventual demise. Its members believe that, while there may be further demands for change, they will come in the indefinite future. This belief alone contributes heavily to a feeling of security, which

TABLE 5.5

The Grands Corps and Their Future Role
in the Society

	Very Solid		Fairly Solid		Shaky			
	%	No.	%	No.	%	No.	Total	N
Public sector	75.8	47	19.4	12	4.8	3	100.0	62
Private sector	57.4	35	27.9	17	14.8	9	100.0	61

itself precludes defensive reactions. If anything, they see themselves as becoming more indispensable to the society. They observe that as the problems facing French society become more complex and acute, the reliance on a trained elite whose loyalty, dedication, and competence are incontestable will increase. The elite views itself as representing a stable element in the society, and stability and order are what all societies seek. This explains why they do not even feel threatened by the possibility of the advent of a left-wing government. As one of the respondents explained, "If a Left government were to come to power tomorrow, they would need us as much as any other government, so I think it very unlikely that the Left would want to abolish such institutions as the grandes écoles and the grands corps." Another respondent made much the same point when he noted, "What could a left-wing government actually accomplish for itself by doing away with the so-called

143

elitist institutions? It would be buying trouble. Everyone recognizes that they have to criticize such institutions, but that's not the same thing as actually doing something drastic about them." Yet another respondent suggested that "some of the Left's leaders are really far too intelligent to want to abolish institutions that would provide them with their only source of order when they took power." In fact, many members of the elite expressed the view that it was highly probable that a left-wing government would actually increase the elite's role in the society. The elite's power is closely tied to the existence of a centralized state,[28] and a Left government would be likely to undertake only those measures that would increase the state's role and powers. Hence, this could only add to the elite's power. The vast nationalization program that was put into effect after World War II and the consequent increase in the elite's power serve only to confirm the elite's view that a Left government poses no danger to its integrity. This example was often cited by our respondents.

Now, all this does not mean, of course, that the elite would welcome a left-wing government or that it would not look with grave suspicion on such a government, particularly if it included the Communist Party. But a Left government that excluded the communists would be looked upon pretty much like any other government. Many of the respondents pointed to the fact that many of their colleagues are members of the Socialist Party and play important and active roles within this party. One can, of course, legitimately speculate as to whether the fact that some members of the elite are active in the opposition does not lead the Left to temper its criticism of the elite institutions and to make it more reluctant to undertake far-reaching reforms if it should come to power. That certain members of the elite find themselves prominent in the opposition only serves to add to the legitimacy of the elite as a whole, for it reflects a considerable degree of openness on its part. That Michel Rocard, the former secretary-general of the P.S.U. and now a deputy of the Socialist Party, has been for the past several years integrated into the corps of the Inspection des Finances may appear paradoxical. But from the elite's point of view, it is by no means a wholly disadvantageous situation. It is not altogether surprising, therefore, that when graduates of the grandes écoles and members of the grands corps who are

[28] See Jean-Claude Thoenig, *L'Ere des technocrates: le cas des ponts et chaussées* (Paris: Les Editions d'Organisations, 1973).

associated with the Left attack the institutions in which they were trained and nurtured, these attacks never seem to be translated into serious projects for reform.[29]

This sense of security, which is what gives the elite its self-confidence, is shown by the fact that it regards itself as having become indispensable (Table 5.6). While many respondents prefaced their remarks by observing that "nothing is indispensable," or noting that "other societies function perfectly well without our system," they nonetheless expressed the belief that, in France, the grands corps have become so useful that it is difficult to conceive of their replacement by something that would be equally distinctive and reliable. Why does the elite see itself as having become largely indispensable? What are its peculiar qualities, as it sees them?

First, the quality most often stressed is that of personal independence. The members of the grands corps are assured from the moment they enter their corps of a considerable measure of prestige, of rather unusual career opportunities in both the public and private sectors, and of a job security that is scarcely known outside of this elite. Regardless of their competence, or of attempts at other careers that may not always be wholly successful, they can always return to the bosom of their corps. Indeed, when asked what the chief advantages were for them personally of belonging to a grand corps, the career opportunities afforded by such a membership were, as Table 5.7 shows, most often cited. The members of this elite are given a chance to occupy diverse posts because they belong to a grand corps and are therefore assumed to be endowed with certain qualities. From the viewpoint of the individual member, the possibility of an ever-present alternative to his current position is what endows him with the independence that is so highly cherished. For example, members of the grands corps who hold high-level administrative posts claim that they are able to act more objectively and give more disinterested advice to ministers because their careers are not connected with the general considerations of promotion as are the careers of others in the ministry. They see themselves as being free to be more objective and to render unpopular advice because the security of their careers is ensured. This feeling of security is common to all the

---

[29] The immediate impact of a left-wing government on France's elitist structures is discussed in Ezra N. Suleiman, "La Gauche et la haute administration," *Promotions*, No. 100 (November 1976), pp. 43-45.

Table 5.6

Indispensability of Grands Corps[1]

	Totally %	Totally No.	Quite %	Quite No.	Somewhat %	Somewhat No.	Not At All %	Not At All No.	Don't Know %	Don't Know No.	Total %	Total No.
1. For the functioning of the administration												
Public sector	68.9	42	21.3	13	4.9	3	0.0	0	4.9	3	100.0	61
Private sector	40.0	24	35.0	21	16.7	10	8.3	5	0.0	0	100.0	60
2. For the industrial sector												
Public sector	16.4	10	41.0	25	13.1	8	13.1	8	16.4	10	100.0	61
Private sector	31.7	19	40.0	24	20.0	12	8.3	5	0.0	0	100.0	60
3. For the government and the political system												
Public sector	50.0	31	33.9	21	8.1	5	3.2	2	4.8	3	100.0	62
Private sector	39.7	23	39.7	23	12.1	7	8.6	5	0.0	0	100.0	58
4. For the society as a whole												
Public sector	45.9	28	31.1	19	6.6	4	8.2	5	8.2	5	100.0	61
Private sector	33.9	20	33.9	20	16.9	10	15.3	9	0.0	0	100.0	59

[1] Question: Do you think that the grands corps are indispensable for the functioning of the various sectors and for the society?

TABLE 5.7

Advantages of Belonging to Grands Corps[1]

	Prestige	Career Opportunities	Material Advantages	Confidence in Self	Assurance of Success Regardless of Post	Don't Know	Total	N
Public sector								
1st choice (top)	8.3 (5)	71.7 (43)	5.0 (3)	0.0 (0)	5.0 (3)	10.0 (6)	100.0	60
2nd choice (bottom)	5.1 (3)	15.3 (9)	5.1 (3)	8.5 (5)	39.0 (23)	27.1 (16)	100.0	59
Private sector								
1st choice (top)	10.2 (6)	83.1 (49)	3.4 (2)	3.4 (2)	0.0 (0)	0.0 (0)	100.0	59
2nd choice (bottom)	20.7 (12)	10.3 (6)	3.4 (2)	10.3 (6)	37.9 (22)	13.8 (8)	100.0	58

[1] Question: From a purely personal point of view, what are the two most important advantages that you enjoy as a result of belonging to a grand corps?

Note: The pairing of cells indicates 1st choice (top) and 2nd choice (bottom).

members of the elite, whether they are in the public, semipublic, or private sectors; and because it is not granted to others, it sets the elite apart by giving them a sense of superiority.

Second, this independence leads, it was often noted, to greater effectiveness. It allows them to take a larger view of problems and it allows them to plan in a way that others, bogged down by immediate considerations, cannot. As one respondent observed, "The important thing about the members of the grands corps is their independence and their capacity for objective actions. Take the domain of transport. To think about the problems of transportation over the next ten or twenty years, the state needs a reserve of men who can think clearly and objectively. It can't leave such a task up to the Ministry of Transport because that would be leaving it to the SNCF, RATP, etc. Each of these has a niche to protect. The independence of the members of the grands corps allows them to transcend petty considerations." Because they escape the constraints imposed by normal promotions through the ranks and are therefore guided entirely by considerations other than those having to do with careers, the members of the elite believe that their advice is more willingly sought. This is no doubt more true for the public and semipublic sectors than it is for the private sector. Nevertheless, they see their advice as being sought because of their efficacy, because they can do things that few others can.

This self-image reveals that the members of the elite have set themselves off in important ways from those they work with who do not belong to this group. In other words, they have produced a self-image that is in marked contrast to the image they hold of others. Thus, where others are preoccupied with petty career problems, they themselves are not in the least concerned with such mundane matters. Where others cannot transcend the narrow interests of a particular agency, they themselves are always able to adopt a more global view that allows them to survey and to solve the entire problem. Where others constantly find themselves in subservient situations, they, in contrast, always find themselves in commanding positions. Where others are generally less effective and less influential, they themselves always manage to translate their independence into effectiveness.

The third reason which is seen as accounting for the elite's indispensability has to do with the fact that it constitutes a well-defined group that is immediately recognizable. As one respondent put it, "Being a member of the grands corps is a visiting card;

it allows you to situate people right away." This means that each member is endowed with advantages simply because he can call on other members of the group. This facilitates communication among the various sectors of society. "I have all the advantages of belonging to caste and there's no sense denying it," said one member of the elite. Another noted that the "grands corps could have no influence without the solidarity of their members." Thus, belonging to the grands corps, because it allows one to call on a vast network of personal relations, is assumed to be one of the key ingredients of the elite's competence.

In addition to seeing itself as indispensable to the society, the elite also views itself as the repository of certain qualities that are generally in short supply—reliability, incorruptibility, hard work. It is not that "the others" lack these qualities; rather, it is that one can always find them in the elite.

AUTHORITY

The view that an elite holds of the nature of authority is an extremely important aspect of its self-image, for it indicates something about its belief in its capacity for leadership. Its view of authority can suggest another part of, as well as act as a support for, its self-image. In an era such as ours, when greater demands for participation are made, it may well be that a strong belief in authority runs counter to the general tenor of these demands, just as the self-image of the elite is hardly compatible with the precept that "all men are created equal." At this point there is no need to enter into a discussion of the degree to which the self-image of the elite is incompatible with democratic norms. For the moment we wish to continue viewing things through the eyes of the elite itself.

The elite has a strong sense of hierarchy. It regards hierarchy in organizations as indispensable for their proper functioning. Table 5.8 shows clearly that if given a choice between collective decision-making and a more traditional, hierarchical setup, the elite would prefer the latter.[30] For any institution to function, it was maintained, it is always essential to know who is responsible for what. The dispersion of responsibility is incompatible, according to the elite, with the smooth functioning of an organization. This

[30] The questions posed in Tables 5.8 and 5.10 are derived from questions used in the survey, *Recherche sur la mise en place du Ministère de l'Equipement,* carried out in 1969 by the Centre de Sociologie des Organisations.

TABLE 5.8

Hierarchic vs. Collective Decision-making[1]

	Public Sector		Private Sector	
	%	No.	%	No.
For an organization to function effectively, a strong hierarchic structure, with only one person at the top, is necessary.	76.3	45	87.9	51
Strong hierarchic structures are inefficient. More collective arrangements are necessary.	23.7	14	12.1	7
TOTAL	100.0	59	100.0	58

[1] Question: Some people question the utility of having strong hierarchical structures within a firm or an organization. With which of the following statements do you agree?

is as true of a public agency as it is of a profit-oriented firm. Table 5.9 indicates that whereas a number of possibilities can be envisaged insofar as the participation of workers in their enterprises is concerned, the one possibility which entailed collective decision-making—that workers should be permitted to run the enterprises in which they worked—was the one least acceptable to the elite.

TABLE 5.9

Workers' Participation in Industry

	Public Sector		Private Sector	
	%	No.	%	No.
They should be able to share the profits	45.0	27	13.8	8
They should be represented within the directorate of the firm	21.7	13	20.7	12
They should be permitted to run their own firm	0.0	0	0.0	0
They should have no role whatsoever in the management of their firm	10.0	6	36.2	21
Don't know	23.3	14	29.3	17
TOTAL	100.0	60	100.0	58

"Workers running their own enterprises—we hear a great deal of such claims these days—that is pure demagogy," said one respondent. Another noted that "this is in the interest of neither the workers nor the society. The workers have neither the interest nor the capacity to run a business enterprise, and the society can only function properly when it has at its helm men trained for and dedicated to this task." Still another expressed the common view that "the moment you cannot pinpoint who is responsible for a specific task, you have only chaos." That it is in the nature of things that society be organized along strictly demarcated lines of authority is a view widely held by the elite. "I may sound like something of a Fascist," said one respondent, "but I firmly believe that authority cannot be shared." Table 5.10 shows that the elite believes that organizations function best when each one knows the limits of his authority. Moreover, it is clear that the elite does not merely believe that things have always been like this; they believe that this is how things should be. "When I was young," said one respondent who was not much in favor of the elitist institutions, "I thought that everyone was equal. But you soon get to realize that when one gets on a plane one doesn't ask for the pilot's seat. Of course, a method has to be found for giving workers the impression that they're being given greater consideration, but the pilot's seat is always for the pilot. Everybody is better off this way." The elite, in other words, must be left in a position of leadership, unencumbered by constant challenges to its leadership, for the adverse consequences of such challenges fall not only on the elite but on the society as a whole.

The views that members of the elite hold with regard to the importance of authority and responsibility reflect not only an acceptance of tradition—"that is the way things have always been" —but a particular view with respect to the division of society into those who are "fit" to rule and those who must accept to be ruled. This is indicated in Table 5.11, which shows an outright rejection of the belief that social background is what determines, or what ought to determine, one's place in the occupational hierarchy.[31] As

[31] Items 1, 2, and 3 in Table 5.11 were first used in the University of Michigan's multination study of bureaucrats and politicians. For comparisons with Britain, Germany, and Italy, see Robert D. Putnam, "The Political Attitudes of Senior Civil Servants in Britain, Germany and Italy," *British Journal of Political Science*, III (1973), 257-290. This essay is reprinted in Mattei Dogan, ed., *The Mandarins of Western Europe: The Political Role of Top Civil Servants* (Beverly Hills: Sage Publications, 1975), pp. 87-128.

TABLE 5.10
Hierarchy and Authority[1]

	Totally Agree %	Totally Agree No.	Somewhat Agree %	Somewhat Agree No.	Somewhat Disagree %	Somewhat Disagree No.	Absolutely Disagree %	Absolutely Disagree No.	Total %	Total No.
1. Hierarchical organization allows each person to take initiative within clearly defined and unambiguous limits										
Public sector	58.1	36	35.5	22	4.3	3	1.6	1	100.0	62
Private sector	66.7	40	26.7	16	5.0	3	1.7	1	100.0	60
2. In all organized life, there are those who command and those who obey. This is how it should be										
Public sector	64.5	40	29.0	18	4.8	3	1.6	1	100.0	62
Private sector	68.3	41	23.3	14	5.0	3	3.3	2	100.0	60

[1] Question: Here are two widespread views concerning hierarchy. For each one, could you say whether you are in agreement?

TABLE 5.11

Authority and Elitism

	Totally Agree %	Totally Agree No.	Rather Agree %	Rather Agree No.	Rather Disagree %	Rather Disagree No.	Totally Disagree %	Totally Disagree No.	Total %	Total No.
1. In every country some people are more qualified than others to rule because of their background										
Public sector	3.3	2	0.0	0	18.0	11	78.7	48	100.0	61
Private sector	3.3	2	3.3	2	16.4	10	77.0	47	100.0	61
2. Few people know what their real long-term interests are										
Public sector	50.8	31	23.0	14	21.3	13	4.9	3	100.0	61
Private sector	45.9	28	29.5	18	16.4	10	8.2	5	100.0	61
3. Every citizen should have an equal chance to influence the affairs of his country										
Public sector	8.5	5	25.4	15	33.9	20	32.2	19	100.0	59
Private sector	11.7	7	45.0	27	23.3	14	20.0	12	100.0	60
4. Some people are born with leadership qualities; others will never have these qualities										
Public sector	77.4	48	17.7	11	4.8	3	0.0	0	100.0	62
Private sector	71.0	44	22.6	14	3.2	2	3.2	2	100.0	62

we noted earlier, social background per se is generally opposed, in the view of the elite, to merit, which is attained through rigorous competition and which is seen as being perfectly compatible with democracy. The elite justifies its elevated position in the hierarchy on the basis of its qualifications which have been tested, and it rejects any suggestion that it is a social elite. As a consequence of this belief, it holds the view that its competence entitles it to its position, a fact that is of great importance in the self-confidence of the elite.

The attitude toward the nature of authority also reveals, as Table 5.11 shows, the distinction between the elites and the rest of society. The elite believes that people rarely know what their long-term interests are. This clearly creates a gap which some members of society need to fill. Because of the position it occupies and because of the way it came to occupy this position, the elite regards it as its duty to show the nonelite what its interests really are. Moreover, despite the fact that the members of the elite justify their privileged positions on the basis of largely acquired qualities, it is striking to note that they regard leadership as an inherent quality, one that some are fortunate enough to be born with. One cannot develop leadership qualities because of their ascriptive nature. Consequently, the elite sees itself as occupying its enviable position by virtue of merits that are both acquired and innate. It is difficult to imagine a combination of such merits leading to modesty or to a view that "all men are equal." For just as we might expect, although the elite is generally in favor of the sentiments expressed by the statement that everyone ought to have an equal chance to influence decisions, they believe that these sentiments are merely "abstract" and "utopian." Societies, for them, are justifiably divided into a group that is capable of leading and into the rest of society which needs to be led. The only question that arises after one accepts this ineluctable truth is how society selects its elite. In France, it is argued, the state has devised a system that ensures the selection of the best elements. "It is the way in which the state recruits and trains its executives, in the public and private sectors, that makes it possible to produce an elite that is highly competent," noted one respondent. Another respondent, echoing similar sentiments, observed that "the reason our elitist system, with all its faults, has become indispensable is that one knows precisely what to expect from its products, who are the most highly selected and who possess a combination of qualities that are hard to find in a single individual."

The self-image of the elite clearly distinguishes it from the rest of society, and one needs to comprehend the elite's views with respect to leadership, hierarchy, and authority in light of the growing demands for participation and decentralization. The self-image of the elite suggests that in France the elites do not share, are in fact fundamentally hostile to, the aspirations which those demands embody. Shedding one's illusions about equality is a gradual process. This is shown by another survey of grandes écoles students who, not having yet reached a position of authority, are considerably more inclined than the elite in power to envisage the possibility of workers' participation in their own enterprises (Table 5.12). The general hostility to workers' participation is due to two factors. First, as we have seen, the self-image of the elite is such as to endow it with paternalistic attitudes vis-à-vis the society. The elite

TABLE 5.12

Participation in Private Industry
(percent)

	Yes	No	Don't Know	Total
1. Co-management of enterprise by workers	36	49	15	100
2. Participation of workers in the management of their enterprise	76	18	6	100
3. Allowing representation of workers in the Conseils d'Administration	82	14	4	100
4. Allowing representation of consumers in the Conseils d'Administration	43	44	13	100

Source: Adapted from *Les Informations*, No. 1462 (May 1973), p. 68.

sees itself as being best equipped to formulate the directions in which the society should move because it alone can perceive the society's real interests. It does this while acting independently of any interests of its own. Table 5.13 shows that the elite even sees ordinary citizens as having little interest in politics, whereas it has a great deal. This, of course, is not surprising, for

TABLE 5.13

Interest in Politics: French People and Elite

	A Great Deal		Fair Amount		Little		Not At All		Total	
	%	No.	%	No.	%	No.	%	No.	%	No.
*People**										
Public sector	23.7	14	26.3	16	39.5	23	10.5	6	100.0	59
Private sector	28.6	17	22.9	13	42.9	25	5.7	3	100.0	58
Elite†										
Public sector	86.8	51	13.2	8	0.0	0	0.0	0	100.0	59
Private sector	88.6	51	8.6	5	2.9	2	0.0	0	100.0	58

* Question: Generally speaking, do you think that the French people are interested in politics?
† Question: Are you yourself interested in politics?

it merely shows, as with the other dimensions that we have analyzed, the elite's attempt or need to distinguish itself from the mass.

The second reason why the elite does not share the aspirations for greater participation and decentralization is of a slightly different order. It has to do with the defense of interests that are specific to the elite, a matter about which we have said little so far and to which we shall return in subsequent chapters. The point is that the elite's position is inextricably linked to a centralized form of organization. We noted earlier the elite's belief that a left-wing government would inevitably augment state intervention and therefore could not really be considered a threat to the elite. Consequently, the elite itself does not deny that centralization serves to maintain and even to enhance its power. As Thoenig rather scathingly noted:

> The grands corps and the centralized state have become indissolubly linked. On the one hand, the centralized state is a prisoner of the grands corps and cannot rid itself of them. On the other hand, the grands corps are totally dependent for their privileges and their prestige on the centralized state. The present crisis of the grands corps is thus due to the crisis of the centralized state, which can no longer deal with the multiple aspects of collective life but which refuses to abandon its powers and its privileges. The collective tasks which the state assumes and for which the grands corps were conceived are

becoming more and more difficult to carry out. As long as there were other institutions besides the state to carry out the indispensable functions and as long as these functions were relatively simple, there was a countervailing force to the administrative elite. Today, however, the state alone occupies the field and at the same time the grands corps are getting overwhelmed by the complexity of the problems involved in governing society.[32]

Now, the fundamentally undemocratic norms that characterize the elite's self-image may be judged on their own grounds and may be regarded as constituting sufficient justification for the elite's overthrow. On the other hand, they in no way weaken the ability of the elite to endure. On the contrary, the belief in its superiority, its distinctive self-confidence, and its search for legitimacy or for what Weber called "imperative co-ordination,"[33] are essential factors accounting for the elite's survival. They are not the only factors, nor are they sufficient by themselves, but they are indispensable. In order to explain more fully the survival of elitist institutions in France, we need now to turn to an examination of the elite's organizations, of the conception of their functions, and of their ability to adapt their organizations to changing demands made by the society.

[32] Jean-Claude Thoenig, "L'Exemple Français des grands corps," paper presented at the Eighth World Congress of the International Political Science Association, Munich, August 31-September 5, 1970, p. 12.

[33] Weber, *The Theory of Social and Economic Organization*, p. 325.

Chapter Six

NONSPECIALIZATION
AND ORGANIZATIONAL DEXTERITY

THE previous chapters have illustrated the diversity of posts which the elite has come to occupy and examined the elite's belief that its competence entitles it, and prepares it, to direct almost every activity within the public and private sectors. The question that we must now try to answer is how the elite's multifarious activities can be reconciled with the general view that one of its distinguishing features is its specialized competence. Certainly no country has been more admired (or criticized) than France for the manner in which it trains specialists and technicians destined to occupy the highest posts. It is the country where, as David Granick noted some years ago, the "technocrat has the strongest position," where he in fact reigns "supreme."[1] The grandes écoles are held chiefly responsible for the training of the French specialists, and they have naturally come to be seen as the breeding ground for the technocracy that is believed to dominate French society. Because the whole question of technocracy—and, in the French case, of the role that the specialized schools play in fostering it—is more complex than has been supposed, we need to examine it rather closely. The problem of technocracy is of particular interest to our central theme because an analysis of it will enable us to understand how an ostensibly specialized elite is able to embrace, and to insist upon its acquisition of, generalized skills, and thus legitimize its diverse roles in the society. In this way, the elite comes to enjoy the advantages associated with specialization and those associated with generalized skills.

THE TECHNOCRATIC PROBLEM

"Technocracy" is one among a number of terms (or, occasionally, epithets) that are often employed to describe contemporary indus-

---

[1] David Granick, *The European Executive* (New York: Doubleday Anchor, 1962), p. 72. Also see the same author's *Managerial Comparisons of Four Developed Countries: France, Britain, United States, Russia* (Cambridge, Mass.: The M.I.T. Press, 1972), pp. 178-191.

trial societies. It usually goes hand in hand with others such as "technotronic," "managerial," "elitist," "organizational." These terms, as they are apt to be used today, are supposed to give us snapshots of the dominant mode of organization of modern industrial society. They are not haphazardly chosen, because they all succeed in conveying, as of course they are intended to convey, an image of a society that is rationally directed and dominated by an elite group.

This is especially true of the term "technocracy," which may be taken to refer to the application of science to every aspect of society. In *The Technological Society*, Ellul employs the term "technique" to refer to rational methods that are used to attain a particular end, and notes that "today no human activity escapes this technical imperative."[2] The rationalization and standardization of all that affects our life is a prospect that leads many an apolitical or antipolitical person to, in Bernard Crick's words, the "defense of politics."[3] I will return presently to this theme, but it needs to be emphasized here that the widespread and successful application of science is generally seen as being in direct opposition to politics, much as science and religion were once seen as being in irremediable conflict. Science implies objectivity, precision, proof, whereas politics implies ambivalence, conflict, compromise.

The application of science to all forms of human endeavor has had many champions. In the early part of the nineteenth century, Saint-Simon lauded the productive function of industrial society and was convinced that putting industry in the hands of the industrialists and technicians would be for the benefit of the entire society. But the reaction to positivism was not long in coming, and for the past century the champions of an efficient, more rationally directed industrial order have always had to face severe critics. The main contention of these critics, perhaps never more numerous than today,[4] has been that such a society is fundamentally incompatible with the ideals of a democratic society, and is so for three

---

[2] Jacques Ellul, *The Technological Society* (New York: Vintage Books, 1964), p. 21.

[3] Bernard C. Crick, *In Defense of Politics*, 2nd ed. (Chicago: University of Chicago Press, 1972).

[4] See Theodore Roszak, *The Making of a Counter-Culture* (New York: Doubleday Anchor, 1973), Jean Meynaud, *Technocratie et politique* (Lausanne, 1960); Henri Lefebvre, *Position: contre les technocrates* (Paris: Gonthier, 1967), J.-A. Kosciusko-Morizet, *La "Mafia" polytechnicienne* (Paris: Editions du Seuil, 1973).

related reasons: it is elitist; it is oblivious to social problems; and it denies the virtues of participation and self-expression.

First, insofar as elitism is concerned, it is undeniable that many of those who addressed themselves to the problems posed by modern industrial society generally put their entire faith in a single group. For Saint-Simon it was the industrialists and the planners who held the key to progress; for Veblen, it was the technicians. In fact, Veblen had nothing but contempt for the "lieutenant of finance," who, in any case, had long "ceased being a captain of industry."[5] He wanted to see an end to "the industrial dictatorship of the captain of finance"[6] so that the technician could take his rightful place. "The expert men," he wrote, "technologists, engineers, or whatever name may best suit them, make up the indispensable General Staff of the industrial system; and without their immediate and unremitting guidance and correction the industrial system will not work. . . . The material welfare of the community is unreservedly bound up with the due working of this industrial system, and therefore with its unreserved control by engineers, who alone are competent to manage it."[7] That one group is singled out as being the most competent to make society's decisions is not easy to square with democratic notions of ruling.

Second, in addition to domination by an elite, a technocratic society inspires fears because it appears under the guise of an objective, nonideological society. Those in power claim to be concerned with objective solutions to society's problems and not with social conflicts. In rejecting all ideologies, it is argued, they mask their own ideology. James Burnham's *The Managerial Revolution* presented a universal thesis: "At the conclusion of the transition period the managers will, in fact, have achieved social dominance, will be the ruling class in society. This drive, moreover, is worldwide in extent, already well advanced in all nations, though at different levels of development in different nations."[8] Burnham's anti-Marxian argument was important because it deemphasized the role of politics and to that extent presaged the celebrated thesis according to which the distinction between capitalism and socialism was no longer important. Consequently, in a rationalized soci-

[5] Thorstein Veblen, *The Engineers and the Price System* (New York: Viking Press, 1921), p. 66.

[6] *Ibid.*, p. 82. [7] *Ibid.*, p. 69.

[8] James Burnham, *The Managerial Revolution* (Bloomington: Indiana University Press, 1966), pp. 71-72.

ety, many social conflicts are likely to be ignored and policy is likely to be made without reference to these conflicts. This is why many groups have never accepted the "end of ideology" thesis; for these groups, the allocation of resources remains an indisputably political problem, one that does not lend itself to a strictly objective, rational, and nonideological solution.

Third, when instrumental problems are seen as the most important ones in a society, then not only are social conflicts negated but mass participation becomes superfluous. Technocracy and elitism are fundamentally nonparticipatory. It is hardly surprising that those who believe in participatory democracy are among the staunchest critics of technocracy. And one can well understand the belief that perhaps the most serious conflict in the second half of the twentieth century is between democracy and bureaucracy.[9] In attempting to explain the uprisings that occurred in France in May 1968, Alain Touraine argues that the revolutionary movment was not directed against the capitalist system. "The struggle was not against capitalism, but first and foremost against technocracy. . . . Its revolutionary prospect was anti-technocratic, while its critique of bourgeois and capitalist society could only have led to modernization or a purely negative rejection of society."[10] As Touraine succinctly put it: "The password of the technocrats who run society is adaptation. The May Movement replied, self-expression."[11] Thus, to the extent that society aims at rationality and is forever searching for the "one best" solution, it precludes the presentation of alternative solutions. It also precludes a general participation in the formulation of the solutions. When societies come to assume —as Saint-Simon, Comte, Veblen, and others once assumed—that there is only one solution and then act upon this solution, then we can say that technocracy has triumphed over democracy. As Daniel Bell notes, "Technical decision-making, in fact, can be instrumental, the other [nontechnical] emotional and expressive."[12]

Because the term "technocracy" figures in so many polemical works, it has become difficult to separate its conceptual and analytical uses from its normative and pejorative ones. In Theodore

[9] Seymour M. Lipset, *Political Man* (New York: Doubleday Anchor, 1961), p. 9.

[10] Alain Touraine, *The May Movement: Revolt and Reform* (New York: Random House, 1971), pp. 28-29.

[11] *Ibid.*, p. 24.

[12] Daniel Bell, *The Coming of Post-Industrial Society* (New York: Basic Books, 1973), p. 34.

Roszak's *Where the Wasteland Ends,* for example, one finds that technocracy exists "just about everywhere on earth."[13] We have "the suave technocracies" (United States, Western Europe, and Japan), the "vulgar technocracies" (Soviet Union), "the teratoid technocracies" (Nazi, Fascist, junta-led countries), and, finally, the "comic opera technocracies" (underdeveloped countries). If Roszak's taxonomy is not very illuminating, this should matter very little, for eventually, according to him, "the differences between the several technocratic styles are very likely to diminish,"[14] at which point we will all simply be living in a technocratic world. While Roszak's use of "technocracy" illustrates the polemical battering this term receives, it is also possible to find instances where it means nothing at all.[15] If every society sooner or later becomes technocratic and if everyone somehow turns into a technocrat, we are not likely to come close to defining the properties of a technocratic society. Most studies that have addressed themselves in a serious vein to the technocratic phenomenon have tried to pinpoint the technical experts who possess important decision-making powers and have attributed specialized skills to them.[16] Technocracy is usually taken to mean the application of "technique" to the solution of societal problems. We must now examine the extent to which specialization and expertise are characteristics that the French elite shares and believes in.

TRAINING AND WORK

The experts who hold power—the technocrats—are generally believed to be those who have received specialized training in the elite institutions of higher learning and who occupy the executive posts in the various sectors of society. Most studies that touch on

[13] Theodore Roszak, *Where the Wasteland Ends* (New York: Doubleday Anchor, 1973), p. 34.

[14] *Ibid.,* p. 45.

[15] See, for example, Marshall E. Dimock, *The Japanese Technocracy* (New York: Walker/Weatherhill, 1968). Dimock's is a rather old-fashioned book that has little to do with technocracy and one suspects that the title was supplied by a subtle editor who knew that the term "technocracy" is one capable of drawing attention.

[16] See Jean Meynaud, *Technocracy* (New York: The Free Press, 1968). See also Charles P. Kindleberger, "Technical Education and the French Entrepreneur," in Edward C. Carter, Robert Forster, and Joseph N. Moody, eds., *Enterprise And Entrepreneurs in Nineteenth and Twentieth Century France* (Baltimore: The Johns Hopkins University Press, 1976), pp. 3-40.

the subject of technocracy usually dwell in some detail on the French case, which is generally regarded as exemplary. Since the French possess specialized schools, it is logically assumed that they produce specialists. As Anthony Sampson put it some years ago, "The French elite are the arch-technocrats of Europe."[17] The schools that train the French elite have long been envied by other nations.[18] The Fulton Report on the British civil service attacked the "amateurishness" of the British civil servants and extolled the professionalism of their French counterparts:

> The French system produces highly professional elites on both the administrative and technical sides; their professionalism is maintained and constantly renewed by the flow of recruits who have undergone a high-powered, modern training. The elites are exclusive. It is difficult to enter them from within the service except at the start of a career; and to do so requires intense preparation and a particular kind of higher education. . . . [As] to the quality of the elites themselves there is no doubt. They offer a highly attractive career, so eagerly sought after that the service can pick from the cream of the educational output.[19]

The Fulton Commission did no more than reinforce the popular image of the French official: a man familiar with the slide rule and the computer, accustomed to applying strictly rational criteria to the solution of problems, and unencumbered by an education in Greek and Latin. This is an important image, not because it has anything to do with reality, but because it is widely believed. In effect, it would be difficult to imagine an elite maintaining a monopoly over such a remarkable diversity of posts and for such long a period if it were the technical, specialized elite it has been made out to be. At the heart of its success lies its profound belief in generalized skills, which are the only kind of "skills" that enable one to move from one sector to another without prior technical training for a particular post.

The training that the graduates of the grandes écoles receive may

---

[17] Anthony Sampson, *Anatomy of Europe* (New York: Harper & Row, 1968), p. 331.

[18] Britain, Germany, and Italy have long toyed with the idea of creating institutions modeled on the French grandes écoles.

[19] The Fulton Report, *The Civil Service Today*, Vol. I (London: H.M.S.O., 1968), p. 137.

be fairly specialized, but it has little to do with the posts that these graduates will later occupy. It does not and it cannot train them for the diverse posts that they will come to hold in the public and semipublic sectors, or in the large industrial enterprises and banking institutions. The members of the Conseil d'Etat, the Inspection des Finances, and the Cour des Comptes all receive the same training at ENA, just as the members of the Corps des Mines and Corps des Ponts et Chaussées receive the same training at the Ecole Polytechnique. The important question that needs to be asked is: in what way is the training acquired at these schools a specialized type of training?

At ENA, the training consists of a year's on-the-job work (*stage*) in a prefecture or in an embassy. This is then followed by a year and a half of course work at the school. The work done at the school revolves around the study of administrative and judicial matters, economics, international affairs, and social problems. Apart from the *stage*, with which the students' training begins, little fresh knowledge is acquired by the civil servants whose years at the Institut d'Etudes Politiques have already familiarized them with these subjects.[20] At the Ecole Polytechnique, there is likewise a uniform scientific training given to students in mathematics, physics, chemistry, and the like. The most successful students at both ENA and Polytechnique enter into one of the grands corps. For those who graduate from Polytechnique and enter into the Corps des Mines and the Corps des Ponts et Chaussées, there is an additional two years of training at the Ecole des Mines and at the Ecole Nationale des Ponts et Chaussées. Even at these schools, however, the emphasis tends to be placed on *stages*. This is especially the case in Ecole des Mines where there is little formal training, since the students spend most of their time as *stagiaires* working in various branches of the private sector. The significance of the *stage* should not be underestimated because it illustrates most clearly the value that is assigned to on-the-job training. This is thought to provide, far more than a purely formal training is able to do, an acquaintance with general problems associated with decision-making at a high level. It is also believed to give the student a particular kind of experience which will have a far wider applicability than formal training in a narrow area. The *stage*, then, is

[20] William R. Schonfeld, *Obedience and Revolt: French Behavior Toward Authority* (Beverly Hills: Sage Publications, 1976), pp. 235-241.

ideally suited to a group of leaders that does not wish to circum-
scribe the area over which it exercises decisive influence.

To the extent that the members of the technical and nontechnical
corps acquire a degree of specialized knowledge in a particular
sector, this is largely due to the relatively short time they spend
working in their corps. The members of the corps are obliged to
spend a minimum period (usually two to four years) working
within the corps, each of which is, lest it be forgotten, a part of the
administrative structure with a particular sphere of jurisdiction.
After having spent this obligatory period working within the corps,
the new recruits generally request a leave of absence. They then
go on to occupy posts in a wide variety of institutions for which
neither the formal training nor the *stage* have particularly prepared
them. Consequently, even if we were to conclude that the training
of the members of the grands corps is of a "specialized" kind, we
would still have to confront the fact that the members of these
corps occupy a wide array of posts which are scarcely tied to a
specialized training. In sum, the work that the members of the
corps perform is, at best, tenuously linked to the training they have
received.

It may well be that the ambiguity about the training dispensed
by the grandes écoles is what gives them an unrivaled aura of
prestige, if not a certain mystique. "The Ecole Polytechnique,"
noted Michel Debré, "is neither a school which gives a specific
professional training nor a university with an indeterminate orientation. It is a school of a very particular type."[21] Maintaining
a certain ambiguity about the elite's training is important because
it allows its members to exploit the advantage associated with expertise and with more general (or amateur) skills. The society
may attach a certain importance to expertise, so that this may
render the elite more legitimate. On the other hand, if expertise is
defined too narrowly, it makes it more difficult for the elite to justify its hold over such a wide diversity of posts. This is why the
elite rarely claims what others have claimed for it, namely, that its
chief virtue lies in its possession of technical skills. It believes very
firmly, much as the British civil service has believed since its creation, that a general preparation for leadership positions is the
most desirable. Behind the façade of specialization, behind the ra-

[21] Michel Debré, "Allocution de M. Debré," *La Jaune et la Rouge*, No.
266 (January 1972), p. 4.

tionale that has underpinned the parallel system of higher education, one finds unmistakably not a specialized, utilitarian elite, but,
on the contrary, an elite that has made something of a cult of
amateurishness. It is on this that the elite's monopoly on the key
positions in the society largely depends, for generalized skills enable the elite to occupy posts that have little connection with its
prior training. The members of the elite become politicians, bankers, industrialists, international civil servants; and even when they
remain in the public sector, they occupy posts for which their
training has not prepared them. This has led some writers to define
technocracy in a way that divorces it from technical specialization.
As Bon and Burnier write:

> The technocrat fixes the goals and the means of the techni-
> cians' work. He is in a position to effect a synthesis of the re-
> sults obtained, to choose between different options, and to de-
> fine the priorities. Nine times out of ten, he is incapable of
> taking the place of any of the technicians whose skill he relies
> on. The technocratic culture is not a technical culture: it inte-
> grates the principal results of administrative, financial, indus-
> trial and other techniques in order to be able to utilize them
> as a factor in policy-making.[22]

Thoenig likewise observes that "It is not high specialization that
characterizes the engineer of Ponts et Chaussées, but his *polyvalence*, the fact of being the 'generalist' of technique."[23] This is as
true of the scientifically trained official as it is of the one who receives a nonscientific training. The graduates of the Ecole Polytechnique occupy equally important and equally diverse posts
throughout French society. As a recent entering class of the Ecole
Polytechnique was informed: "The scientific training you receive
will not give you the knowledge in any branch that the specialists
have, but it will give you the aptitudes and the methods such as to
allow you to be on top of everything."[24] The Cot Commission,
formed to study the role of the engineering corps in modern
French society, noted much the same thing in its report:

[22] F. Bon and M.-A. Burnier, *Les Nouveaux intellectuels* (Paris: Editions
du Seuil, 1971), p. 107.

[23] Jean-Claude Thoenig, *L'Ere des technocrates: le cas des ponts et chaussées* (Paris: Les Editions d'Organisations, 1973), p. 220.

[24] Cited in Bon and Burnier, *Les Nouveaux intellectuels*, p. 112.

What will be required of the Ecole Polytechnique? . . . It will have to supply the Nation with two types of men, imbued with the sense of public service, the capacity for flexibility and adaptation, and intellectual rigor:

—First, a certain kind of researcher with a polyvalent training and concerned with practical problems;

—Second, a certain kind of engineer who is neither a "technician" (that is, the specialist of a technique who does not exercise the functions of synthesis and decision-making), nor a "technocrat" (who sometimes arbitrarily attributes to himself these functions), but a "technologist." This is the term we propose to use to define an executive in a high-level scientific position who is also concerned with practical problems, who has experience working with people, and who is capable of synthesizing and making decisions.[25]

The commitment to a general orientation and the fear of too narrow a specialization are important for several reasons, not the least of which is the suggestion that those who occupy the key posts in the society, the recipients of the elite education, are not the masters of technique or the true specialists. The true specialists are to be found, it might be suggested, a notch or two below the holders of the key posts. At this level the specialists are more distant from the political arena; they are less concerned with overviews and more concerned with the solution of specific problems, and finally, their tenure in office is probably considerably longer than that of their superiors. Above all, the middle-level executives in France are not endowed with that aura of elitism which fosters, or perhaps even makes a necessity of, a belief in generalized skills.

SPECIALISTS VS. GENERALISTS

It was suggested earlier that it is not always to the advantage of the elite to view itself as being too narrowly specialized. What is striking, however, is that it has raised the need for "polyvalence" or "general" skills to a level of an ideology. Table 6.1 shows, among other things, that technical competence is not considered

[25] Rapport de la Commission de l'AX présidée par P. D. Cot, "Le Rôle des grands corps d'ingénieurs dans la société moderne française," *La Jaune et la Rouge*, No. 230 (October 1968), pp. 22-23.

TABLE 6.1

Qualities of Elite Training

	Public			Private		
	1	*2*	*3*	*1*	*2*	*3*
1. Rigor of work methods	73.7	0.0	0.0	71.4	0.0	0.0
2. Leadership capacity	16.7	5.3	0.0	11.4	2.9	0.0
3. Capacity to grasp rapidly essentials of a problem	13.2	71.1	2.6	17.1	71.4	0.0
4. Technical competence	2.6	2.6	7.9	0.0	8.6	8.6
5. Capacity for hard work	2.6	15.8	31.6	0.0	17.1	25.7
6. Political sense	0.0	0.0	0.0	0.0	0.0	0.0
7. Sense of reality	2.6	2.6	15.8	0.0	0.0	17.1
8. Initiative and capacity for taking risks	0.0	0.0	10.5	0.0	0.0	11.4
9. Desire to succeed and competitive spirit	0.0	0.0	26.3	0.0	0.0	31.4

one of the qualities that is developed by the corps. Rather, the corps are seen as instilling as much as possible a general capacity to grasp any problem, a quality that is considered essential for leadership and that the elite believes itself unquestionably to possess. This is equally true of all the corps. As a member of the Ponts et Chaussées noted:

> Our role as engineers of the Ponts et Chaussées does not consist in making calculations (this is the task of the forecasting engineers and of their collaborators), but to verify their legitimacy, to weigh the consequences of their eventual deviation from reality, to determine how much can be left to chance . . . there too, there is a place for works of SYNTHE-SIS, which is perfectly worthy of the level of our corps.[26]

The ability to synthesize, to adopt global views and to make global decisions is considered to be the hallmark of the elite. To possess an "esprit de synthèse" is to be blessed with the most desirable quality, a quality that is in contradiction with that of nar-

[26] J. Mante, "Réflexion sur l'orientation du corps des ponts et chaussées," *Bulletin du PCM,* Vol. 64 (March 1967), p. 27. Emphasis in original.

row specialization. The extent to which the qualities of a generalist have been elevated to the level of a cult can be seen from the arguments which the members of the elite themselves advance in support of lack of experience and knowledge:

> I have the opportunity of changing posts every three or four years. Let's say that I'm offered a post at the Caisse des Dépôts—and this post would only be offered to a member of the grands corps (I don't have to explain why—friendship, corporatism, the telephone, etc.)—I come to it, as to other posts, with the great merit of ignorance. This is what allows for a new view of things. The general and relative incompetence of members of the grands corps is a great advantage: it allows them to take a fresh view, which the others cannot.

> My great advantage as head of this bank is that I never had a modest job in a bank, so I knew nothing about banking before coming to this post.

> To be a good director of a firm, or of any organization, it's good not to have been involved in any particular aspect [of the organization]. It allows you to arrive at an objective synthesis.

The advantages that inhere in a generalist orientation do not mean that all posts of leadership require the same qualities. Table 6.2 shows, for example, that the elite does not regard the same qualities to be important for four different posts—member of a ministerial cabinet, director of the central administration, director of a nationalized industry, and director of a private enterprise. The table also shows, however, that there is one quality which the elite views as being crucial to all these posts: that of being able to grasp rapidly the essentials of any problem. No amount of technical competence, which is credited with little importance, endows one with this quality. What one needs is a general, *polyvalent*—as it is referred to by the elite—capacity. This the elite believes itself to possess, and it uses it to justify the spectacular career mobility of its members.

Technocrats are generally seen as being overly concerned with the technical aspects of problems to the detriment of social and political considerations. The problems that a modern industrial society faces are scarcely seen as technical problems by the elite. They are seen unquestionably, as Table 6.3 shows, as political

TABLE 6.2

Key Qualities Required for Different Posts[1]

	Rigor of Work Methods	Leadership Capacity	Capacity to Grasp a Problem Rapidly	Technical Competence	Capacity for Hard Work	Political Sense	Sense of Reality	Initiative and Capacity for Taking Risks	Desire to Succeed and Competitive Spirit
1. Cabinet									
Public sector	18.4	10.5	84.2	7.9	23.7	73.7	39.5	7.9	5.3
Private sector	34.3	2.9	85.7	5.7	17.1	85.7	37.1	0.0	14.3
2. Higher Civil Service									
Public sector	73.7	28.9	75.8	7.9	65.3	2.6	13.2	5.3	13.2
Private sector	85.7	37.1	82.9	2.9	62.9	0.0	5.7	5.7	2.9
3. Nationalized Sector									
Public sector	39.5	60.5	31.6	13.2	10.5	5.3	39.5	44.7	2.6
Private sector	45.7	80.0	65.7	2.9	2.9	5.7	37.1	17.4	2.6
4. Private Sector									
Public sector	7.9	86.8	13.2	2.6	5.3	2.6	50.0	84.2	28.9
Private sector	0.0	91.4	8.6	2.9	2.9	14.3	62.9	77.1	31.4

[1] Question: What are the three most important qualities necessary for holding posts in these different sectors?

Note: Because of multiple choices, rows do not total 100 percent.

TABLE 6.3

Are Problems of Modern Societies Technical?[1]

	Totally Agree		Rather Agree		Rather Disagree		Totally Disagree			
	%	No.	%	No.	%	No.	%	No.	Total	N
Public sector	3.4	2	10.2	6	28.8	17	57.6	34	100.0	59
Private sector	3.5	2	0.0	0	19.3	11	77.2	44	100.0	57

[1] Question: It is often said that the problems of modern societies are more political than technical in nature. Do you agree with this?

questions. This does not accord well with the popular image of French technocracy, but it does accord well with the elite's general view that the growing complexity of society's problems requires, above all, men whose breadth of view, and understanding of a vast set of interdependent problems that involve the entire society, enable them to transcend the limitations of technicians.

The belief that technical knowledge is relatively unimportant for the directors of both public and private enterprises is, as we shall see, highly significant insofar as the movement of the elite from one sector to another is concerned. What is implied is that the task of management is idenitcal for *any* large enterprise, whether it is private or whether it is run by the state. This view was first introduced in France by Henri Fayol, who entitled his influential work *Administration industrielle et générale*. Fayol maintained that although there was no doubt that the complexity of modern organizations implied a greater importance of technical knowledge, this tended to obscure the fact that the well-being of enterprises ultimately depended on other than technical considerations.

The number, the variety, and the importance of technical operations; the almost exclusively technical education of our professional schools; the jobs offered to our technicians—all these factors converge to give to the technical function and, as a consequence, to the *technical capacity*, an importance that leaves in the background other capacities that are equally necessary, and sometimes more useful, for the functioning and the prosperity of business enterprises.[27]

[27] Henri Fayol, *Administration industrielle et générale* (Paris: Junod, 1920), p. 8. Italics in original.

The administration of an organization, then, is an activity that calls for certain capacities that are separate from the possession of technical expertise. Administering involves, above all, according to Fayol, "foreseeing, organizing, commanding, coordinating, and supervising."[28] More important, such capacities are indispensable for those charged with the responsibility of directing an enterprise, for "As one goes up in the hierarchy, the relative importance of the *administrative capacity increases*, while that of the *technical capacity diminishes*."[29] This represents a rather accurate view of the elite's preparedness for directorial posts. It is a view that the schools themselves foster so that their graduates can in fact accede to positions of responsibility in all sectors. The members of the elite see themselves as leaders who parcel out their talents to the various sectors. What is at question is never the suitability of one's talents for a particular post, but rather the suitability or prestige of a particular post for a member of the elite. Table 6.4 indicates that the elite does not view its talents for leadership as being confined to a particular sector. The tasks of directing a public or a private enterprise are seen as being fundamentally similar, since both require an ability to grasp quickly the essentials of a problem, to command, to coordinate, and to solve problems by going to the appropriate people and decision-making centers. Obviously, the

TABLE 6.4

Training for Public or Private Sector[1]

Training	Public		Private	
	%	No.	%	No.
Equally well for both public and private sectors	50.8	30	78.6	44
Better for the public sector	42.4	25	14.3	8
Better for the private sector	3.4	2	0.0	0
Neither for the public nor for the private sector	3.4	2	3.6	2
Don't know	0.0	0	3.6	2
TOTAL	100.0	59	100.0	56

[1] Question: For which sector would you say that your training has best prepared you?

[28] *Ibid.*, p. 11.
[29] *Ibid.*, p. 15. Italics in original.

view of the elite that its training and experience are such as to permit it to take on leadership positions in both the public and private sectors is one that has certain implications for the relationship between the two sectors and for the formulation of policies. We will return to this theme in Chapter Eight, when we come to discuss the manner in which the once-sacred notions of state service and the defense of the general interest have undergone a profound transformation in the wake of the drive to industrialization in France.

That there is a perfect concordance between the aims of the specialized schools and the views of the elite is hardly surprising in view of the link that binds them. It is evident that if the schools were to provide only the narrowest technical training, they could not prepare their graduates for the leadership positions to which they are destined. Consequently, the schools have always had to tread a narrow path between maintaining that they were preparing the elite of a particular sector and maintaining that they were preparing the elite of the nation as a whole. The latter view is now the more accepted one, having in effect become a part of the elite's ideology. It constitutes an important aspect of the elite's strategy to maintain its hold over the various sectors. How accepted the view has become that the schools do and ought to provide general rather than specialized training can be seen from the remarks of Roger Martin, one of the leading industrialists in France. As a product of the Ecole Polytechnique and the Ecole des Mines, he could proclaim before an audience of the former school that the technical aspect of his training was totally useless:

> In 1948, with much nostalgia, I left public service for private enterprise. For ten years, I asked myself what I was doing in the firm that had hired me. Between what I was taught at the Ecole Polytechnique and at the Ecole des Mines, I can solemnly attest that nothing was ever of any use to me. I must admit that I never cared for mathematics or for research. The education I had gave me no ideas, and hence no preconceived ideas, about the science of management. If I have a few today, they can only be the fruits of a pure autodictaticism, and yet I owe much to this institution.[30]

[30] Roger Martin, "Ouverture," *La Jaune et la Rouge*, No. 261 (July 1971), p. 8.

That the president of an industrial giant like Saint-Gobain-Pont à-Mousson could affirm, on the occasion of his speech as president of the general assembly of the Ecole Polytechnique, that his arrival at his present grandiose position had been largely due to his "auto-dictaticism" rather than to the training he received at France's leading technical schools is, for future generations of the elite, more than sufficient proof that a technical training or professional specialization is likely to limit one and, ultimately, to reduce one's chances of reaching the summit. As Martin put it, "It is obvious that the first training must aim at allowing men to be free to adjust to ongoing changes, and that from retraining to retraining, one's whole life will have to alternate between periods of training and of activity." He then went on to observe that the "generalist option appears to respond better to this problem of constant change." He did note, however, that "it risks leading to a superficial, 'muddling through,' kind of approach."[31]

We cite Martin's words not because they are particularly original, but rather because they are particularly representative of the elite's views and because they are addressed to future members of the elite by one who represents the model of success. Martin, in effect, reinforces what future members of the elite are constantly told: in order to derive the maximum benefit from the privilege of a grande école education, it is important to be able to adapt to changing conditions, environments, posts, and not be cornered into a specialized activity. As one of the respondents of our study put it: "The rule is to be mobile, intellectually and in your career. You have to move on from post to post. You have to show that you can adapt to situations, to people, to posts. This is the real secret of success." Another respondent put it equally succinctly, "God help you if you're known as an expert who's spent so many years in the _____ area. They'll always say 'he only knows such and such' and you'll never get the marvelous opportunities that are really at your fingertips. If you want to succeed, the rule is: don't get too attached to a particular post or sector. Keep on the move."

Specialization and technical expertise—technocracy—which have often been seen as the defining characteristics of the French elite are important only insofar as they provide a justification for the elite's monopoly on important posts in the society. While the elite rationalizes its power and privilege on the basis of its training and competence, it must also deny that it is a specialized elite so

[31] *Ibid.*, p. 7.

that it may maintain and extend its position. Hence the invocation of the importance of being a generalist. Indeed, among the elite—ostensibly the graduates of specialized schools that give a practical, useful training—it is scarcely regarded as a compliment to be known as a technician. It is often a term of opprobrium, for the ambitious and successful seek above all an escape from technical work. One member of the Ponts et Chaussées working in an executive position in Paris spoke with derision of those colleagues of his "who liked the good, quiet life of *province*." He noted that "they are excellent technicians, they really know their métier, but they are really *ratés* (failures) also. Think of all the things someone in their position could have done, but, no, they preferred to be good road builders instead."

Merit and a general polyvalent aptitude justify to the elite that it properly belongs in all the positions it occupies. It does not see itself as usurping that which belongs to any other group. To the extent that the top positions in any society should be filled on the basis of qualifications, the elite feels that its merits have been severely and objectively tested. As one member of the elite noted: "If the corps did not exist, would it be necessary to create them? This would probably not be necessary since something else would already exist. Ultimately, the corps are the consequence of a belief in merit. At a moment when everything is questioned, one can also question the corps. But since a criterion of selection has to exist, if the present one is done away with, a new one certainly risks being based on nepotism—and merit seems a wholly better criterion."[32]

Since our study is concerned with those members of the elite who *do* make full use of their positions, we need to understand the mechanism that allows them to reach the kinds of positions that they occupy and that we described in Chapter Four. In order to do this, it is not sufficient to look only at their self-image and their rationalizations of their competence. Important as these are, they cannot alone explain why a particular elite is able to preserve certain of the key positions in the society for its members. To understand this, one must look closely at the networks that the elite establishes through its organizational structures.

[32] P. Daunesse, "A Propos des grands corps d'ingénieurs," *Association des cadres dirigeants et l'industries pour le progrès social et économique*, No. 241 (March 1969), p. 134.

NETWORKS AND ORGANIZATIONS:
THE CORPS AS PLACEMENT BUREAUX

The corps are institutions that were originally established to fulfill specific functions on behalf of the state, but they are "distinguished from ordinary departments by the fact that legally and in practice they are corporate bodies as well as branches of government."[33] If the corps had merely stuck to their originally designated spheres, their importance would have remained limited to certain sectors. That this is not the case is due to the organizations of the elite, the preoccupations of these organizations, and their ability to modify their tactics.[34] The problems associated with the study of elite organizations have proved intractable in large part because no formal organizations (like the corps in France) exist. Aside from broad categories of "strategic elites"—civil servants, businessmen, engineers, intellectuals—it has been difficult to obtain a concrete grasp of the interaction among the strategic elites, even though the sociometric technique has gone some way toward measuring elite interactions.[35] In France, many of these problems do not exist because elite interaction is assured by the elite's organizations. By examining what has become the central preoccupation of these organizations (i.e., the corps)—obtaining posts for their members and maintaining these posts for future members—we shall be able to see the degree of solidarity and differentiation that exists among the different organizations.

In explaining the revolutions that occurred in France between 1814 and 1870, Theodre Zeldin notes that "Immediately after every revolution the ministers were besieged by place hunters seeking the booty of victory. . . . And this search for jobs was as much the cause as the result of revolutions."[36] The "fever of ambition," to use Zeldin's phrase, the clamor for the cherished posts, is a central preoccupation of the elite's organizations. The corps compete

[33] John A. Armstrong, *The European Administrative Elite* (Princeton: Princeton University Press, 1973), p. 24.

[34] When we refer to the organizational structure of the elite or to the elite's organizations, we are referring to a juridically defined corporate entity—the corps.

[35] See Frank Bonilla, *The Failure of Elites* (Cambridge, Mass.: The M.I.T. Press, 1972), and Allan Barton et al., *Opinion-Makers in Yugoslavia* (New York: Praeger Publishers, 1973).

[36] Theodre Zeldin, *The Political System of Napoleon III* (New York: W. W. Norton & Co., Inc., 1971), p. 7.

fiercely with one another when certain posts open up because obtaining glorious posts satisfies the ambitions of the individual members and affects the corps' prestige, or its "image de marque."

The competition for posts may appear as not highly significant in explaining the *raison d'être* and the influence of the elite's organizations. However, the importance of the drive and ambition of the elite should not be underestimated, especially when one examines its degree of integration and differentiation. In the first place, the spreading of its tentacles assures for each corps the capture of yet another sector. Second, the imperialistic nature of the corps allows them to obtain a foothold in newly created areas and thus makes it more difficult for them to become obsolete. This, as will be seen, is a key factor in explaining the adaptation of the elite to changing conditions. Third, the personal drive of the individual members of the elite, whose desire to climb high and rapidly has long been nurtured by their schools and by the corps themselves, is an extremely important factor. To a very considerable extent, then, as the corps have essentially become placement bureaux for their members.

To regard as an essential function of the corps the placement of their members in suitable posts may appear to trivialize their role. But it must be clearly recognized that the work that the corps themselves do is, in most cases, highly routine and devoid of interest to an ambitious person. Indeed, one's career is considered a failure if most of one's professional life is spent working in the corps itself. And the corps themselves recognize this perfectly well. Consequently, the only way that they can attract the best products of the grandes écoles is by offering them a wide range of career opportunities. The elite attaches considerable importance to the preservation of the corps' *image de marque* and to the career advantages it derives from its membership in a corps. Now, defending the corps' image means, in effect, assuring that its prestige is not eroded. The most important sign that such a situation may actually be taking place is the loss of crucial posts to another corps. Hence the importance attached also to the defense of the corps' own sphere of influence.

We observed in the previous chapter that the possibility of having a choice of high-level positions in any number of areas was generally regarded as the greatest advantage that could be derived from belonging to one of the grands corps. In fact, entry into one of these corps even gives one the liberty of doing little for the rest of one's life. One person who had been received first in the entrance examination to the Ecole Polytechnique and who was critical of many aspects of the school, particularly the ranking system, wrote in a magazine article: "I had decided not to choose under any circumstances the first corps of the *'botte,'* that of the Mines. Now I see things more objectively: I am weighing the advantages. Without a doubt, I will choose the Mines which offers a large range of possibilities, and which will leave me a greater degree of freedom for the future."[37] This person simply came to the realization that in choosing a particular corps one was in no way choosing to work in a particular sector, nor was one manifesting a predilection for the particular type of work that the corps was engaged in. Rather, one was simply entering an elite organization that offered the maximum liberty insofar as the choice of a career was concerned. In other words, one had to understand that in entering a corps one was in effect joining a corporatist group that facilitated the acquisition of certain advantages. It in no way entailed the choice of or a commitment to a particular career. This is recognized by all the members of the elite, as the following statements attest:

> The corps are indispensable for advancing careers. If it wasn't for my corps, how else would I have been in Matignon [the Prime Minister's cabinet] ordering ministers around at the age of thirty?

> I cannot imagine anyone having the power I have in my present post and at my young age who does not belong to one of the grands corps.

> I'm at the moment representing our government in certain negotiations with a foreign government. If I had not belonged to one of the grands corps, I certainly would not have been chosen.

The preoccupation with posts and careers comes early to the members of the elite. It is, in fact, part and parcel of their socialization experience. While still students, they are made fully aware of the availability of posts and of the advantages that accompany these posts. One of the ENA students interviewed by Maria-Antonietta Macciocchi describes the process in these terms:

[37] Robert Brunck, "L'Horizon d'un élève de l'X," *Preuves*, 4ᵉ trimestre (1971), p. 16.

In the final year, we are bombarded by hundreds of pieces of paper describing the vacant posts, which make our mouth water, with an appendix detailing the economic advantages, the extra bonuses, the flexible hours, the vacations. And everyone begins to make his calculations. Aside from the top ten [who enter one of the grands corps], everyone has to transform himself into a kind of electronic brain in order to calculate his future. Look at these tons of printed paper— their function is to turn on the red lights of our self-advertising careerist radar. The state, for us, is a colossal employment agency.[38]

Because of the position that the grands corps have assumed in society, they are constantly solicited by ministers, by private firms, and by all types of agencies. Consequently, the openings for key executive posts in the public, parapublic, and private sectors are distributed through a narrow network that includes the major corps. The corps themselves are interested only in posts that reflect well on themselves, and it is considered one of the chief duties of the head of a corps "to eliminate requests that are not prestigious" or to dissuade a member from "taking a position that would reflect badly on the image of the corps." As one head of a corps put it: "I receive all kinds of requests for all sorts of jobs and I have to eliminate immediately those, important as they may seem to some people, that are unbecoming to members of this corps. Sometimes it happens that a member insists on taking a particular position that we think would do harm to our reputation, and here we have to bring all the pressure to bear—which also includes denying him a leave—to prevent him from taking this post." The firms and agencies who ask the corps to supply them with one of their members understand the needs of the corps and so are not likely to offer low-level posts. Indeed, for high-level directorial posts in the public and private sectors recruitment is often done exclusively through the corps. "It is true," said the president of one of the largest industrial enterprises in France, "that when we look for talented people we do not place ads in newspapers or anything like that. We go to our corps and we try to find someone who fits the job we're trying to fill." The president of this enterprise was a member of the Corps des Mines, as was another who said, "You

[38] Cited in Maria-Antonietta Macciocchi, *De la France* (Paris: Editions du Seuil, 1977), p. 294.

179

know, our corps is very small and until recently, even now actually, you called M. _____, who has always been considered the Pope of the corps no matter what post he happened to be occupying himself, and he would indicate your man." There is little doubt that the man referred to as "the Pope" of the corps has had a considerable influence over a great many careers. He was able in a large number of cases to channel careers in particular directions because he considered it the correct training for crowning posts. This was often done without regard for the desires of particular individuals who may have manifested interests in other directions. One such person noted that he was always interested in going into a particular type of industry but this was never possible because "M. _____ had always destined me for this particular post and in order to arrive at this post he thought it important I have such and such an experience."

The extent to which the grands corps have come to have a hold over the key positions in the various sectors has given rise to a particular type of network system which ensures that such positions do not go beyond a limited circle. To gain entry into this network, it is not merely sufficient to have entered a grande école, it is necessary to gain entry into a corps. Having done that, one enters into a network through which pass all the lucrative and prestigious positions. The importance placed on finding posts in the parapublic and private sectors for the members of the grands corps becomes comprehensible when one takes into account the fact that this elite arrives at the top of the administrative hierarchy at a remarkably early age. The need to find outlets for them outside the administrative sector therefore comes to assume paramount importance. In addition, there is a strong feeling among the elite that it ought to be compensated materially for its years in public service. Hence, the shift to a post in the semipublic or private sector always entails an extremely lucrative remuneration. One cannot underestimate the material factor involved in the circulation of posts, for even though these men have been brought up on the notions of "duty" and "service," they also demand a compensation that is not out of keeping with their self-image.

The move from one key post to another involves a most orderly game of musical chairs: when a vacancy is about to occur, for example, in a top post in one of the major banks, an Inspecteur des Finances in the bank is likely to call up a friend who is still in the administration and ask him whether he is ready for "le grand saut" (the big jump from the public sector to a major post in the private sector). Alternatively, the one who is still in the administration might begin to inform the head of his corps and his camarades in both sectors that he is ready for "the big jump." Now, the principle of "le grand saut" is that it can generally only be a move from a major post to a major post. Hence, it is normally thought advisable to reach the summit in the public sector in order to reach the summit in the private sector equally rapidly. A very early move from the public to the private sector often means having to make your way up the executive ladder—the opposite of making "le grand saut." On occasion one may be fortunate enough to make a remarkable jump very early in one's career, as happened in the case of a young member of one of the grands corps who was asked to join a major corporation by a friend who had recently left the administration and taken up the top position in the corporation. The young man indicated that since he was only thirty-four years old he still had time before leaving the administration, so that extraordinary circumstances would be required to induce him to make a move at that point. The "extraordinary circumstances" were forthcoming within a matter of weeks, and these included the second highest post in the corporation and a salary of $15,000 per month. As the man in question explained, "What was the point of waiting any longer? Even if I had waited another four or five years, I would never have gotten a post like this. And one has to seize opportunities as they present themselves!" To be sure, this is a rather unusual case, but what is not unusual is the move in search of material compensation, the monopoly on the major posts which the elite exercises, and the purely personal element in recruitment to the top posts.

The members of the elite naturally put the greatest emphasis on their abilities to assume the onerous tasks of managing public and private enterprises. They believe that because they "circulated" a great deal and always at high levels, they are the most competent for such positions. They are not unaware, however, of the importance of personal relations in this type of network. As one Inspecteur des Finances explained: "Baumgartner [former Minister of Finance] used to tell the young Inspecteurs des Finances he was training: 1) it is indispensable to be eloquent; 2) it is useful to be intelligent; and 3) it's not at all bad to have good contacts." Another member of the elite belonging to the Corps des Mines put it this way: "The reason that members of the grands corps go right to the top in the private sector is that those who do not belong to the grands corps have 1) no contacts; 2) a limited horizon; and 3) limited experience." Obviously, there is a circularity in this explanation since all three depend on one's membership in the grands corps. Nor does this circularity escape the elite, for as one respondent observed, "Those who enter the grands corps may not be better than others at the very beginning of their careers, but after three or four years, they *are* better. This is because of their career experiences which are open to them because they belong to the grands corps. The others are stuck with working on the same problems, so they can't possibly become as experienced. It's a vicious circle."

In seeking to fill a high-level post, in either the public or private sector, a member of a grand corps will generally call for one who belongs to the same corps. The solidarity of the members of a corps and the attachment of all members to their own corps are extremely pronounced. One member of the Conseil d'Etat said: "I try daily to be an asset to my corps. The other day the Director of Criminal Affairs [in the Ministry of Justice] told me that a member of the Conseil d'Etat had just been arrested for drunken driving. This hurt me terribly, not because of the man involved whom I didn't know personally, but because I suddenly realized that a member of the Conseil d'Etat could be caught in this terrible situation." A member of another corps observed that "I never forget that I am member of my corps." The corps is forever present, even for those who maintain that they have nothing but contempt for these "corporatist" institutions. As one such member noted: "I don't believe in these old-fashioned, elitist castes, but they never let go of you and so you end up having to be a part of them."

Nowhere is the degree of solidarity better manifested than in the belief that one has a duty to preserve one's post for a member of one's corps. Table 6.5 shows that members of the grands corps feel inclined to name someone from their corps as their successor, even when they do not know him personally. This is considered nothing less than a duty, the minimum that is expected from them. One respondent said, "There is absolutely no question that I would name the person who belonged to my corps over anyone else." Why? "Because that's the way it is. Those are the rules and you have to play by them." The term *"renvoyer l'ascenseur,"*—sending back the elevator so that a camarade can climb up just as the elevator was sent down to you—was frequently used. "I would name someone from my corps to succeed me," said one respondent, "because that is what is expected of you. You have to *renvoyer l'ascenseur* because you yourself have benefited from the system and

TABLE 6.5

Choice of a Successor[1]

	Public Sector		Private Sector	
	%	No.	%	No.
1. A member of your corps whom you do not know personally but who is highly recommended by the corps	65.0	39	53.4	31
2. A member of another corps who is personally known to you	13.3	8	3.4	2
3. Someone who is not a member of a grand corps but whose qualities you appreciate	18.3	11	39.7	23
4. Don't know	3.3	2	3.4	2
TOTAL	100.0	60	100.0	58

[1] Question: Suppose that at the time of leaving your present post you have the possibility of proposing the name of a successor. Three people are, a priori, especially qualified to succeed you. Whom would you choose?

you're expected to do as much for others. It's ridiculous but that's the way it is." Another respondent observed that it was really a question of competence, so that "It's impossible to imagine someone not from my corps occupying this post, which does after all call for certain skills." While this particular respondent said that it had never occurred to him that his post could ever be occupied by someone who did not belong to the Corps des Mines, others noted that they did not believe in assigning posts on the basis of corps but that, in the final analysis, the persons likely to possess the necessary qualifications for their posts would all probably be members of their respective corps. As one such respondent said: "I believe that whoever has the best qualification, regardless of whether he belongs to a corps or not, should get the post. I would add, however, that this post requires a solid familiarity with legal matters, an ability to synthesize, a knowledge of the administrative machine, an ability to get things done, so in all likelihood the best qualified person would come from my corps." A member of another corps occupying a high-level executive post in the private sector said: "I think it totally absurd to allocate posts on the basis of one's corps. I would pick whoever was most qualified. It is true nonetheless that if I start to look around and try to find the person who combines 1) a mastery of fiscal matters; 2) wide administrative and managerial experience, and 3) an ability to cut through the maze of documents and people and go right to the heart of a problem, I think that an Inspecteur des Finances would probably be the best qualified person. It has nothing to do with his being a member of my corps, it's just that the members of my corps receive the kind of training and experience that fits them best for these posts."

Monopolistic Competition

Just as the fact of holding on to particular posts and sectors evidences the remarkable solidarity of the members of a corps, so it divides the various corps among themselves. Each corps tries to cling to its own posts and seeks to capture others, for all have the same goal of maintaining their prestige and their image. The various corps are generally seen as a unit rather than as competing institutions by their own members (Table 6.6). However, even when they are seen as rival institutions, their rivalry rarely extends beyond competition for posts. It is always a question of jurisdiction, of turf, and scarcely ever a question of policy that divides the corps. One member of the elite said, ". . . actually, there is no rivalry among the corps." Another said "Yes, there is rivalry, if

TABLE 6.6

Solidarity vs. Rivalry Among Corps[1]

| | Public Sector | | Private Sector | |
	%	*No.*	*%*	*No.*
Solidarity and cooperation	81.7	49	79.3	46
Rivalry and conflicts	13.3	8	13.8	8
Don't know	5.0	3	6.9	4
TOTAL	100.0	60	100.0	58

[1] Question: According to some people, there is a profound solidarity that links the different corps. According to others, there are deep rivalries and divisions which hinder the efficient functioning of institutions. From your own experience, which would you say is the more correct view?

you consider competition over posts a form of rivalry." "Ultimate-ly," a leading member of the elite observed, "there is one funda-mental interest that all the corps share, whether they are conscious of it or not: to maintain the present system."

The evidence suggests that although one's loyalty is, above all, to one's own corps, there is nevertheless a very high degree of solidarity among the various corps. Table 6.7 shows that when a member of one of the grands corps is confronted by some impor-tant problem, he will usually choose to consult someone who is a member of the grands corps over someone who does not belong to any of the elite corps. The intracorps solidarity is also shown by the fact that a member of a corps will most often consult some-one from another corps whom he knows personally rather than someone in his own corps whom he does not know (Table 6.8). The answers to these projective questions are rather telling be-

TABLE 6.7

Would You Rather Consult a Member
of a Grand Corps or a Noncorps Person?

	Member of a Grand Corps		Noncorps Person		Don't Know			
	%	No.	%	No.	%	No.	Total	N
Public sector	71.7	43	15.0	9	13.3	8	100.0	60
Private sector	69.0	40	12.1	7	19.0	11	100.0	58

TABLE 6.8

Would You Rather Consult a Member of Your
Own Corps or Member of Another Corps?[1]

	Member of One's Own Corps		Member of Another Corps		Don't Know			
	%	No.	%	No.	%	No.	Total	N
Public sector	10.0	6	86.7	52	3.3	2	100.0	60
Private sector	5.2	3	94.8	55	0.0	0	100.0	58

[1] Question: Suppose that you find yourself confronted by a rather delicate problem and that you are in need of help. Two people are equally competent to help you: one is a member of your corps but you do not know him personally; the other is a member of another corps but you have had occasion to meet him. Whose help would you seek?

cause they indicate more than mere attitudes toward a particular situation. The use of a more rigorous sociometric technique to measure more precisely the degree of intracorps and intercorps interaction would almost certainly have led to the same conclusions that are indicated by the use of the projective questions of the type that we have employed.

Nor should the evidence of interelite solidarity appear surprising. The differences that divide the elite are short-term tactical differences that the members consider as being no more than "healthy competition." When it comes to questions of long-term interests, competition within the elite ceases and the defense of its interests takes precedence over everything. What was once considered as healthy competition becomes dangerous. Events seem to bear this out, for if one examines the periods during which the elite institutions and their privileged position in French society came under severe attack—prior to World War I, in the 1930s, at the Liberation, in 1968—all differences among the elite vanished and they banded together to preserve as much as possible of the existing structure. Even the relatively minor crisis at ENA in 1970, which posed a momentary threat to some of the grands corps, was sufficient to lead to a remarkable demonstration of unity among these corps, which came to speak with one voice. Just as in an oligopolistic market where price fixing is more advantageous to the few firms involved, so the elite in France knows when to control competition that appears to threaten the entire elite.

The reason for the solidarity that exists within a corps, and even between corps, is not difficult to understand when one considers the advantages that accrue to each individual member as a result of this particular form of elite organization. As Thoenig put it, "The individual is nothing or almost nothing without the corps. His personal status, his chances for success, his ability to carry out tasks all depend on whether or not he belongs to a corps."[39] Entry into a corps endows one with considerable prestige and opportunities from the outset of one's career, and because it allows one to occupy important posts early in one's career, it follows that a corps member's professional experience is different from one who is not fortunate enough to belong to a corps. Whether this justifies the grands corps' predominance in the major posts is another matter and one that obviously transcends the sole criterion of qualifications. Ultimately, the hold on the key posts, which has become

[39] Thoenig, *L'Ere des technocrates*, p. 244.

such an important preoccupation of the corps, must be seen for what it is: a method by which each corps extends its sphere of activity, attracts the ablest products of the grandes écoles, legitimizes itself, and allows its members to accede to positions that are influential, prestigious, and highly remunerative. The corps is able to do this because it has created a system that excludes the possibility of real competition. It is important, therefore, to stress the mundane, materialistic aspect of the scramble for positions on the part of the elite because behind all the justifications of talent, qualifications, incorruptibility, and so on lie the ambitions that dominate the upper bourgeoisie, ambitions that are chronicled in Balzac's novels—the desire to make it, "the fever of ambition which devours every head and which excites every mind."[40] These ambitions are fostered and nurtured by the elite institutions, which from the outset seek to set the new recruits apart from society. A recent survey of two grandes écoles shows that few ever expect to experience unemployment (Table 6.9). But what is sought is more than

TABLE 6.9

Expectation of Unemployment

	Polytechnique	Central	Both Schools
Yes	13.0	27.0	21.0
No	77.0	60.0	68.0
Have been unemployed	3.0	4.0	3.0
Don't know	7.0	9.0	8.0
TOTAL	100.0	100.0	100.0

Source: *Les Informations*, No. 1,462 (May 1973), p. 61.

security of employment, it is security at a level that few in the society can aspire to. Hence, the individual who enters a grand corps is offered rewards which few ever turn down and which, more importantly, ensure his support for the institutions without which he could not have enjoyed these rewards. This explains why even those members of the grands corps who expressed hostility to the system were so ready to *"renvoyer l'ascenseur."* To be sure, not every member of this elite arrives at the top, and some were quick to point out that many of their camarades had fallen by the wayside, which means no more than that they continue to enjoy

[40] Zeldin, *The Political System of Napoleon III*, p. 8.

prestigious positions that may be no more than sinecures. But the fact that not all members of the grands corps come to occupy exalted positions is surely not the correct way of viewing the problem. The problem should be looked at in the following terms: what are the chances of one's reaching the highest positions in the society if one does not belong to one of the elite institutions? The statistics presented in Chapter Four provide the answer to this question.

That an institution should seek to act in its interest, however it chooses to define it, is surely understandable. It is therefore not difficult to comprehend the elite organizations' preoccupation with securing and preserving their hold over the key posts in the society. We have seen that the corps do all they can in this respect. Their members have even been successful in intellectually rationalizing their rapid accession to society's major posts: their generalized skills enable them to acquire wide-ranging experiences and their "specialized" skills seem to become important when the need for a successor arises. However this may be, our task demands that we go one step further and examine the consequences, intended or otherwise, of the elite organizations' tactics. In other words, it is possible that, as a result of their competition for control of various sectors, these organizations acquire a certain flexibility which facilitates their adaptation to changing conditions and which, ultimately, explains their survival.[41]

DISCRETION

Pareto and Mosca both emphasized the extent to which rapacity and greed contribute to the downfall of an elite. They both observed that it ill-behooves an elite to flaunt its privileges. To some extent, the institutional structure within which French elites function has helped to introduce not only a measure of pride among the members, but also a keen awareness that the privileges they enjoy will generally be envied by others.

If the French elite sees itself as legitimate because it is chosen on the basis of merit, because it exercises responsibility on behalf of the state, because it believes in order and hierarchy, because it is incorruptible, these beliefs must also be accepted, to a very large extent, by the society. The elite does not remain secure simply by projecting an image. It must itself *believe* in the image and it must

[41] This is discussed in the next chapter.

convince others that it fulfills an indispensable function for the society. It is often forgotten that even charisma requires constant renewal, and that it is based only in part on a mystical relationship. Equally important are the tangible results, the leader's ability to deliver what he has promised. As Weber put it: "If he is for long unsuccessful, above all if his leadership fails to benefit his followers, it is likely that his charismatic authority will disappear. This is the genuine charismatic meaning of the 'gift of Grace!' "[42]

It is possible for an elite to benefit from general ignorance about its activities. Certainly the French elite has considered it important to avoid flamboyance and the open display of power. It has always preferred to act discreetly, which explains in part why it has not hitherto been the subject of objective studies. Except for Thoenig's study on the Corps des Ponts et Chaussées, we remain relatively ignorant of the functioning and the power of the elite. When asked whether they believed that the elite was in general admired, rare was the person who did not begin by saying that outside of a small segment of the population few people knew or cared about what it meant to be an Inspecteur des Finances or a member of the Corps des Mines. Table 6.10 shows that the majority of the elite in both the public and private sectors believe that the grands corps are either not admired at all (because they are envied, feared, or not known) or simply not known in anything but the vaguest way. This ignorance was generally held to be a salutary thing because, as one of our respondents put it, "to know something about this elite system is likely to lead to misinterpretation." All the people need to know—all they, in fact, vaguely know—is that these people are very good at passing exams, that they are *"grosses têtes."* As a member of the Corps des Mines who had been in Michel Jobert's cabinet at the Ministry of Foreign Affairs expressed it, "The less people speak about us, the better it is."[43] The imperative of discretion has a long tradition among the elite. A former polytechnician, General Maurin, advised the students of the Ecole Polytechnique in 1945: "Do not forget that the day you have forced your way through the rather narrow gate of the Ecole Polytechnique, you risk bearing the brunt of envy. Certainly, it is better to be envied than pitied, but it serves no purpose to excite the envious. . . .

[42] Max Weber, *The Theory of Social and Economic Organizations* (New York: The Free Press, 1964), p. 360.

[43] Cited in Josette Alia, "Les Agents secrets du pouvoir," *Nouvel Observateur,* 11 March 1974, p. 34.

TABLE 6.10

Are the Grands Corps Admired by the Society?[1]

	Very Much %	No.	Rather %	No.	Little %	No.	Not At All %	No.	Unknown %	No.	Don't Know %	No.	Total	N
Public sector	19.4	12	11.3	7	3.2	2	25.8	16	38.7	24	1.6	1	100.0	62
Private sector	16.1	10	8.1	5	3.2	2	22.6	14	45.2	28	4.8	3	100.0	62

[1] Question: Do you think that the grands corps are admired in France?

Therefore, speak of the Ecole Polytechinique only among your-selves or in a small family circle."[44]

Is the penchant for discreetness merely an innocuous tradition or is it intended to shield the elite from public wrath because of the monopoly it has on the key posts in the society? The members of the elite readily acknowledged, almost to a man, that they were probably more envied than admired. Moreover, even among those who believed most strongly in the corps, some sounded a certain note of caution (Table 6.11), indicating that the corps were still

TABLE 6.11

The Preponderance of the Grands Corps
in French Society[1]

	Public Sector		Private Sector	
	%	No.	%	No.
A phenomenon with great advantages	31.0	18	26.8	15
A phenomenon whose advantages still outweigh the disadvantages	41.4	24	35.7	20
A phenomenon whose disadvantages are becoming evident	19.0	11	26.8	15
A phenomenon against which it is necessary to react	5.2	3	10.7	6
Don't know	3.4	2	0.0	0
TOTAL	100.0	58	100.0	56

[1] Question: All things considered, how do you view the growing pre-ponderance of the members of the grands corps in the diverse directorial posts of French society?

viable, but that it would be a mistake to assume that this will nec-essarily always be so. Hence, the *need* to be both vigilant and as discreet as possible.

But discretion may become less and less possible precisely as a result of the intensive competition among the members of this elite and the consequent success of the members of the elite in

[44] General Maurin, "Allocution prononcée devant les élèves de l'Ecole Polytechnique," *La Jaune et la Rouge*, No. 2 (March 1946), p. 79.

securing the important posts. One can see a process which involves competition among the corps, which leads to the adaptation of the corps to new conditions, but which also leads to an imperialism. Hence, the very nature of the elite system, which requires each elite not merely to fight for its presently held turf but to extend itself, has been a key element until now in the survival of the elite, but may in the end bring it into question. One member of the Corps des Ponts et Chaussées explained the difference between his own corps and that of the Corps des Mines in this way: "We have always been grounded in reality. We do tangible things, such as building roads. We are in touch with people at the national and at the local level. The Corps des Mines is always searching for something, that's why it extends itself here and there and everywhere. And when the day of reckoning comes, the Corps des Ponts et Chaussées will always be able to say that we are needed just to build roads."

Chapter Seven

ADAPTATION

"L'X est vieille, et en même temps, elle est toute neuve."
Charles De Gaulle[1]

"En somme, l'Inspection a évolué en restant elle-même."

THE institution that is able to change and yet remain intact has clearly achieved a remarkable feat. Such, at any rate, are the aims and the habitual self-characterizations of any well-organized institution that seeks to preserve its position over a long period. The church, no less than communist parties, has always tried to see itself as "evolving" while not deviating from its dogma in the least. One can regard the twin aims of change and stability as an attempt to stand still and walk at the same time. However, rather than being antithetical, it is also possible that each is an indispensable complement to the other. For an institution to survive, that is, to preserve its functions, roles, missions, privileges, it must demonstrate a certain degree of flexibility. Consequently, in trying to understand the survival of France's elite, we must try to understand its capacity to adapt to new conditions and environments. It should be made clear that adaptation refers here not to the impact of the elite on the society, but only to the ability of the elite to preserve itself. For the moment, we are concerned only to round off our analysis of the problem of elite transformation.

THE SCOPE OF ELITE ENDEAVORS

Mosca suggested that with adequate foresight an elite could last indefinitely.[3] To do so, it must have the ability to transform itself

[1] Charles De Gaulle, speech at Ecole Polytechnique, *La Jaune et la Rouge*, No. 129 (July 1959), p. 44.
[2] F.-L. Closon and J. Filippi, *L'Economie et les finances* (Paris: Presses Universitaires de France, 1968), p. 106.
[3] Gaetano Mosca, *The Ruling Class* (New York: McGraw-Hill, 1939), p. 462.

continually. The transformation and adaptation of elites are central to Mosca's analysis of elite survival. They are important to Pareto, too, though he attaches perhaps a greater importance to the elite's will to fight to preserve its position. Elites decline, according to Pareto because "they become effete,"[4] and because they become "weighed down by sentimental and humanitarian tendencies."[5] No less than Mosca, Pareto shared a profound admiration for Taine's analysis of the French Revolution. If Louis XVI and the French aristocracy went down, it was because, as Taine put it, "they forgot that the primary objective of government, as it is of the police force, is the preservation of order through force."[6] And like Pareto, Mosca juxtaposes, at many points in his study, political developments in nineteenth-century France and Britain. "One should note," he wrote, "that in the course of the nineteenth century England adopted peacefully and without violent shocks almost all the basic civil and political reforms that France paid so heavily to achieve through the great Revolution. Undeniably, the great advantage of England lay in the greater energy, the greater practical wisdom, the better political training, that her ruling class possessed down to the very end of the past century."[7] This emphasis on the "energy," "wisdom," and "training" of a ruling elite distinguishes Mosca's analysis from Pareto's, for the latter more often adopted what may be characterized as a "hard-line" position when it came to a discussion of the preservation of an elite's position. Just as Mosca put a greater emphasis on the need for the elite to legitimize itself, so he also placed a greater stress on its self-transforming ability and capacity for adaptation. Indeed, adaptation was a necessary aspect of the elite's need to renew its legitimacy, for without a capacity to renew and transform itself, which entailed a considerable degree of openness, an elite could not long expect to remain legitimate. "Ruling classes," wrote Mosca, "decline inevitably when they cease to find scope for the capacities through which they rose to power, when they can no longer render the social services which they once rendered, or when their talents and the services they render lose in importance in the social environment in which they live."[8]

---

[4] Vilfredo Pareto, *The Rise and Fall of Elites* (New York: Bedminster Press, 1968), p. 60.

[5] *Ibid.*, p. 62.

[6] Cited in Mosca, *The Ruling Class*, p. 119.

[7] *Ibid.*   [8] *Ibid.*, pp. 65-66.

Mosca is here referring not merely to the loss of willpower and talent, but rather to what Schumpeter called "the pressure of the objective social situation,"[9] which may render an elite obsolete. An elite establishes its importance in large part because it fulfills a specific and badly needed function. Once that function becomes, objectively, of little importance, inactivity and flagging energy results. However, some elites will overcome this and strike out for new ground, while others may not. "But it is precisely because a decline in the social importance of a class function—the inadequate exercise and ultimate surrender of that function—*sets the members of the class free* that the decline in class position which might be expected occurs only if the class is unable to adapt itself to some other function that rates the same social importance as the old one."[10] As long as the elite is able to adapt in such a way as to continue carrying out what Schumpeter calls "socially necessary" functions, it will continue to survive. "And every class that has once enjoyed an elevated position is greatly aided in seizing new functions, because the sources and gains of its prior function survive."[11]

Now, Schumpeter spells out more clearly than Mosca what the process of adaptation entails and how this contributes to elite, or class, survival. "Classes themselves rise and fall according to the nature and success with which they—meaning here, their members—fulfill their characteristic function, and according to the rise and fall in the social significance of this function, or of those functions which the class members are willing and able to accept instead. . . ."[12] In addition, Schumpeter notes "the connection between class efficiency and adaptability to altered circumstances," indicating that those who cannot adapt because of rigidity and too narrow a specialization cannot long continue to exist. "There is the aristocrat, for example, who hurls himself into an election campaign as his ancestors rode into battle; and there is the aristocrat who says to himself: 'I can't very well ask my valet to vote for me.' Here, in fact, is the measure of two radically different types of European aristocrat. *The class situation may so specialize members of the class that adaptation to new situations becomes all but impossible.*"[13] It follows that adaptation involves the abandonment of

[9] Joseph Schumpeter, *Imperialism and Social Classes* (New York: The World Publishing Company, 1971), p. 151.

[10] *Ibid.* Italics in original.   [11] *Ibid.*

[12] *Ibid.*, pp. 159-160.   [13] *Ibid.*, pp. 167-168. Italics added.

what is no longer a "socially necessary" function and a willingness to assume other functions, which themselves come to assume an importance if for no other reason than that they are taken over by the elite. "Social leadership," notes Schumpeter, "can express itself in many different concrete activities, and those which are chosen by a once-dominant group will thereby achieve higher social evaluation."[14] But if an elite does not begin to exhibit this diversity, or imperialism, it is not likely to be able to attract the most talented and energetic elements, and thus it will become infected by a "flagging will power." To be imperialistic, to be constantly in search of new functions, is a sign not only of the vigor of the elite but also of its unwillingness to become narrowly specialized. This type of activity is what enables an elite to renew its legitimacy in the society.

ORGANIZATION AND STRATEGY: A RECAPITULATION

"The minority is organized for the very reason that it is a minority."[15] Small organized groups are also more likely to pursue shared goals; they are more likely to elicit a commitment from the total membership.[16] Such is the case of the elite organizations (the grands corps) in France.

Entry into these organizations is severely restricted, so that they have experienced no noticeable increase in their membership, which is determined purely on the basis of academic qualifications.[17] Each member recognizes his colleagues as having similar qualifications, a factor which leads to mutual respect and to a "sense of affinity" with one another. All the members are profoundly conscious of the fact that they have been "chosen" to belong to an elite that is universally recognized for its intellectual capacities. All along, the feeling of having achieved more than others is confirmed by their experiences. As one elite member put it, "there's no doubt that all the members of the grands corps share a certain reflex of superiority. It's not a bad thing either." This "reflex of superiority" is fostered by their organizations which

[14] *Ibid.*, p. 158.

[15] Mosca, *The Ruling Class*, p. 53.

[16] See Mancur Olson, *The Logic of Collective Action* (New York: Schocken Books, 1969), pp. 22-35.

[17] Most of the grands corps have about 300 members. The one exception is the Corps des Ponts et Chaussées, which has close to 2,000 members.

take it upon themselves to secure prestigious posts for their members. Once an individual's career is launched, he may depend less directly on his organization to secure new posts for him than on other members of his organization with whom he is in contact in many sectors.

There is thus an internal and an external aspect to the elite organizations. The internal aspect consists of the work that they are juridically empowered to carry out, and this is normally done by a small minority, either the beginners or the older members who have been unable to make a career in the "big world." The external aspect consists of the success that the members of each corps achieve in various sectors. This is the larger, more important, and more visible aspect of the corps. Indeed, the internal aspect, downgraded as it is in most elite organizations (Mines, Inspection des Finances), is important to the extent that it serves as a base from which the external function can be better approached. This is why we were led to characterize these organizations as placement bureaux. No individual enters the Inspection des Finances just to inspect finances, and no individual enters the Corps des Mines so as to be associated in any capacity with mines. This is less true of the Conseil d'Etat and of the Cour des Comptes, though the members of these corps enjoy the same possibilities for using their corps to acquire positions in other sectors.

Now, a link is always maintained between the individual working outside the corps, regardless of the sector, and the corps itself. For one thing, the elite member owes his posts, to a large extent, to his membership in the corps. This reflects on the corps itself, so that the corps always have an interest in seeing that their members accept only prestigious posts. This was stressed by all the heads of the corps. "One of my main functions," said one, "is to make sure that no member accepts a post that does not carry sufficient weight." Another head of a corps noted, "I only intervene when one of our boys contemplates taking a position that we don't consider sufficiently dignified." Still another head of a corps observed that "my responsibility is not to tell the members to go here and there. I don't have that power. I consider a larger part of my responsibility fulfilled, however, when I channel our members into posts of the first order only." Not unimportantly, he added, "what would become of the grands corps if their members started taking any post?" But a link is also maintained between the individuals on leave from their corps and the corps to which they belong, and among the members of the corps, regardless of the sector in which they are working, by a series of informal meetings. In one corps, it was the responsibility of one senior man to invite different members of the corps to a lunch once a week. In another corps it was the responsibility of the head of the corps to persuade an illustrious member of the corps to invite some of the younger members to lunch. "These kinds of meetings, which I arrange all the time," he explained, "are very important. The young make their contacts. The old get to know the kind of people they can later call on. And the solidarity of the corps benefits because there's no such thing as a generation gap. All this is possible because the corps is small."

The elite, then, is highly structured and organized. Its members, no matter how critical they may be of the system as a whole, support and defend their organizations. Moreover, differences within the elite are put aside when the elite as a whole is under attack. We have suggested that these differences are scarcely of an ideological nature. Since all the corps have an imperialistic nature, they tend to clash over terrains, but such clashes are always tempered by the fact that there is a certain mutual respect insofar as basic terrains are concerned.

Now, the organizations of the elite ensure that their members will be highly mobile and highly sought after within and beyond the state apparatus. This has had a profound impact on the adaptability of the elite to changing conditions within the society. Adaptation involves a reorientation, if not a total change, of direction. It involves branching out, curtailing emphasis in one area and concentrating on another area. Hence, it involves conscious, deliberate policies. It rarely depends on chance. The adaptation of an elite to a particular set of circumstances means that change was seen, or foreseen, on the horizon and that a set of policies was instituted to meet them. Successful adaptation requires not only the avoidance of obsolescence, but the need to fulfill continually "socially necessary" functions. As Schumpeter wrote, "In particular there now emerges . . . the sense in which we speak of a socially necessary function, of class activity and orientation to activity which we, the observers, understand to be necessary for the survival of the social group, under a given set of circumstances and with a given disposition on the part of the people, and which the group itself senses to be vital for survival."[18] We turn now to an examination of specific aspects of the French elite's adaptation.

[18] Schumpeter, *Imperialism and Social Classes*, p. 157.

From State to Nation

The overriding original aim of the grandes écoles was to train people for state service. It was an aim that the schools themselves embraced but that came gradually to be put into question as a result of the changing pattern of career choices of their graduates. The Ecole Polytechnique, for example, was clearly created to train officials for various state activities. The decree of 22 October 1795 stated that the "Ecole Polytechnique is created for the purpose of training students for service in the Artillery, in military engineering, civil engineering and civilian construction, in Mines, in shipbuilding and naval construction and Topography, as well as for the free exercise of professions which require knowledge of mathematics and physics." While the decree left room for training people for other than state service, it was clear that its principal aim was to train engineers for the state. Under Napoleon, the school's aim was even more narrowly defined: it was to train military officers. Table 7.1 shows that the graduates of the school have gradually ceased to choose the military as a career. As Gérard Grunberg notes:

> More and more members of the technical grands corps are leaving their corps after a few years of service. More serious still was the phenomenon of resignations occurring immediately upon graduation from the school at the end of the last century. The armament sector no longer attracted the young polytechnicians. This trend was slowed down by a ruling that obliged those who resigned to reimburse the state for the expenses incurred in educating them free of charge. It was to become more widespread again at the Liberation. The recruitment into the armament sector dried up completely and even certain engineering corps, notably the corps of military engineers, experienced a certain disaffection.[19]

How did the school, committed as it was to state service, react to the disaffection of its graduates from the military? The reaction was not slow in coming and it was unequivocal: it entailed a complete change in the notion of "state service." The Ecole Polytechnique did not abandon this notion; rather, it redefined it. It now saw itself as training people to serve the nation as a whole. "The

---

[19] Gérard Grunberg, "L'Ecole Polytechnique et 'ses' grands corps," *Annuaire international de la fonction publique, 1973-1974*, p. 385.

TABLE 7.1

Distribution, by Sectors, of Ecole Polytechnique Graduates

	Class of 1935 & 1936		Class of 1956 & 1957		Class of 1964 & 1965	
	No.	*%*	*No.*	*%*	*No.*	*%*
Military						
Army	279	60.5	16	3.0	5	0.8
Military engineers	82	18.0	139	24.0	125	21.4
Total Military	361	78.5	155	27.0	130	22.2
Civil						
Civil corps	84	18.0	181	32.0	194	32.6
Research	—	—	19	3.0	81	13.6
Resigned	16	21.5	213	38.0	190	31.9
Total Civil	100	21.5	413	72.5	465	77.8
GRAND TOTAL	461		568		595	

Source: L'Expansion (June 1967).

notion of service was extended in such a way as to legitimize the school's new orientations."[20] As early as 1926, a member of the alumni association, attempting to justify the wave of resignations, could declare:

The Ecole Polytechnique was created for the purpose of providing the state with the engineers or civil technicians that it needed, as well as with a certain number of officers for particular branches of the military. Has this recruitment system succeeded? The history of the school suggests an affirmative answer. . . . One has to take a broad perspective. The state is not the nation, it is only its principal servant. When the complaint is made that polytechnicians are deserting state service, is it not possible to reply that they are in no way ceasing to render service to the nation? One has but to look around to see that the former officers contribute as much to the life and prosperity of the nation as their *camarades* who have remained in the ranks. Need one protest against this fact? On the contrary, if we look at the matter from the point of view of the nation's interest, could we not justly define the aim of

[20] *Ibid.*, p. 386.

the school by saying that its mission is to prepare the technical elite of the nation?[21]

The "nation" thus replaces the "state," and the Ecole Polytechnique takes on the responsibility of training the technical administrative elite and the industrial elite. This shift required a considerable adjustment, for the school might conceivably have responded to the pressure of the military and insisted on remaining the principal training school for officers.[22] But the school followed the sentiments of its student body who no longer preferred the military as a career. In so doing, it established itself as the training ground for an even more important elite, for industry now clearly superseded the military.

This adjustment entailed a shift from military training to a great concentration on the corps, which recruited their members from the Ecole Polytechnique. To maintain its position, the Ecole Polytechnique has come to link its fate more and more to the technical grands corps. The school's top graduates make their way into the grands corps via their specialized schools, the Ecole des Mines and the Ecole Nationale des Ponts et Chaussées. Now, there has been a movement to open these corps to nonpolytechnicians. In recent years, both Ecole des Mines and the Ecole des Ponts et Chaussées have admitted engineers who enter these schools directly by passing an examination. Of course, these engineers do not have the same stature or prestige as the polytechnicians. But this does indicate that the specialized schools might, if they wished, be able to divorce themselves entirely from the Ecole Polytechnique.

In effect, the opening of the corps to nonpolytechnicians constitutes something of a challenge to the Ecole Polytechnique. Thus far, the proportion of those who gain lateral entry into the technical grands corps is too small to have a significant impact on the relationship between the grands corps and the Ecole Polytechnique. However, as Grunberg notes:

> This type of recruitment [lateral] benefits a very small number of persons and has a distinctly corporatist tinge, but its significance is great to the extent that the Ecole Polytech-

[21] Cited in *ibid*.

[22] The Ecole Polytechnique remains to this day under the tutelage of the Ministry of Defense.

nique, even if it maintains a distinct predominance, is no longer the only top-level school capable of insuring recruitment
into the most prestigious of the technical corps. This innovation came at a moment when the members of the technical
grands corps participated in the debate that took place on the
reform of the corps and on the role of "X" in their recruitment.[23]

This kind of adjustment, small as it may appear, is important
from the corps' point of view. It constitutes an attempt, however
modest, to meet the criticism of elitist impenetrability that has been
directed at the corps and at the specialized schools. As a director
of one of these schools observed: "I confess that admitting a few
nonpolytechnicians to a specialized school will not be construed
as a revolutionary reform. But it is a reform on which others will
build. The important thing is that it sets a direction, it opens new
avenues. Even the Inspection des Finances admitted a non-ENA
person to its ranks this year." A director of another school noted
that "For the moment, the specialized schools will continue to recruit predominantly from the Ecole Polytechnique, but this only
because the Ecole Polytechnique gets the best scientific brains. But
now that other roads are being opened up for entry into the grands
corps, the pressure to open these roads still further will probably
intensify—and the corps will respond!" The corps will respond,
partly because they will adapt to changing requirements and notions of democracy, and partly because they would like to "develop
their strategy with total independence."[24]

It may well be, as Grunberg notes, that the technical grands
corps now have less of a need for an exclusive relationship with
the Ecole Polytechnique than at any time in the past. Certainly, if
we consider the relationship between the nontechnical corps and
ENA, we find that the corps vehemently objected to the school at
the outset. When ENA students put the grands corps into question
in 1972, the corps lost no time in making a case for a totally independent policy of recruitment, one that would not in the least be
tied to ENA. The independence which the corps desire extends not
only to the recruitment of their members, but also to their training,
for each corps has its own strategy which can be accomplished
only by giving their members a certain type of training. Hence, the

[23] Grunberg, "L'Ecole Polytechnique et 'ses' grands corps," p. 400.
[24] *Ibid.*, p. 401.

corps cannot rely wholly on the general curriculum of the Ecole Polytechnique. Nevertheless, there is no doubt that the link between the corps and the Ecole Polytechnique remains strong, though a certain adjustment has taken place. This is well analyzed by Grunberg:

> The privileged link between "X" and the technical grands corps is certainly still alive but its meaning has changed. "X" has been able to give up, without great difficulty, the role of being above all a school for public service. The corps are and will be called upon to develop a strategy that will require them to take their distance from it. This change notwithstanding, "X" and the corps both have an interest in maintaining a close relationship with each other. As long as certain of the technical corps retain their elevated positions, "X" will have an interest in playing a preponderant role in their recruitment. . . . But the corps no longer need all the polytechnicians nor Polytechnique all its corps. Does not the fact that the two partners no longer have as great a need of each other as in the past constitute for both a proof of success?[25]

FROM PUBLIC TO PRIVATE

The adaptation of the Ecole Polytechnique to a new image of its role was, as we indicated, not exceptionally difficult to accomplish. For one thing, because the school provided a fairly general scientific education, it was possible for it to move in a number of directions without totally overhauling its curriculum. Second, the adaptation called for was one that entailed few risks. The school had merely to recognize the fact that it ought now to accept openly its responsibility of training other than military leaders. The school, then, did not abandon its obligation of training people for state service, it merely added to this the responsibility of training the nation's—both public and private—leaders.

For the specialized schools who recruited directly from the Ecole Polytechnique, a more radical adaptation was called for. Since these schools were more intimately linked to the grands corps, they had a responsibility of gearing their curriculum to the needs of the corps, whose capture of certain sectors necessitated knowledge in a particular area. Moreover, it mattered a great deal to the special-

[25] *Ibid.,* pp. 406-407.

ized schools whether their graduates went on to occupy prestigious posts. Hence, both the specialized schools and the corps had to manifest a considerable degree of flexibility in order to adapt to the changing nature of the state's activities, as well as to the changing economy.

In retrospect, the most obvious, and the most profound, change that was occurring, particularly after the First World War, was that France was becoming an industrial society. The technical corps were quick to accept the industrial trend, more quick perhaps than the nontechnical corps. The reason for this is not that the technical corps had greater technical expertise, but rather that the areas under their jurisdiction up to that time were fast declining in importance. They now found, in other words, that their scope for expansion within the public sector was severely limited. This was not the case for the nontechnical corps. Thus, whereas industrialization and economic development greatly diminished the Corps des Mines' scope in the public sector, it entailed the reverse for the Inspection des Finances, for the state was to assume a greater role in the economic and financial sectors. The declining importance of the mining sector obliged the Corps des Mines to find outlets and to seize opportunities beyond the public sector in order to preserve its position. What is important is that the corps did not abandon the public sector or the mining sector. It used its prestige in these areas to move into the industrial sector in much the same way it was to use the success in the industrial sector to gain a reputation for economic wizardry and so launch itself into the public economic sector. The corps thus acted in accordance with Schumpeter's precept that "every class that has once enjoyed an elevated position is greatly aided in seizing new functions." But the class is only "aided"; more important is the fact that it must recognize, accept, and act in accordance with the changes that call for the "seizing of new functions."

Such has been the case of the Corps des Mines, and the changes in the corps' orientation are reflected in and buttressed by the training which the Ecole des Mines now offers its students. It is a training that destines the select few to key posts in industry, in the public sector, and in research. The school regards these as the key areas into which it must move if it is to preserve its position and if the Corps des Mines is to remain a leading corps. The principal aim of the school, as a high official of the school put it, "is to constitute an independent center of reflection on our society. This includes three principal areas: (a) economic and industrial policy; (b) relations between industry and education; and (c) research."

The emphasis which the school places on the importance of industry may strike one as being rather surprising, given the fact that this is a public institution theoretically training people for state service. But the school, like the corps whose recruits it trains, has succeeded in transforming its original goals while keeping itself intact. The relationship which the school enjoys with industry is something of which it is especially proud. In part, this is because it has become a most rewarding relationship: the school trains people specifically for industry, from which it receives large research contracts in return. In part also, the relationship of the school with industry serves to distinguish even more the grandes écoles from the universities. As one member of the Corps des Mines closely associated with the school put it: "For the universities, industry doesn't exist. They want nothing to do with it. This has only helped us. Let's be clear about it, our students are assured of excellent jobs, of an excellent training for these jobs through the *stages* they do in the industries, and the industries themselves know that they can rely on us. Also, the school is extremely well off financially, as a result of its relationship with industry." Another official maintained that industry had been rebuffed so often by the universities that any kind of close relationship between them is all but ruled out. The educational reform of 1976, which sought to professionalize university training and which was bitterly opposed by the students, was yet another confirmation that industry cannot count on the universities in France.

The direct consequence of this divorce between industry and the universities is to be found not only in the area of employment, where university graduates may be less than welcome, but also in the area of research. Fully two-thirds of the Ecole des Mines' research funds come from industry (private and nationalized). However, it should be noted that the research funds which industry makes available to the school are in the form of contracts and thus are used almost entirely for applied research. But even if the research carried out by the school is of an applied nature, it nonetheless remains true that the Ecole des Mines, together with the Ecole Polytechnique and the Ecole Normale (where pure research is carried out) are the only grandes écoles where significant research is pursued. Most of the lesser grandes écoles recruit students of a high caliber but are essentially engineering schools. The professors of these schools have neither the facilities nor the training to undertake serious research.

Both the Ecole des Mines and the Corps des Mines have made efforts in recent years to encourage some of their recruits to choose research as a career. In certain cases, they have sought to dissuade those desiring a career in research from entering the C.N.R.S. by offering them better facilities and salaries. Why should these institutions attach such an importance to research? It is not simply in order to be a better handmaiden to industry. Rather, it reflects a recognition of the growing importance of science in all areas; to turn their back on future scientific developments would be to make future adaptations difficult. As the Cot Report on the role of the technical corps in modern French society noted:

> In the coming decade, our society, it is said, will seek a continual and rapid economic growth. For the Administration and for the enterprises, public and private, this trend implies:
>
> —the development of the capacity for innovations—which supposes a great emphasis on scientific and technical research —combined with the effect of this, directly or indirectly, on the diverse sectors;
>
> —the collection and rapid analysis of information;
>
> —the application, in the preparation of rational decisions, of highly elaborate procedures of scientific study. . . .[26]

The Cot Report goes on to emphasize that "les équipes efficaces" of tomorrow will have to include in particular:

> —pure mathematicians, people who continually define new methods and new means of action, and mathematicians who have a more diverse training and who will apply these means of action to specific goals;
>
> —engineers of diverse disciplines capable of thinking as doers;
>
> —high-level executives capable of understanding the different aspects (technical, economic, sociological, juridical) of a given situation.[27]

[26] Pierre D. Cot, "Le Rôle des grands corps d'ingénieurs dans la société française d'aujourd'hui," *La Jaune et la Rouge*, No. 230 (October 1968), p. 18.

[27] *Ibid.*, pp. 19-20.

The emphasis which the school and the corps have put on research can be seen from Table 7.2, which shows the increasing number of members of the Corps des Mines going into research. This is regarded by the corps as an attempt to increase its strength.

TABLE 7.2

Members of Corps des Mines in Teaching and Research

	1949		1961		1970	
	No.	%	No.	%	No.	%
Teaching (grandes écoles and faculties)	23	33.3	26	26.5	36	33
Industrial research (IFP, CEA, CER-CHAR)	—	—	15	15.3	26	23.9
TOTAL	23	33.3	41	41.8	62	56.9

Source: D. Desjeux and E. Friedberg, "Fonctions de l'état et rôle des grands corps," *Annuaire international de la fonction publique, 1972-1973*, p. 571.

The Cot Report indeed can be seen as an example of an elite looking into itself and asking: what is the future going to be like and how can the technical grands corps assure their place in it? It is a question that is continually posed and that preoccupies the leaders of the corps. Thus, the current and former directors of the Ecole des Mines write: "It was necessary to ask ourselves what was the function fulfilled—and that would be fulfilled in the future—by the engineers of the Corps des Mines (I). Then to determine the objectives of the school as far as they were concerned (aim of better training the young people for carrying out these functions) (II). To define a program (III) and to implement it. . . ."[28]

The result of such analysis has clearly led the school to a greater association with industry. Does this mean, then, that it is now no more than a training ground for industry, a type of business school? To a very large extent, it sees itself as fulfilling the functions of a business school, and it can scarcely be denied that, in terms of its size and of the positions occupied by its graduates in industry, it is probably the most successful business school in

[28] M. R. Fischesser and M. P. Lafitte, "La Formation des ingénieurs du corps des mines," *La Jaune et la Rouge*, No. 238 (June 1969), p. 3.

France. How, one might ask, is this possible of a school whose ostensible purpose is to train "mining engineers"? Some within the corps have argued that it no longer makes any sense to speak of a "corps" when the corps itself denies the importance of its original function and when it continually seeks new functions.[29] One Polytechnique engineer argued that "the technical grands corps were necessary as long as there was an identity between the corps and the service it rendered. As the services grew in complexity, the corps tried to adapt themselves to the new situations, but it is clear today . . . that this adaptation is no longer possible because the corps are in fact opposed to the services. To convince oneself of this, one has only to glance at the administration of tomorrow: all the corps have to become 'interministerial' and all the teams have to be 'interdisciplinary'—which is the same thing as saying that the very notion of corps has disappeared."[30] This analysis of what has actually taken place is essentially correct, but it misses the point that this is precisely what has allowed the corps to survive. As the two most recent directors of the Ecoles des Mines note: ". . . the functions of the Corps des Mines have completely evolved with the changes brought about in the nationalized sector by the new requirements of the economy: the current functions have only a tenuous relationship with those of the Corps des Mines of the nineteenth century, or of the first half of the twentieth."[31] The members of the corps thus do not deny the changes that have taken place in the society and which have affected the corps. They merely maintain that the corps has had to adjust itself to these changes.

This is how the orientation toward industry is explained and defended. Indeed, the ties with industry now form the cornerstone of the school's training program, which involves *stages* in industry and little classroom teaching. The first two years at the school, which comprise three distinct phases,[32] are spent outside the school. Only after having spent these two years "in the field" does

[29] See the discussion on this point elicted by the publication of the Cot Report, in *La Jaune et la Rouge*, No. 246 (March 1970).

[30] R. Poitrat, "Utilité des corps," *La Jaune et la Rouge*, No. 246 (March 1970), p. 12.

[31] Fischesser and Lafitte, "La Formation des ingénieurs du corps des mines," p. 2.

[32] The three phases are: 1) two months of initiation in industry; 2) twelve months working in a specific industry; and 3) ten months doing a *stage* in a research center.

a student return to the school, and then only to take part in preparing dossiers on actual problems. This last phase is described
as "studies of the scientific bases of modern management and administration with programs of the Business School or School of
Management type."[33] This type of training is perfectly consonant
with the principal tasks, "present and future," that the Corps des
Mines had defined for itself. These tasks are clearly formulated by
the two most recent directors of the Ecole des Mines, and it is
worth quoting them at length:

1) *Industrial policy of the state.* Initiate and above all
stimulate governmental strategy within a certain number of
important technical and economic ministerial divisions: for
example, initiate and stimulate (which means "defend and illustrate") French energy policy, policy of acquisition of raw
materials, etc. This role which has always existed in countries
where public authorities do not practice pure and simple
laissez faire is tending to take on greater importance in all
industrialized societies.

2) *Strategy of large enterprises.* Industrial policy can under no circumstances be limited exclusively to the planning
stage. To defend and illustrate a policy in an economic sector
is also to implement it at the level of the productive sector—
that is, in the public enterprises and in the large private enterprises (the differences between these two sectors, as far as
management is concerned, being less important than the
points in common). The functions fulfilled within the teams
whose role is to defend and illustrate industrial strategy are
therefore a corollary of the functions indicated in #1.

3) *Technical and economic innovation.* Modern industry
is more and more directed by innovation. The future is forged
in the research centers, the spearheads of future expansion.
All strategies and all policies are bound to the dynamism of
the spearheads. The second corollary is so important that it
could have been placed at the top.[34]

[33] Fischesser and Lafitte, "La Formation des ingénieurs du corps des
mines," p. 4.

[34] *Ibid.*, p. 3. What of those members of the corps who do not share these
objectives? This is point number 4: "Every group, of course, has its 'deviants.'
The Corps des Mines has them too. Whenever possible, the latter must
be encouraged to develop their potentialities to the utmost. This means, for

The industrial orientation, whether it involves determining the state's industrial or energy policies or taking an active part in industrial management in the private sector, is the most important aspect of the Corps des Mines' strategy. Hence, it is not surprising that the orientation of the Ecole des Mines should be toward a highly practical training, one that eschews theory altogether. There is little doubt that the Ecole des Mines sees itself as paving the way for a reorientation of higher education. As Fischesser and Lafitte observe: "Such is the essence of the training now dispensed by the Ecole des Mines. It is intended for a small number of 'X' [Ecole Polytechnique] graduates. But it can clearly be transposed to other corps and other schools."[35]

IMPERIALISM AND SURVIVAL

The declining importance for the Corps des Mines of its traditional domain of competence and the corps' orientation toward the industrial sector (Table 7.3) need to be seen as a strategy for adapting to changing economic conditions. In the last analysis, it is a strategy for survival and for maintaining a position of preeminence. Consequently, the corps is not in the least defensive about this strategy. "The real quality and advantage of the Corps des Mines,"

TABLE 7.3

Distribution, by Sector, of Members of Corps des Mines

	1949		1961		1970	
Activity	*No.*	*%*	*No.*	*%*	*No.*	*%*
Civil servants in corps	109	43.4	115	37.1	120	35.9
Public and semipublic sectors	69	27.5	98	31.6	109	32.6
Private sector	73	29.1	97	31.3	105	31.5
TOTAL	251	100.0	310	100.0	334	100.0

Source: Desjeux and Friedberg, "Fonctions de l'état et rôle des grands corps," p. 569.

example, allowing those who wish to be biologists to do the most advanced kind of biology. But these are special cases that must be treated as such, and we shall speak of them no more" (p. 3).

[35] *Ibid.*, p. 7.

said one member of this corps, "is that it embodies the values of industry." A leading official of this corps noted that "there is no doubt that the relationship we now have with industry is very important for the future of the corps. All we try to do is to give 'une formation adaptable, plastique.' But we also insist on a specific training; that is why the *stages* play such an important role. These two things are the chief elements of the training we give and they are really what explain the success of the corps." The Corps des Mines has thus fashioned a strategy for training its recruits in diverse specialties and for being able to orient itself in different directions. As two students of this corps have noted: "The analysis of its recent history brings out the Corps des Mines' remarkable capacity for adaptation to current needs and to the changing priorities that affect the state's activities. It is through this capacity that the corps has been able to maintain, if not increase, its role and its influence in the state apparatus, indeed in French society as a whole."[36] They explain the success of the Corps des Mines by its independence, by what they call its capacity "de s'auto-gérer,"[37] which allows it to train its own recruits and place them in key sectors. This does not explain, of course, why the corps opted in the first place to orient itself toward other sectors. It might just as easily have opted for a larger role within the public sector, or it might even have chosen to remain narrowly specialized.

The ability to adapt is in part the result of the form of organization, but, as every student of organizations knows, organizations have a tendency to become rigid and to be overly preoccupied with defending their own turf. But this has not been wholly the case with the elite organizations that we are discussing. Why? The answer lies in the imperialistic nature of these organizations, which itself is the consequence of competition among the organizations. In other words, these corps are obliged, like Marx's capitalists, to search constantly for other markets. In so doing, they inevitably create a certain element of diversity within themselves. The aptitude of polyvalence, to which the elite attaches so much importance, is closely linked to the strategy of the corps to colonize diverse posts in diverse sectors of society. As we noted, if each corps

[36] Dominique Desjeux and Erhard Friedberg, "Fonctions de l'état et rôle des grands corps: Le cas du corps des mines," *Annuaire internationale de la fonction publique, 1972-1973*, p. 577.

[37] *Ibid.*

were merely to specialize in the sector that falls under its jurisdiction, it could not provide its recruits with interesting and remunerative careers, a preoccupation that, as we have seen, has become central to all the corps. The generalist philosophy becomes, in large part, an arm in the strategy of the imperialism of the corps. Every proposed reform, every suggestion within the elite for ameliorating recruitment, training, efficiency, and so on has as its central aim the diversification of the elite. This results mostly from the competition among the corps themselves, but it has been, as we shall see, an important element in the survival of the elite. Ultimately, competition, diversification, and imperialism call for a certain degree of adaptation, without which this elite would have long become extinct. "The word 'corps,' " notes a former president of the organization that groups the Corps des Mines and the Corps des Ponts et Chaussées (PCM), "also evokes the diversity of members, of cells. . . . A 'corps' will be all the more valuable if its members have diverse activities, and various fields of specialization. It will have all the more prestige if it can offer careers to—and hence attract—men of different profiles. It will have all the more influence if it incorporates within itself a perpetual dynamism, an unceasing desire for questioning, for progress, and for action, through the permanent confrontation of diverse minds."[38]

Diversity is important because it offsets the uniformity which the training imposes on the members of the corps. As M. Boilot notes, "If this condition is not fulfilled; if homogeneity is not counterbalanced by diversity, the corps stagnates, the best people leave while the less good remain. Not being subject to internal criticism, the corps' homogeneity gradually leads it down a narrow path which soon becomes a dead end. Criticism comes to it from the outside, provoking a defensive reaction which accelerates even more the process of self-isolation and conservatism."[39] There is an explicit recognition here that the corps must *anticipate* criticism, and rather than concentrate on defending themselves against such criticism, the corps must take measures to undercut their bases, for the greatest danger is not the criticism from the society but the conservative and defensive reflexes within the corps that these attacks would engender. This is not at all different from Mosca's belief that a

---

[38] Pierre Boilot, "Réflexions sur les corps," *Bulletin de PCM*, Vol. 64 (September 1967), p. 11. One needs to bear in mind that such "reflections" are addressed only to colleagues and *not* to the outside world.
   [39] *Ibid.*

nation, a civilization, an elite, can survive indefinitely "provided it learns how to *transform itself continually without falling apart.*" Boilot goes even further and suggests that for the corps to continue to deserve their existence, it is necessary for them to encourage the contradiction between their homogeneity, "the characteristic that defines them," and their diversity, "the characteristic that justifies them."[40] The corps are thus advised, by one who has been deeply involved in the strategy of adaptation and survival, to maintain a careful balance between homogeneity and diversity.

> They must . . . watch carefully over the quality of their re-
> cruitment in order to keep their homogeneity and main-
> tain an equilibrium between the various career opportunities
> that they absolutely must offer their members in order to sat-
> isfy the imperatives of diversity. Thus, for example, the scien-
> tific grands corps must, all at the same time, produce ad-
> vanced researchers who will bring progress to their field and
> whose prestige will reflect on the corps; offer a field to the men
> of action through a dynamic policy of employment in public
> service and in the private sector; finally, provide an attractive
> springboard to the highest posts of responsibility for those
> who have a taste for synthesis and for power.[41]

The *consciousness* of the need for adaptation and the adoption of a strategy that appears best at a particular moment and that is ultimately followed suggest that little is left up to chance. André Thépot shows in his historical study of the Corps des Mines that the corps always attempted to be on the right side after changes in regimes during the nineteenth century. Indeed, they took advantage of the moments of turmoil to draw up plans whose only purpose was to enhance the corps' position. The leaders of the corps, notes Thépot, "demonstrated rather extraordinary opportunism."[42] One must not suppose, however, that there is always one strategy that presents itself and that is immediately agreed upon. Anyone patient enough to go through the periodicals, journals, alumni magazines, reports, and other "house publications" will immediately see that long debates take place on the direction that a corps ought to take. For example, a debate has been going on for many

[40] *Ibid.*   [41] *Ibid.*

[42] André Thépot, *Le Corps de Mines*, Thèse de Doctorat d'Etat, forthcoming, p. 21.

years within the Corps des Ponts et Chaussées concerning whether the corps ought to follow and compete with the Corps des Mines or whether it ought to recognize that it has a specific sector of its own which it ought to stick to. Some argue that the Ponts et Chaussées is a large corps with important jurisdictions that it must never ignore. Others maintain that the Corps des Mines, which is a much smaller corps, is making serious inroads into all the important sectors and that this can only harm the Ponts et Chaussées in the long run; hence, it has no choice but to challenge the Corps des Mines and seek other territories to conquer. No firm decision has been taken, but the strategy that is being followed suggests that the Ponts et Chaussées has decided both to remain a "concrete" corps and to preserve its "image de marque" by going into other sectors. As one of the leaders of this corps observed: "One of the reasons that our corps is so sure of itself is that it has control over tangible areas. Take the area of urban planning—it's vast and it belongs to the Ponts et Chaussées. Take transport—that too belongs to the Ponts et Chaussées. This is the stuff of people's lives. That's why no one can ever think of doing away with the Ponts et Chaussées. A few years ago people talked about our losing ground. No one can speak about us in this way any longer because we've succeeded in going into other areas."

Even within the Corps des Mines, which appears so unified, there is not always agreement on the direction that the corps ought to take. One side has maintained that the corps, now firmly in control of the energy sector, should branch out into the environmental sector. When the Ministry of Environment was established, the Corps des Mines lost no time in jumping in to occupy all the key posts in this ministry. Some saw this as merely another conquest, while others saw it as simply a logical extension of the areas in which the corps normally had expertise. Nevertheless, a strong case was being made within the corps for concentrating the corps' resources in this area. First, it was argued that the environmental sector was the sector of the future because it affected people's lives in numerous ways and so would ultimately involve the Corps des Mines in numerous activities.

Second, some argued that this gave the Corps des Mines the opportunity finally to anchor itself in a concrete area. The corps has always been criticized for essentially being all over the place, for having no specific sector to which the bulk of its members were devoted. Consequently, it was argued that concentration on the

214

environmental sector would stem these attacks, for just as the Ponts et Chaussées always point to their "contact with reality" (the building of roads, the close relationship with local officials) so now the Corps des Mines would be able to do likewise. In other words, it was essential for the corps to be associated with a specific sector for no matter what the future of the corps in the other sectors was going to be—who could tell, it was argued, what things would be like in ten, twenty years of time—the corps would always be able to fall back on, because it would become indelibly associated with, the environmental area.

Third, it was argued that ecological issues would come to dominate the political scene in the years ahead, so that to be associated with, or better still, to be in the vanguard of the movement, would have a profoundly salutary impact on the image of the corps. It was the perfect antithesis to the elitist image of the corps which was so much under attack nowadays. Some clearly saw this as an opportunity to improve the image of the corps, and at the same time to put it at the center of the political stage. The corps would come to be associated with an issue that was popular with the "people" rather than with the industrialists, with the prevention of pollution rather than with the production of energy. In short, the move into the ecological area was to be, among other things, a public relations venture.

Finally, some members of the corps saw the opportunity to move into the environmental sector as their chance for competing with their archrivals—the Ponts et Chaussées. The latter corps had recently moved into the urban sector and now considers that anything that touches on urbanism is in its province. Some in the Corps des Mines believed that by taking charge of the environmental sector it was only a question of time before they could make forays into transportation, urban development, and the like.

There were, then, many motives—the desire to ensure survival by establishing a more concrete base, imperialism, public relations —propelling the Corps des Mines in the direction of "settling down," as it were, to one sector, or if not settling down, then at least anchoring itself to a very specific domain.

But there was another side to these arguments, one consistently supported by some of the more illustrious members of the Corps des Mines. They argued that to anchor the corps in one domain would be a defensive and defeatist policy, one that would ultimately spell the doom of the corps. "Unless we intend to become a corps like the mailmen or those who take care of our forests, we should abandon this absurd idea," said a member of this corps in the nationalized sector. Another equally illustrious member of this corps put it this way: "For sometime now I have been consistently arguing with many members of our corps that if we were to confine ourselves to one specific sector we would no longer be the same corps. We could no longer exercise influence in all the sectors that we now occupy key positions in. We would lose our liberty to move around from one sector to another. We would give way to other, more ambitious corps. We would cease to attract the best people. The Corps des Mines would no longer be the Corps des Mines." This same member of the corps went on to note that "the very discussion of this question troubles me a great deal. It shows that we have an identity crisis. I don't believe we do because I think the others will quickly come to their senses. When you engage in this kind of discussion you are inevitably putting into question the very reasons for your success, or even existence. And if there is really no agreement on the direction to be followed, then the corps can have no common purpose. Its will, its dynamism, are sapped. Look at the Corps des Ponts et Chaussées, they have been unsteady and unsure of themselves and the reason is that they have a serious identity problem."

If some of the key figures in the Corps des Mines were against entering the environmental sector, they took that position partly because they believed that its importance was ephemeral, partly because it might put them in too great an opposition to industry, and partly because it would confine the corps to a narrow domain.[43] This last was undoubtedly the most important, and it constituted a shrewd analysis of the reasons for the survival and extension of the corps. As one member of the corps put it: "We survived the mines, now they want us to clear up the soot!" Another member expressed the same point, though somewhat differently: "What these people who are all wrapped up with ecology don't understand is that the success of a corps is directly proportional to

[43] By "key figures in the corps" I do not mean that they occupy positions within the corps. The corps has a very light administration and those most influential in it are usually the ones most influential outside it. To cite but one example: Pierre Guillaumat, until last year president of ELF-ERAP oil company, has long been regarded as the key figure of the Corps des Mines. This is due in part to his high status outside the corps and in part to his strong attachment to and belief in the corps system.

its ability to adapt to new problems. Granted the ecology problem is a new one; granted it's a new opportunity—well, it is just *one* opportunity. We mustn't miss it, but we mustn't put everything into it either. The moment they understand that, they will understand everything." Friedberg and Desjeux, who have studied the Corps des Mines, concluded, with respect to the corps in general: "In fact, it seems evident today that the power and the important role of the grands corps is due less and less to their exclusive mastery of a certain sector, a specific area, or a narrowly defined function; rather, what is involved is much more their ability to constitute networks of expertise and action appropriate to the new problems with which the state apparatus finds itself confronted."[44]

The Corps des Mines, as we have seen, has lost few opportunities to escape its own narrow sector and to launch itself into other areas whose importance has grown in recent years. It has done this perhaps more succesfully than the Ponts et Chaussées in part because it is a far smaller corps and hence lacks a rigid structure. One should not, however, underestimate the adaptation of the Ponts et Chaussées whose power traditionally resided in rural France. The country's rapid industrialization and the consequent growth of large cities called for a shift in the corps' orientation and necessitated an adjustment to the new opportunities provided by urbanization.[45] The Ponts et Chaussées sought also to gain entry into important decision-making centers as part of an attempt to avoid losing further ground to the other corps. Here the corps has perhaps been less successful than in the area of urbanization.

It should be noted that it is only when conditions change radically that a corps is obliged to adapt or face stagnation. The Inspection des Finances has not experienced a crisis of identity in recent years because it had, from the outset, a firm grip on all the major economic and financial institutions. Since this corps was generally giving direction to events, it certainly could not have been left behind by them. Its control of the major economic posts in the administrative sector, its importance in the political sector, and its monopoly of the credit and banking institutions enable it, more than any other corps, to direct events rather than react to them.

This is not the case with the Cour des Comptes, whose prestige

---

[44] Desjeux and Friedberg, "Fonctions de l'état et rôle des grands corps," p. 579.

[45] See Jean-Claude Thoenig, *L'Ere des technocrates: le cas des ponts et chaussées* (Paris: Les Editions d'Organisations, 1973), Chapters 2 and 3.

is far ahead of its power, and which has made no determined efforts to take over other sectors. This is because it finds itself willy-nilly in the economic sector, which is the only logical area that it could seek to move into. However, to do this would be to confront the Inspection des Finances. The corps therefore continues to verify expenditures of central and local authorities, of nationalized enterprises, and of the social security system. It continues to attract those who graduate at the top of their class at ENA in part because it makes little demands on their time. Although it is rare for a member to criticize his corps publicly, one of the corps' own members said recently that "La Cour des Comptes est un organisme désuet et faussement redoutable."[46]

The corps which find themselves at the center of the key areas in the society today are the Corps des Mines and the Inspection des Finances. Both saw their original *raison d'être*—the mines and the verification of expenditures—decline in importance. Both were quick to offer careers to their members that were not connected with their original functions. Both devised strategies for making of the corps a launching pad to other sectors. Both had the additional advantage of being relatively small (300-odd members in each). The Conseil d'Etat has also been extremely successful in extending its hold on certain key areas (labor, health, education, culture) within the public sector, as well as within the politico-administrative sector (ministerial cabinets) and within the nationalized sector. It has largely avoided the economic sector, preferring instead not to stray too far beyond a set of well-defined boundaries.

Conclusion

I have discussed at some length the bases of the elitist system in France and the principal factors accounting for the survival of elitist institutions. We have seen how the elites have consciously and systematically extended their position in French society and how the educational system which nurtures these elites has remained intimately linked to the maintenance of elitist institutions. I have not, to be sure, felt it necessary, when referring to the strategies of the various corps, to examine the differences among the corps. The reason for this is that all the available evidence indicates that the similarities are far more important than the differences. That is why I have not discussed in any detail the Conseil

[46] "A quoi sert la Cour des Comptes?" *L'Express*, 10-16 July 1972, p. 26.

d'Etat or the Cour des Comptes which, while they differ in some important respects from the other corps, also share a great many characteristics in common—degree of corporatism, advantages provided to their members, search for outlets, prestige and legitimacy bestowed upon those who enter their ranks.

In addition, I have also suggested that the elite is not without legitimacy, and that it is essentially able to legitimize itself through its capacity to get its own standards of competence and expertise accepted by the outside world, at least by the influential public. The tacit support which the Left accords to the elitist system testifies to the relatively strong position these institutions enjoy in the society.

In accounting for the stability of the elites in France, I have laid particular emphasis on their capacity for adaptation. However, the capacity for survival and adaptation can be regarded as virtues only if one looks at the problem from the angle of the elite. In effect, I have said little more than that the flexibility and adaptability of the elite have no other goal than the survival and enhancement of the elite's position in the society. I have so far said little about the extent to which the elites, in managing to survive, respond to the needs of society. I have attempted only to underline the fact that survival is an overriding and *conscious* goal of the elite. The Cot Report, which resulted from a study of a commission set up by the technical corps, significantly and appropriately has as its epigraph the following quotation from Raymond Aron: ". . . and we sociologists know that there exist societies that prefer to die rather than reform themselves."[47] The elites have preferred to "reform" themselves in a manner that leaves them intact and that prevents the erosion of their power and privileges. We must now attempt to examine some of the consequences for the society of the elitist structures that we have analyzed.

[47] Cot, "Le Rôle des grands corps d'ingénieurs dans la société française d'aujourd'hui," p. 1.

Part Three

❧ ❧

CONSEQUENCES

❧ *Chapter Eight* ❧

THE ELITE AND THE NEW ECONOMY

THIS study has thus far been concerned with the elitist institutions in France and the ways in which these institutions have preserved themselves. To explain the coexistence of the powerful elitist system with democratic institutions, we have had to concentrate on the problems and strategies of the elites and of their institutions. As we noted at the outset, the imperative of analyzing the problem from the point of view of the elite is dictated by the nature of the questions that underlie this study. There is simply no way to treat the problem of the stability and transformation of elites other than by looking into the attitudes, strategies, and adaptability of the elites.

It is evident, however, that a study of elite stability cannot stop at an analysis of the factors that are of concern only to the elite. It becomes necessary to situate the elite within the larger society and to examine its impact on the society. This is the aim of the present and the following chapter. What follows is not only a necessary complement to the preceding analysis but will enable us to examine the policy consequences of a trans-sectoral and quasi-monopolistic elite.

Transformation of the French Economy

Traveling through France today, one is bound to be struck by the general wealth and industrial activity of the country, so much so that many surely ask themselves whether this is the same country they knew twenty, or even fifteen, years ago. And if they did not know the country firsthand two decades ago, they probably wonder whether this can be the same country that they had been used to reading about in the most pessimistic terms. Most analyses of the French economy written during and before the 1950s sought to explain the reasons for the static nature of the French economy. The future, it was generally believed, could not be radically different from the past. In his 1951 essay, "French Business and the

Businessman," David Landes concluded: "Thus the urgent, the critical dilemma hangs over France today: to change and, in changing, die; or not to change, and risk a swifter death."[1] Landes' analysis was essentially Schumpeterian, for just as Schumpeter had argued that the disappearance of the entrepreneurial function would spell the doom of capitalism,[2] so Landes maintained that the bourgeois ethos prevented the rise of the entrepreneurial type in France. In France, according to Landes, there was no real distinction between the interests of the family and a business strategy.[3] Consequently, the distinctive precapitalist mentality of the French businessman hindered the development of a competitive, production-and-profit-oriented economy. France was destined to remain a nation of shopkeepers. As Landes noted in a passage that is worth quoting at length:

> The concept of free enterprise as developed in England of the nineteenth century and transplanted to the United States with its postulate of a competitive struggle for markets and drastic penalties for failure, and with its emphasis on earning more and more through producing more and more for less and less, has never really been accepted in France. Instead, France . . . has continued to cherish the precapitalist ideology that underlay the guild organization of the pre-Revolutionary period. This ideology may be summed up briefly as follows: every man has his place in society, should produce enough goods and services of quality to maintain his place, and has a right to the living earned in this manner. In other words, the justification of survival lies not in the ability to make a profit, but in the correct performance of a social function.[4]

Whereas Landes stressed the connection between cultural values and entrepreneurship, others, following the thesis expounded by

[1] David S. Landes, "French Business and the Businessman: A Social and Cultural Analysis," in Edward Meade Earle, ed., *Modern France: Problems of the Third and Fourth Republics* (Princeton: Princeton University Press, 1951), p. 353.

[2] Joseph A. Schumpeter, *Capitalism, Socialism and Democracy* (New York: Basic Books, 1961), pp. 121-124.

[3] For a discussion of Landes' thesis and the debate it engendered, see Dean Savage, "Founders, Heirs, and Managers in France: A Business Elite in Transition" (unpublished Ph.D. dissertation, Columbia University, 1975), pp. 4-16.

[4] Landes, "French Business and the Businessman," p. 348.

Max Weber in *The Protestant Ethic and the Spirit of Capitalism*, placed the emphasis on the religious factor to explain the abhorrence of profits and hence the static nature of the French economy. Being a Catholic country, France lacked the Protestant "profit ethic."[5]

Still a third popular explanation for France's economic backwardness centered on the effects of the centralized state. The high degree of administrative centralization in France which, according to Tocqueville, antedated the Revolution of 1789, brought under the state's net all aspects of the economic and social life of the country. Centralization, in other words, sapped much of the energy of a potentially dynamic private sector.[6] If the state took on greater and greater responsibilities during the course of the nineteenth century, it could be expected to fill still more vacuums. In this way, it discouraged the development of private initiative.

Bourgeois values, religion, and the Jacobin tradition have been seen as the key factors impeding the development of a modern economy in France.[7] Most analysts of France's backwardness did not expect many changes to occur in any of these factors and so could not foresee the day when France would take its place as a leading industrial nation. Yet, no one any longer denies that a profound transformation has taken place in France's economy. It is even common to speak of France's "economic miracle." In fact,

[5] Octave Gelinier, *Morale de l'entreprise et destin de la nation* (Paris: Plon, 1965). For a recent popular statement of the Weberian thesis and its application to France, see Alain Peyrefitte, *Le Mal français* (Paris: Plon, 1977). For a refutation of the thesis based on a case study of Catholic entrepreneurship, see David Landes, "Religion and Enterprise: The Case of the French Textile Industry" in Edward C. Carter, Robert Forster, and Joseph N. Moody, eds., *Enterprise and Entrepreneurs in Nineteenth and Twentieth Century France* (Baltimore: The Johns Hopkins University Press, 1976), pp. 41-86.

[6] This thesis has a large following and one can do no better than turn to its originator for a succinct statement. See Alexis de Tocqueville, *The Old Regime and the French Revolution* (New York: Doubleday & Co., 1955). For a popularization of the thesis, see Peyrefitte, *Le Mal français*, particularly Chapters 8, 9, 10, 29, 31, 33, 45.

[7] Economic historians no longer take as a given that French industrial development was, in fact, as sluggish as most people have been led to believe. Maurice Levy-Leboyer suggests the contrary—that "the sustained growth of the French economy is a datum to be reckoned with" (p. 93). See his "Innovation and Business Strategies in Nineteenth and Twentieth Century France," in Carter, Forster, and Moody, eds., *Enterprise and Entrepreneurs in Nineteenth and Twentieth Century France*, pp. 87-135.

attempts to explain the country's economic stagnation have now given way to attempts to explain its rapid industrialization. As the Hudson Institute noted in its study of France's future economic potential: "It could be said, in summary, that the image of 'la bonne vieille France' represents a cast of mind acquired over the past 150 years—a cast of mind that gradually became a tradition as the France of the pre-revolutionary, revolutionary and Napoleonic eras receded into oblivion."[8]

The Hudson Institute study completely reverses the picture of the static French economy, arguing in effect that few modern economies are or will be as dynamic. This study notes that France has, since the late 1950s, experienced the highest rate of economic growth in Western Europe, has known the highest rate of growth (5.8 percent per year) in the world except for Japan and the Soviet Union, has a labor force that can be considered as the most hard-working, best educated, and most productive in Europe, and, finally, has a higher rate of investment than even Germany. Projecting from these trends into the next decade, Stillman and his associates maintain that by 1985 France will become, with Sweden, the richest country in Europe. The Hudson Institute projections are certainly open to challenge and their euphoric nature is of little relevance to us here. Whether France will or will not be the richest country in Europe within a decade is not a question that ought to detain us. Let it simply be stated that France is anything but a *société bloquée*, that the old analyses of the French economy have been shattered, and that within a period of less than twenty years France has moved from being an agricultural country to one of the most industrialized. My purpose is not to attempt to explain the reasons for this transformation.[9] Rather, it will be of greater interest to see the way in which the relationship between the state and the private sector has affected, and has been affected by, industrial development.

"PANTOUFLAGE"

"The key fact in French planning," wrote David Granick some years ago, "is that the same type of men are sitting in the manage-

---

[8] Edmund Stillman et al., *L'Envol de la France dans les années 80* (Paris: Hachette, 1973), p. 35.

[9] The debate on the transformation of the French economy continues. For a summary, see Savage, "Founders, Heirs, and Managers in France," pp. 17-28.

ment and civil service posts in this cartel: men of the grandes écoles, present and former civil servants who consider themselves technocrats."[10] Another writer has argued that these are the men who "penetrated the centers of public decision-making and turned the state into an instrument for industrialization."[11] Whether these are the true technicians on whom modernization has depended is perhaps debatable. What is less debatable, however, is the fact that the large industrial enterprises in France, the nationalized industries, and the public sector are to a very large extent run by the members of the grands corps.

A recent study of industrial managers in France concluded that "the most characteristic trait in the careers of the sample studied is the frequency of the P.D.-G. [President Director-General] coming from the public sector."[12] The author of this study concludes that this type of career does not simply involve the seduction by the private sector of an elite whose sense of public service has been diluted. Rather, it ought to be seen as "an essential element in the training (acquisition of competence, or relations) of the industrial managers in France."[13] Another study has shown that France differs somewhat from other countries in this respect. This can be seen in Table 8.1. Equally important is the fact that those leaving the public sector for the private almost always enter large enterprises.

We have seen [notes the *L'Expansion* study] that a considerable proportion of French P.D.-G.'s—a proportion that is higher in the bigger than in the smaller firms—come from the public sector. This interpenetration of business and government, resulting from the mobility of high-level directors from the public to the private sector, is one of the particularities of French society.[14]

The educational attainments of the executives of French industries are extremely high. As Granick notes in his comparative study

[10] David Granick, *The European Executive* (New York: Doubleday & Co., 1964), p. 147.

[11] Richard F. Kuisel, "Technocrats and Public Economic Policy: From the Third to the Fourth Republic," *The Journal of European Economic History*, Vol. 2, No. 1 (1973), p. 54.

[12] Dominique Monjardet, "Carrière des dirigeants et contrôle de l'entreprise," *Sociologie du Travail*, No. 2 (1972), p. 1,411.

[13] *Ibid.*

[14] "Portrait-Robot du P.D.-G. Européen," *L'Expansion* (November 1969), p. 137.

TABLE 8.1

The Professional Background of
European Corporation Presidents

(percent)

	France	*G.B.*	*Italy*	*Belgium*	*Holland*
General administration	75.3	56.6	69.2	64.2	65.2
Marketing	3.9	16.4	16.5	7.5	13.0
Finance	2.6	9.0	2.2	—	2.2
Manufacturing	13.6	7.4	8.8	22.6	13.1
Other (law, etc.)	4.4	10.6	3.3	5.7	6.5

Source: "Portrait-Robot du P.D.-G. Européen," *L'Expansion* (November 1969), p. 137.

of business managers, "Thus one sees that at least 68 percent of the top executives of all the leading 475 nonnationalized firms, and 74 percent of the subgroup in prestige industries, had an education equalled by only 2 percent of the French male population of their age group."[15] Here the role of the grandes écoles, and particularly of the Ecole Polytechnique, is of special importance. "Of Frenchmen with higher education degrees, only about 2.8 percent had degrees from Polytechnique—as contrasted with 42 percent of the top managers with higher educational degrees in the very large, nonnationalized firms in the prestige industries."[16]

The homogeneity of the educational and professional background of the directors of French industrial enterprises implies three things: first, they have usually been trained in state professional schools (the grandes écoles); second, at least a part of their career has been spent in the public sector; and third, they graduated in the top 15 to 20 percent of their class. It is this last factor that enables them to choose entry into one of the elite corps. Entry into technical and administrative corps, as we have seen, is regarded as of the utmost importance not only for a successful administrative career but for a successful career in the private sector. What indicates above all that the hostility between the public and private sectors is a relic of the past is that the grandes écoles no

[15] David Granick, *Managerial Comparisons of Four Developed Countries: France, Britain, United States, and Russia* (Cambridge, Mass.: The M.I.T. Press, 1972), p. 187.

[16] *Ibid.*

longer see themselves as training only agents of the state. They have come to have closer relations with the private sector and they have willingly accepted as a fact of life that a considerable proportion of each class will enter the private sector immediately after graduation. Indeed, the percentage of those who resign from the public service immediately upon graduation and choose employment in the private sector has been continually on the increase. As Levy-Leboyer has shown, whereas only 1.9 percent of the total number of polytechnicians resigned their commissions upon graduation in order to enter a business career in the first half of the nineteenth century, the figure had reached 78.8 percent for the class of 1918-1919.[17] Thus, it is not surprising that the training that the heads of French enterprises receive distinguishes them from their European counterparts. As the comparative study carried out by *L'Expansion* observes:

> It is immediately apparent that the directors of French industries are the most educated, whereas the English directors are the least educated. A detailed examination shows that more than half of the French P.D.-G.'s included in this study were trained in grandes écoles, and of these, half were trained at the Ecole Polytechnique. In France, the educational level is the measure of one's worth and a polytechnician is considered to be of superior and broader intelligence.[18]

In his study of the Inspection des Finances, Lalumière has shown that the phenomeon of *pantouflage* (the move from the public to the private sector) has been a normal career move for the members of this corps.[19] During the past eighty years, the percentage of Inspecteurs des Finances moving into the private sector has not varied much. While the variation has been between 25 and 50 percent, it has averaged about 30 percent, which is about the same as the Corps des Mines. We have already shown (Chapter Seven that the number of members of the Corps des Mines who are at any given time civil servants has been declining, whereas departure from the corps to the semipublic and private sectors has been increasing.

[17] Levy-Leboyer, "Innovation and Business Strategies in Nineteenth and Twentieth Century France," pp. 107-109.

[18] "Portrait-Robot du P.D.-G.," pp. 139-140.

[19] Pierre Lalumière, *L'Inspection des Finances* (Paris: Presses Universitaires de France, 1959), p. 72.

The available data suggest a clear pattern: grande école———→ grand corps———→ the administration———→ high executive post in the private sector. This pattern has been repeated so often that it has led to a reorientation of the aims of the grandes écoles, particularly the Ecole Polytechnique, and to a career model to which the most ambitious aspire. A recent survey of Ecole Polytechnique students documents this. The students were asked how they regarded entry into the grands corps upon graduation, and how they look on the possibility of an eventual post as a president of a company. The results showed that "those who are most attracted to directorial posts in firms are those who desire to gain entry into the grands corps. [This] paradox disappears as soon as we realize that the best way to attain the post of director in the largest firms is to enter a grand corps and then, according to the usual expression, to 'pantoufler' or to take advantage of the large possibilities offered by leaves of absence."[20] The data show a clear correlation between desire to enter a grands corps and desire to become president of a company,[21] which suggests that public service is no longer considered an end in itself.

DILUTION OF PUBLIC-PRIVATE DISTINCTION

We have already seen that the once-sacred distinction between the private and public sectors in France is not as rigid as it once was. Indeed, nothing indicates this more than the fact that "a majority (60 percent) of those who wish to enter a grand corps believe that there is no difference between working in the public or in the private sector. Only a very small number wants to remain working as long as possible in the corps which they join."[22] To be able to avow openly that one's eventual goal is a high post in the private sector shows that the French civil servant has come a long way from his hostility to "pecuniary gain" and all that worked against the "general interest." The traditional mutually hostile perception of the two sectors, which for a long time seriously affected their relationship, has been well described by Henry Ehrmann:

> The feelings of the bureaucracy towards organized business are not free from ambivalence. The civil servants admittedly

[20] Gérard Grunberg, "L'Ecole Polytechnique et 'ses' grands corps," *Annuaire international de la fonction publique, 1973-1974*, p. 390.
[21] *Ibid.*, p. 391.
[22] *Ibid.*

need the practicality and the experiences of the business world, especially as long as in their own training an almost exclusive emphasis was placed on rhetoric, mathematics, law, and economic theory of the nineteenth century. But they will criticize quite openly those practices of the trade associations and the cartels that lead to "economic Malthusianism." As long as such practices continue to protect the marginal firms, irrespective of costs, the civil servants hold that big business is hypocritical if it complains about the political demagoguery favoring the "little men." They regret and sometimes ridicule the overcautious attitude of industry towards problems of investment and modernization. They castigate what they consider the employers' slovenliness towards housing and other social problems, and are aware of the need for protecting unorganized interests, especially those of the consumer. They blame many of the difficulties that stand in the way of European economic integration on the reluctance of French business to face the competition of a wider market. Especially the younger administrators who have already reached high positions show an increasing amount of impatience with the ingrained habits of the business community.[23]

What has so far been said in this study, and what remains to be said, indicates that this description, dating back 25 years, may not be applicable to contemporary France.[24] To be sure, administrators continue to claim that only *they* represent the "general interest," that the business community has "selfish interests" and that the administrators, unlike the businessmen, are not motivated by pecuniary gain. Also, the business community continues to claim that the administrative mentality has not yet evolved sufficiently to accept the existence of business enterprises and profits. As one leading businessman recently expressed it:

> It is a question of reeducation and of information that needs to take place. The notion of profit, like that of business leadership, is in France certainly one of the things most attacked and is always presented as something fundamentally

[23] Henry Ehrmann, *Organized Business in France* (Princeton: Princeton University Press, 1957), p. 266.

[24] The research for Ehrmann's study was conducted in 1952-1953 (see *ibid.*, p. xviii). But even then, Ehrmann arrived at the conclusion that this hostility was abating. See *ibid.*, pp. 266ff.

shameful. A very serious effort at demystification is necessary, which is not an easy task, given the enormous weight
of the mental habits of this country.[25]

It is important to bear in mind that there is often a marked discrepancy between rhetoric and reality. If the businessman sees the
civil servant as being somewhat deficient in the "profit ethic," it
does not mean that the latter does not share the businessman's
basic values. The attachment to a set of beliefs is always important to the extent that it provides a framework within which to
operate. Consequently, the ideology of the general interest makes
possible and often legitimizes the catering to particular interests.[26]
Similarly, the businessman's view that the civil servant has still not
sufficiently embraced the "profit ethic" enables him to pursue even
more aggressively the attempt to transform the administration in
his image. Indeed, one observes that M. Duport does not have specific recommendations to make with regard to the rapprochement
of the two sectors. "Personally, I think that the only real reform
lies in the changing of minds and of mental habits, and in becoming aware of the economic, sociological and human realities of tomorrow and not those of yesterday."[27] And Henry Ehrmann did
not, justifiably, exaggerate the hostility that characterized the mutual perceptions between the public and private sectors. He noted
that "the general circumstances surrounding the high civil servant
in present-day France will often either obliterate the differences between his mentality and that of the business leaders, or render
them meaningless because they do not in fact influence the adjustment of competing claims."[28]

Except for the most superficial generalizations, a noticeable
tempering in the hostile rhetoric has taken place between the two
sectors. Table 8.2 shows that even those in the public sector are
ready to avow that there is easy communication between the two
sectors, and that the two sectors are by no means as distinct as
they are often thought to be. This is a remarkable assertion, one
that does not accord with what we know about the administration's
regarding itself with a certain degree of self-righteousness and

[25] Jean Duport, "L'Administration vue par le secteur privé," in *Administration et secteur privé* (Paris: Dalloz, 1973), p. 25.

[26] See Ezra N. Suleiman, *Politics, Power, and Bureaucracy in France*
(Princeton: Princeton University Press, 1974), pp. 222-238.

[27] Duport, "L'Administration vue par le secteur privé," p. 33.

[28] Ehrmann, *Organized Business in France*, pp. 266-267.

TABLE 8.2

Communication Between Public and Private Sectors[1]

	Extremely Difficult		Varies, but Generally Very Difficult		Rather Easy		Very Easy		Don't Know		Total	N
	%	No.	%	No.	%	No.	%	No.	%	No.		
Public sector	1.7	1	6.7	4	46.7	28	45.0	27	0.0	0	100.0	60
Private sector	3.4	2	5.2	3	13.8	8	75.9	44	1.7	1	100.0	58

[1] Question: It is often said that the public and private sectors are two wholly separate worlds and that communication between the two is extremely difficult, if not impossible. Judging from your own experience, do you find communication with the other sector difficult or easy?

claiming to uphold such virtues as "disinterestedness," "unselfish-ness," and the "general interest." We do not have comparable data for an earlier period, but it can be said with a certain degree of assurance that had a similar question been posed even less than twenty years ago, one would have obtained a different answer. Indeed, one is struck by the general willingness of public officials to state that they will soon "pantoufler" to the private sector, something that one did but did not speak of so readily even a decade ago. The extent to which the mutual perception of the two sectors has become less hostile can be seen still further from Table 8.3.

TABLE 8.3

Is Separation Between Public and Private Sector Desirable?

| | *Very* | | *Fairly* | | *Hardly* | | *Not At All* | | | |
	%	*No.*	*%*	*No.*	*%*	*No.*	*%*	*No.*	*Total*	*N*
Public sector	13.3	8	35.0	21	41.7	25	10.0	6	100.0	60
Private sector	3.4	2	29.3	17	62.1	36	5.2	3	100.0	58

One can perhaps reasonably expect businessmen to declare that the public sector should be more responsive to the private sector and that the barriers between the two sectors should come down. But that the officials of a society with such an *étatiste* tradition should today be able to declare that it is not wholly desirable for there to be a separation between the public and private sectors testifies to a profound change in mentalities.

If there has been a change in perceptions, in mentalities, it is because there have been more spectacular and fundamental changes in the structure of the economy. Industrialization may have been slow in coming to France, but it has come and it has been accepted, and, as we shall see in the next chapter, encouraged by the state. Consequently, if the perceptions of the managers of the private sector and those of the public sector diverged in the past, this was to a large extent because the two sectors were indeed different. Today, both the civil servants and the heads of the large industrial enterprises see themselves as managers. The distinction between the art of managing in the private and public sectors is no longer made in France. In fact, whereas the higher civil servants make categorical distinctions between politics and administration, they make no distinction whatever between "managing" in the public and private sectors. The reason for this is that the private sector is no longer composed of small businesses. The managers of the state now feel they have an "interlocuteur valable." They can deal on an equal footing with their counterparts in the private sector whose functions they have come to see as being very much akin to their own. As Ehrmann noted: "Characteristically enough, the views of the high bureaucracy and those of business leaders on the proper organization and the functions of a modern employers' movement are almost identical. Both groups wish to see that solidly organized trade associations in the major branches of economic activity assure the flow of information and control in either direction."[29] Both sides would like to see a high degree of centralization in the organization of the other because each is looking for an "interlocuteur valable." This is what explains the seemingly senseless distinction that administrators draw between *groupes d'intérêt* or *groupes de pression* and professional organizations. The former are looked upon as "lobbies" seeking purely selfish ends whereas the latter are seen to represent the interests of a collectivity. The distinction makes sense only if we bear in mind that one is likely to recognize as legitimate that which most resembles one's image of oneself. Organization implies having a constituency, a degree of representativeness, respectability, and, hence, potential power. A large organization can more easily claim that its demands are made on behalf of a fairly large constituency, even if it cannot claim that it is representing the general interest. The farmer who dumps artichokes to block country roads is interested only in increasing the price of artichokes. Ultimately, of course, the organized and the unorganized seek to have specific demands met. But for the administrator who is all too likely to move into the private sector at a future date, a rationale that facilitates this move becomes necessary. That rationale is always the same. We have seen it utilized in the case of institutions like the Ecole Polytechnique, the Ecole des Mines, the Corps des Mines, and we see it utilized in the case of individuals—the higher civil servants who make the leap to the private sector: the national interest must be more widely conceived than it has hitherto been; it must go beyond the administration, it must include the private sector which has been responsible for bringing the country to

[29] *Ibid.*, p. 271.

where it is today and which has for so long been treated with disdain by the state's agents, etc.

It is paradoxical that those who have been largely responsible for providing the intellectual justifications for the dilution in the public-private distinction have been a number of liberal reformers who believe that a much closer relationship between industry and the state is now called for. Both sectors, it is argued, have common interests, so that it is only a question of doing away with the mutual incomprehension. Indeed, these reformers, most of whom are former higher civil servants occupying important positions in the nationalized and private sectors, believe that the gap between the two sectors will be bridged because of the transformation in the economy. "Growing in size as a result of mergers and concentration, the enterprises are gradually reaching the age of reason."[30] That concentration of industrial enterprises may only superficially indicate that competition is in progress is now generally recognized. However, the arguments presented in *Pour nationaliser l'Etat* provide the intellectual rationale for the civil servants who wish to make the move to the private sector by pointing to the excessive role that the state plays in the economy and by pointing to the respectability of internationally competitive enterprises.

THE MOVE TO DYNAMIC SECTORS

Given that those who would like to tear down the wall separating the public and private sectors are, for the most part, either former civil servants in directorial posts in the private sector or higher civil servants likely to move to the private sector, it becomes important to know what the sectors are that they gravitate toward.

There is no doubt that the graduates of the grandes écoles, and the members of the grands corps in particular, have a predilection for large firms. François Morin notes that "technocratic control, like foreign control, is essentially limited to the large enterprises."[31] This is confirmed in Dean Savage's study, which shows that grandes écoles graduates tend to become managers, as opposed to founders or heirs, of firms (Table 8.4). More important is the fact that the

---

[30] C. Alphandery et al., *Pour nationaliser l'Etat* (Paris: Editions du Seuil, 1968), p. 193.

[31] François Morin, *La Structure financière du capitalisme français* (Paris: Calmann-Lévy, 1974), pp. 68-69.

TABLE 8.4

Education of Different Types of Firm Head
For Destratified Sample
(percentage distribution)

Type of Education	Type of Firm Head			
	Founder or New Owner	Heir	Manager	All
Secondary[1] or less	56.7	49.2	26.7	43.0
University[2]	4.9	7.4	18.1	10.7
Nonscientific grandes écoles[3]	11.9	24.6	20.1	19.2
Scientific grandes écoles[4]	26.5	18.7	35.1	27.1
	100.0	99.9	100.0	100.0
Weighted N =	(85)	(97)	(108)	(290)
Sample N =	(58)	(83)	(150)	(291)

[1] Includes vocational and technical training.

[2] Includes a small number of persons with degrees from foreign universities.

[3] Includes mainly those with degrees from Hautes études commerciales and other business grandes écoles, plus graduates of Sciences Po and a small number from other nonscientific grandes écoles.

[4] Approximately 60 percent of the persons in this group have degrees from Polytechnique, Centrale, or Mines.

Source: Savage, "Founders, Heirs, and Managers in France," p. 145.

graduates of grandes écoles predominate in the largest firms (Table 8.5). As Savage notes, "It is evident that the educational attainments of firm heads increase with company size. . . . There does not seem to be any relation between size and type of education obtained in the case of the *Facultés* and nonscientific *grandes écoles,* but the proportion of elite members having attended the scientific *grandes écoles,* increases rapidly with company size."[32]

A breakdown of the grandes écoles group shows that graduates of different schools and members of different corps have particular preferences. This is in part due to the fact that their training and

[32] Savage, "Founders, Heirs, and Managers in France," pp. 146-147.

TABLE 8.5

Education of Elite Members by Size of Firm
For Destratified Sample
(percentage distribution)

| Type of Education | Firm Size (Number of employees) | | | |
	Small (50-199)	Medium (200-999)	Large (1000 & up)	All
Secondary[1] or less	47.9	36.9	12.0	43.0
University[2]	9.9	11.7	16.2	10.7
Nonscientific grandes écoles[3]	19.7	17.5	19.7	19.2
Scientific grandes écoles[4]	22.5	34.0	·52.1	27.1
TOTAL	100.0	100.1	100.0	100.0

[1] Includes vocational and technical training.

[2] Includes a small number of persons with degrees from foreign universities.

[3] Includes mainly those with degrees from Hautes études commerciales, and other business grandes écoles, plus graduates of Sciences Po and a small number from other nonscientific grandes écoles.

[4] Approximately 60 percent of the persons in this group have degrees from Polytechnique, Centrale, or Mines.

Source: Savage, "Founders, Heirs, and Managers," p. 147.

professional backgrounds predispose them for particular activities. It is also due to a large extent to the access they have to particular sectors as a result of the imprint already made by their *camarades*. Thus, the banking and credit sector is the one most favored by the Inspecteurs des Finances. This is of profound importance insofar as the concentration of industry is concerned. As Michel Drancourt has noted: "The role of the banks here is crucial. It appears that they favor the development of the large enterprises rather than the accession of the medium enterprises to the level of the big ones."[33] That the Inspecteurs des Finances favor the banking and credit sector is by no means a novel situation. As Lalumière notes:

The sector in which private firms needing credit dominated [before 1914] had their preferences. In particular, the institu-

[33] Michel Drancourt, *Les Clés du pouvoir* (Paris: Fayard, 1964), p. 30.

tions of finance capitalism, the financing source for the entire economy, were colonized by those who resigned [from the Inspection des Finances].[34]

The other sectors that attract the Inspecteurs des Finances are the mechanical, chemical, metallurgical, and steel industries, though they do not dominate in any of these. It is the Corps des Mines that colonizes these industries. As Desjeux and Friedberg observe: "The mining engineers in the private sector always concentrate in the heavy industry sector, such as chemicals, mechanics, metallurgy, and steel, the industries that have traditionally welcomed the *'pantouflards'* of the corps and in which the corps has been reinforcing its presence. Moreover, the corps has considerably increased its presence in the sectors that are peripheral to the industrial sector proper, namely, in the banking sector and in the consulting firms."[35] Levy-Leboyer shows that the increasing move on the part of polytechnicians from the public to the private sector was paralleled by a move into the dynamic industries. "The recovery of such sectors as transportation, building, and energy and the development of the basic industries favored some sort of migration into the private sector: in 1877, some 200 polytechnicians held positions in the transport and heavy industries, and their numbers rose to 656 in 1905, and to more than 1,100 in 1930. Before the war, engineers of the Corps des mines were leading some of the main corporations. . . . Finally the use of advanced technology provided the graduates of polytechnique with activities in keeping with the scientific tradition of their school."[36] Lalumière's conclusion regarding the Inspection des Finances can therefore be said to apply to all the grands corps:

> The Inspecteurs des Finances who leave [the Inspection des Finances] gravitate toward the most active sectors of the economy. They maintain a very strong position in the area of finance capitalism whose principal institutions they direct.

[34] Lalumière, *L'Inspection des Finances*, p. 86.

[35] Dominique Desjeux and Erhard Friedberg, "Fonctions de l'état et rôle des grands corps: Le cas du corps des mines," *Annuaire international de la fonction publique, 1972-1973*, p. 579.

[36] Levy-Leboyer, "Innovation and Business Strategies in Nineteenth and Twentieth Century France," p. 109. For more recent data on the industries into which members of the nontechnical grands corps move, see Pierre Birnbaum, *Les Sommets de l'état: essai sur l'élite du pouvoir en France* (Paris: Editions du Seuil, 1977), pp. 142-144.

At present, they are infiltrating the chemical and automobile industries which are experiencing expansion. They tie their fortunes to the most dynamic aspects of capitalism.[37]

In addition to moving into the most dynamic sectors of the economy, the civil servants who enter the private sector move for the most part into directorial posts of French enterprises. Rarely do they find their way into foreign multinational enterprises. In the past, it was a deliberate policy on the part of the corps to discourage their members from taking positions in foreign firms. Also, foreign firms were less likely to seek former civil servants since they were considered to have little managerial or business training. Although there is less hostility today on the part of the corps toward foreign firms, a marked preference continues to be shown for French firms. Entering a French firm keeps one within the *circuit* and extends the influence of the corps over French territory, which is what the corps is interested in. One director of a corps put the matter succinctly: "Yes, we do prefer that members of the corps enter French enterprises, but we no longer object too much when a member wants to join a foreign firm. We make only one requirement: it should be an important position in a respectable enterprise."

State Officials as Businessmen

If the French administration has power and prestige, and if a career in the administration leads to a high-level and well-remunerated post in the private sector, this is by no means a phenomenon that is unique to France. In Japan, for example, public officials take up government service as a route to a career in private enterprise.[38] As in France, "with the rapid growth and bureaucratization of corporations, private industry [in Japan] looks more and more to the civil service to meet the increasing demand for executives at the higher levels."[39] The question that needs to be asked is why this phenomenon should occur in France to the point where it has become institutionalized. What interest does private industry have in hiring people whose training does not, at least in principle,

---

[37] Lalumière, *L'Inspection des Finances*, pp. 87-88.

[38] Chitoshi Yanaga, *Big Business in Japanese Politics* (New Haven: Yale University Press, 1968), pp. 107-119.

[39] *Ibid.*, p. 115.

predispose them to the business world and in whom, as is often argued, there persists "a certain mental structure which summarily condemns, on the basis of a certain ethic, all that involves economic gain, everything that has to do with profit?"[40]

Many answers could be, and have been, given to this question. To some, the question ought never to be posed because it has no meaning since it is oblivious to class interests that are shared by the holders of power. Those who hold this view suggest that even the distinction between the owners of production and the managers is meaningless.[41] To others, it is a simple question of cooptation whose ultimate purpose is to strengthen the enterprise's position in its dealings with the state. The more general question that is posed by the relationship between business and the state, and one that we will treat more explicitly in the next chapter, is to what extent the two share overlapping interests and to what extent they are independent of one another.

The question that is of immediate concern to us is: why does the business community seek to attract state officials? Schumpeter's analysis may help provide an answer. "A genius in the business office," he wrote, "may be, and often is, utterly unable outside of it to say boo to a goose—both in the drawing room and on the platform. Knowing this he wants to be left alone and to leave politics alone."[42] Beyond the search for profits, in other words, the businessman exhibits a remarkable incompetence. He is unable to defend himself in the political arena and his social vision is practically nonexistent. The need to compensate for this lack is what accounts to a large extent for the business community's desire to have as its leaders former state officials.

Business in France has lacked the legitimacy and acceptance that have been readily accorded to other professions. We have seen that the organized elites have been able to survive and extend their positions in large part because of the legitimacy they acquire. The private sector has desperately sought to have some part of this legitimacy transferred onto it so that it could defend itself or obtain what it requests from the state more easily. Perhaps no one had a keener awareness of the businessman's lack of vision and

[40] Duport, "L'Administration vue par le secteur privé," p. 25.

[41] Nicos Poulantzas, *Les Classes sociales dans le capitalisme d'aujourd'hui* (Paris: Editions du Seuil, 1974), pp. 189-204.

[42] Schumpeter, *Capitalism, Socialism and Democracy*, p. 138.

legitimacy, as well as of his political incompetence, than Schumpeter who, in comparing the figure of the industrialist with that of the medieval lord, wrote: "The latter's 'profession' not only qualified him admirably for the defense of his own class interests . . . but it also cast a halo around him and made of him a ruler of men. The first was important, but more so were the mystic glamour and the lordly attitude—that ability and habit to command and to be obeyed that carried prestige with all classes of society and in every walk of life."[43] He went on to note that the opposite was true of the industrialist and merchant who had "no trace of any mystic glamour about him which is what counts in the ruling of men. The stock exchange is a poor substitute for the Holy Grail. We have seen that the industrialist and merchant, as far as they are entrepreneurs, also fill a function of leadership. But economic leadership of this type does not readily expand, like the medieval lord's military leadership, into the leadership of nations. On the contrary, the ledger and the cost calculation absorb and confine."[44] Consequently, in seeking men with public backgrounds, business is not seeking any form of specialized knowledge—managerial, financial, technical, or otherwise. It seeks, rather, men who can command respect, within the industry and within society, who symbolize legitimacy and who are therefore able to defend the interests of the business class. Almost every spokesman for business with a national reputation in France is a former high civil servant.[45] Nor can this be a mere accident. Their pronouncements on the state of the economy, their prescriptions for remedying an ailing sector, their views on the role that business can play in a new activity are all listened to carefully. Perhaps no greater understanding of the role of members of the grands corps in business can be attained than by listening to some of the executives of business enterprises explain why such people are recruited for high posts in the private sector:

They have universal respect. They have a large view of the world.

[43] *Ibid.*, p. 137. [44] *Ibid.*

[45] Roger Martin (Corps des Mines), president of Saint-Gobain Pont-A-Mousson; Ambroise Roux (Pont et Chaussées), president of the Compagnie Générale d'Electricité; Paul Jouven (Mines), until last year, president of Pechiney. An exception is François Ceyrac, who heads the Conseil National du Patronat Français (C.N.P.F.). Ambroise Roux is also the vice president of the C.N.P.F. On the C.N.P.F., see Bernard Brizay, *Le Patronat* (Paris: Editions du Seuil, 1975).

It's true that they have no particularly specialized knowledge. But that is not considered a handicap. They have a general knowledge that allows them to deal with most situations.

They know the ropes. They know how to make a case. They know what arguments not to make. These talents are hard to come by.

Yes they tend to be arrogant, to pretend they know everything, but they gain respect for that because they really believe that they're rendering a service that nobody else can give.

They give business an aura of respectability, which it badly needed in the past because this country tended to deprecate commerce and profits. Now that France is industrialized and it has real, if not defenders, at least representatives, the business sector is much more acceptable.

That it should be those who have most often been accused of having little sympathy for profit and for economic gain and whose dedication has been to the "general interest," who should turn out to be the spokesmen for the private sector may strike us as being the ultimate in paradoxes—and one that we will have to explain more fully.

We have already noted that former civil servants provide the business community with an aura of legitimacy that they acquire as a result of having served the state and of belonging to the grands corps. Equally important, they have far more political skills than they have so far been credited with. "Knowing the ropes" is one thing, but "knowing what arguments to make" is another. One must note that ex-politicians, who surely "know the ropes" rather well, have never been accepted as spokesmen for big business in France. If they have political talent, they lack the attributes necessary for acceptance, the symbol of legitimacy that we have referred to. Ex-civil servants have combined legitimacy and political skill, which explains in large part the desire of business to have them as their spokesmen. It explains also why technical knowledge has not been regarded as a necessary attribute for occupying a high-level position in the private sector. In fact, even within the public sector, specialization is discouraged because it is believed that one will become associated with one sector and thus will, when the move is made to the private sector, be put in charge of a similar area rather than be given wide executive responsibilities. Wide executive responsibilities refer to directorships, which call for the polyvalence that the elite considers its hallmark. Schumpeter was to draw a particularly important conclusion from the absence of the leadership qualities of the business class.

> The inference is obvious: barring . . . exceptional conditions, the bourgeois class is ill-equipped to face the problems, both domestic and international, that have normally to be faced by a country of any importance. The bourgeois themselves feel this in spite of all the phraseology that seems to deny it, and so do the masses. . . . But without the protection of some nonbourgeois group, the bourgeoisie is politically helpless and unable not only to lead its nation but even to take care of its particular class interest. Which amounts to saying that it needs a master.[46]

While there may be a slight overemphasis in Schumpeter's analysis on the helplessness of the business class to defend its own interests, the French case would seem to indicate that the use of a group whose background and training have had little to do with business, and in fact been antithetical to it, is closely linked to the need for acceptance, legitimation, and, most important, influence. Certainly, it has little to do with managerial and technical skills.

Commitment to Policies

Can a set of policies be discerned to which the elite shows an unswerving commitment? In the first place, elite members change positions frequently, hence they frequently come to defend conflicting interests. Second, being members of a prestigious elite, they cumulate functions, so that it becomes difficult at times to distinguish the precise capacity in which they are acting. This problem has been well posed in a recent article in which the author treats the problem of identifying even the academic elite of such an institution as the Institut d'Etudes Politiques of Paris. "Take, for example, the case of an Inspector of Finance who teaches at the Institut d'Etudes Politiques and at another prestigious institution, who is a member of the governing boards of several banks and of a real

[46] Schumpeter, *Capitalism, Socialism and Democracy*, p. 138.

estate company, who sits on one of the planning commissions, who is a former member of several ministerial cabinets and international organizations, and who is the author of several social science studies as well as two novels. Among these different activities which is the one that must be considered in determining his social position? Do we say that he is a teacher (in which case he belongs to the category of intellectuals)? Or does he belong to the business world, the higher civil service, or the political sector? Do these various positions imply one another—in which case it would be sufficient to consider only the most inclusive one—or, on the contrary, are they totally independent of one another?"[47]

Many people might tend to regard the posing of this problem as an attempt to deny the existence of a power elite. After all, it has been argued, there is little difference whether one is primarily a businessman or a lawyer or an educator. What matters is one's social origin.[48] But the problem of "positionality" is a real and a very meaningful one, because it allows for a nonstatic type of analysis. Rather than permitting us to assume that one out of many positions defines a person's orientation permanently, it calls for an examination of the *relative* importance of different positions that may or may not be held simultaneously. Meynaud's study of technocrats is oblivious to such questions as positions and roles, and his definition of technocrats ultimately falls back on the common social background of those in elite positions.

The question whether French society is ruled by a cohesive elite does not generally receive a negative answer. And yet France may be more like a society of castes, each of which is closed, impenetrable, jealous of its functions, and noncommunicative. Even the most die-hard elite proponent would not deny that there is a good deal of difference between the "elite" and "caste" theories.[49] The first implies cohesiveness; the second implies autonomy of disparate elites. Consequently, where the first implies cooperation, the second implies rivalry.

---

[47] Luc Boltanski, "L'Espace positionnel: multiplicité des positions institutionnels et habitus de classe," *Revue française de sociologie*, Vol. xiv, No. 1 (January-March 1975), p. 4.

[48] See G. William Domhoff, *Who Rules America?* (Englewood Cliffs, N. J.: Prentice-Hall, 1967), and *The Higher Circles* (New York: Vintage Books, 1971).

[49] See Jean Meynaud, *Technocracy* (New York: The Free Press, 1969). Jean-Claude Thoenig, *L'Ere des technocrats: le cas des ponts et chaussées* (Paris: Les Editions d'Organisations, 1973).

A good example of the "elite" and "caste" theories can be found in the works of Meynaud and Thoenig. Whereas Meynaud presents the elite theory, Thoenig sets forth the caste thesis in his *L'Ere des technocrates*. The title of Theonig's study is a misnomer, for rather than documenting, as its title suggests, the technocratic predisposition of French society, the study in fact shows the contrary. What one fears after reading Thoenig's study is the entrenched power of a small elite, not the rational, scientific, precisely calculated decisions of this elite. Let us see why this is so by looking closely at some of the more important conclusions of this study. *L'Ere des technocrates* is not directly concerned with questions having to do with technocracy. Indeed, the term is scarcely mentioned and the author is certainly not preoccupied with this phenomenon. The study deals with the Corps des Ponts et Chaussées and as such its principal preoccupation is the structure and functioning of this corps. It analyzes the corps' desire to adapt itself to urban society so as to secure a monopoly over the burgeoning opportunities offered by urban development. This involved no less than a shift in the corps' power base from a rural to an urban setting. In attempting to shift its interest, preoccupations and power from rural to urban settings, the Corps des Ponts et Chaussées inevitably came into conflict with another corps (Travaux Publics).

At no point in the study does one have the impression that these "technocrats," all graduates of the Ecole Polytechnique, are concerned with rational objectives of policy. The very contrary appears to be the case. Thoenig writes:

> The monopoly in the field of civil engineering is threatened. The Ministry of Equipment risks being thrown out of the countryside and not sufficient means are at its disposal to succeed quickly in the city. The Corps des Ponts et Chaussées is attacked at its strongest points at the very moment when it is undergoing a subtle transformation. . . .

> It is time to react. The leaders of the Corps des Ponts et Chaussées feel that territorial reorganization is a preliminary that needs to be taken care of without delay.[50]

The problem for the Corps des Ponts et Chaussées is always that of maintaining a monopoly over a domain. It is always a question of

[50] Thoenig, *L'Ere des technocrates*, p. 121.

preserving its power rather than using that power to achieve goals. "The notion of a goal is effaced."[51] When the corps' power base is secure, the elite is able to think of real problems and to get on with solving them. But this is secondary. As Thoenig notes, "The problems of its [the urban policy's] contents will be raised only later; in order to formulate a policy, the corps has first of all to make certain that it alone controls the contested ground. Once the ground is occupied, one can begin to think about the nature and the needs that must be satisfied in the urban environment, to turn one's attention to short-term realities and to proceed with implementation."[52]

Ultimately, then, what emerges from Thoenig's study is that the formulation of public policy in the area of urban development is not based upon any rational criteria of cost-efficiency. Rather, the policy that emerged was the consequence of compromises effected between two contending, and powerful, administrative units. Is there a more powerful refutation of the technocratic decision-making thesis? It is difficult, of course, to be sanguine about the fact that policies are based neither on ideological discussions nor on rational criteria but represent simply an accommodation to an administrative battle. The important point, at least insofar as the French case is concerned, is that the formulation of public policy is a long way from being based on objectively defined criteria.

The example of the Corps des Ponts et Chaussées is not unique. It would be difficult to pinpoint a coherent set of policies that the Inspection des Finances or the Corps des Mines are committed to within the areas of the economy or of energy. It is not difficult to find examples where policies have been abandoned and new ones have been embraced, sometimes smoothly, sometimes after a difficult adjustment period.[53] But the important point is that it is not the policies per se that matter, for policies are judged according to their impact on the power and position of the elite. Table 8.6 shows that the elite denies that its particular organizations have developed specified policies. This is not surprising given that the elite prefers to think of itself as being sufficiently open to include

[51] *Ibid.*, p. 160.   [52] *Ibid.*, p. 102.

[53] The abandonment of the rural sector in favor of the urban centers required an adjustment not only for the Corps des Ponts et Chaussées, but even more so for the agricultural corps. The encouragement of large, competitive enterprises required the relaxation of rigid *dirigiste* policies.

TABLE 8.6

Has Corps Defined a Policy for its Area?[1]

	Yes		Vaguely		No		Don't Know			
	%	No.	%	No.	%	No.	%	No	Total	N
Public sector	13.1	8	39.3	14	42.6	26	4.9	3	100.0	61
Private sector	8.5	5	22.0	13	66.1	39	3.4	2	100.0	59

[1] Question: Generally speaking, has your corps succeeded in defining a policy for the area over which it has jurisdiction?

diverse elements. More important, however, is the fact that the elite believes that to avow that it is defending a particular policy is to deny that it is serving a higher interest than that of its organization—something that it cannot accept. It could still be that the elite does pursue specific policies, though it would be difficult to obtain this from an attitudinal question. But if we view Table 8.6 in conjunction with the data in Table 8.7, we can make some progress toward answering the question: what is paramount for the corps?

The commitment of the elite is to the health and well-being of its corporate organizations, rather than to a set of policies. Policies are looked upon as a means of enlarging a corps' domain, of leaving it unchanged, or of reducing it. The reaction to particular policies depends on such criteria. The corps see themselves as being committed to maintaining and enlarging their "image de marque." The struggle among the technical corps, for example, to gain more ground in ministerial cabinets is nothing less than an attempt to shore up their "image de marque." As the PCM, the Association of the Corps des Ponts et Chaussées and the Corps des Mines, put it:

> The interest of the nation and that of the corps must coincide if the management [of the corps] is good. This supposes, notably, that the corps is sufficiently dynamic so as to guarantee the quality and the mobility which are indispensable to the opening of a *large range of job possibilities* in very diverse sectors, whether it is the public (interministerial), semipublic, or private sectors. The corps must also maintain an equilibrium between different career orientations (top specialists, men of action, "homme de synthèse," managers), all of

TABLE 8.7

What a Corps Defends[1]

	Public Sector	Private Sector
A policy in its own sphere	6.9 (4) / 3.4 (2)	5.4 (3) / 0.0 (0)
Image and prestige of the corps	24.1 (14) / 29.3 (17)	71.4 (40) / 5.4 (3)
Career advantages for its members	27.6 (16) / 27.6 (16)	8.9 (5) / 32.1 (18)
Its own sphere of influence	31.0 (18) / 22.4 (13)	5.4 (3) / 51.8 (29)
Don't know	10.3 (6) / 17.2 (10)	8.9 (5) / 10.7 (6)
TOTAL	100.0 (58) / 100.0 (58)	100.0 (56) / 100.0 (56)

[1] Question: What are the two most important things that your corps defends?

Note: The pairing of cells indicates 1st choice (top); and 2nd choice (bottom).

which are indispensable to the "image de marque" of a corps and of its worth.[54]

The lack of commitment to policies should not be taken to mean that the corps are not guided by certain overriding ideals. On the contrary, we have suggested that the elite is deeply committed to a certain view of the society—centralized, nonparticipatory, and fundamentally conservative. But within this overall context, to

[54] Cited in J.-A. Kosciusko-Morizet, *La "Mafia" polytechnicienne* (Paris: Editions du Seuil, 1973), p. 109.

which all the corps subscribe and which neutralizes conflicts among them, there is an important degree of pragmatism. It is this that enables them to shed one set of policies for another and to maintain an equilibrium between what Mosca called two contradictory and self-defeating tendencies—the tendency to innovate and the tendency toward conservatism. Specific short-range policies are viewed as a means of preserving both the existing structure of the society and the power and prestige of the corps.

The preoccupation with the corps' prestige and image necessitates, as was suggested in an earlier chapter, a degree of both adaptation and imperialism. But imperialism is regarded as a virtue and its synonym is *ouverture*. For imperialism (a term that is never used by the elite in this context) means that the corps is not oblivious to the outside world and that it allows for the utilization of specific talents.[55] The Cot Report on the role of the engineering grands corps is perhaps most revealing in this regard. It notes that "the good use of members of the engineering corps supposes that, during their careers, these members are able to orient themselves toward activities other than those that are traditionally open to the corps only."[56] The report then proceeds to suggest that everything should be done to permit the members of the technical corps to serve in different sectors of the administration, in the public and semipublic enterprises, in the private sector (from which they ought to be permitted to return to the administration), in the diplomatic corps, in the prefectoral corps.[57] The lack of commitment on the part of the corps to a set of definable policies, as well as their overriding need to find outlets and "colonize" sectors, ultimately coincide with the private sector's need for officials who can defend industry's interests through their access to decision-making centers.

[55] See the interesting report by the president of the PCM, René Mayer, *Un P.C.M., pour quoi faire?* (Paris: PCM, 1970). This report was issued as a supplement to the March 1970 number of *Bulletin de PCM.*

[56] The P. D. Cot Commission Report, "Le Rôle des grands corps d'ingénieurs dans la société française," *La Jaune et la rouge*, No. 230 (October 1968), p. 33.

[57] *Ibid.* The report, like so many of the elite's professional publications we have cited, should be read as an exemplary document in the adaptation and survival of elites. There is almost no word about the policies that the corps ought to pursue. This is the report that quotes a well-known sociologist to the effect that "some societies prefer to die rather than reform themselves."

✂ *Chapter Nine* ✂

THE PRIVATE SECTOR AND THE STATE

THE relationship between the private sector and the state is a complex one. It is also a relationship that changes since it is affected by the variations in the society's and in the economy's goals. The drive toward industrialization in France in the last two decades has undoubtedly altered the relationship that the state had established with both big and small business. Indeed, the state used to be criticized in France not so much for its interventionism as for its coddling of the small businessman and its desire to save him from being crushed by the giant corporations. The picture painted by Zola in *La Bonheur des dames* of the little man being crushed and squeezed by large, efficient firms was one that remained very powerful and that was reflected in the state's economic policies. We shall see presently that government policies can be characterized by an element of contradiction, perhaps some would prefer the term "schizophrenia," even when they manifestly appear to be directed toward favoring a particular sector. Even a policy that has as its main aim "industrialisation à l'outrance" is one that is formulated within a political context,[1] so that a closer examination reveals that other policies exist to temper the consequences of the drive toward industrialization. Thus, the small businessman in France cannot be said to have been showered with favors over the past two decades. Nonetheless, if one looks at the level of industrialization attained by French society, one sees that the continued survival of the small businessman and the shopkeeper could not have occurred without the aid of the state. The question that ought to be posed is, therefore, not why has the state allowed the "little man" to go under, but what has the state done to allow the little man to continue to exist despite the fact that it has been committed to a policy of industrial growth? This is not a question that I intend to answer. I raise it because I want to indicate the important role

[1] See Jean Boddwyn, "The Belgian Economic Expansion Law," in Steven J. Warnecke and Ezra N. Suleiman, eds., *Industrial Policies in Western Europe* (New York: Praeger Publishers, 1975).

that the state plays in initiating and changing economic policies, the direction that this policy has taken in recent years and, finally, the complexities that inhere in the relationship between the state and the private sector.

CORPORATE GROWTH AND THE STATE

Just as formerly the state was generally recognized to have played an important role in hindering industrial development, so now it is credited with having played a major role in the transformation of the French economy. Whether through the Plan or through selective policies designed to encourage particular industries, the state has without a doubt played an active role over the past two decades. One writer has recently noted that "one answer to the question of how and why 'dynamic France' overcame 'static France' is that there was a change in elite behavior and popular attitudes."[2] By this, the writer simply means that it was the agents of the state, "the technocrats," as he refers to them, who initiated and took responsibility for the changes that led France into the industrial and postindustrial era. This thesis is well documented but it represents, as we will see, only a part of the answer to the general question of how and why France has overcome its industrial backwardness. Stanley Hoffmann has, in fact, argued that it is outside the civil service that "one finds profound—if not complete changes of behavior,"[3] though he also notes that changes have taken place in the goals which the state has set for the society.[4]

That there have been changes in "elite behavior"—that is, in the behavior of those who are chiefly responsible for conducting the state's activities—can hardly be questioned. Nowhere has the change in the state's attitude been more radical and nowhere has it represented a sharper break with the past than in its desire to encourage the development of large industrial enterprises. To this end, the state has followed a determined policy of encouraging mergers. Although this policy has been pursued relentlessly under

[2] Richard F. Kuisel, "Technocrats and Public Economic Policy: From the Third to the Fourth Republic," *The Journal of European Economic History*, Vol. 2, No. 1 (1973), p. 53.

[3] Stanley Hoffmann, *Decline or Renewal? France Since the 1930's* (New York: Viking Press, 1974), p. 474.

[4] *Ibid.*, p. 450.

the Fifth Republic, it was initiated under the Fourth Republic by the governments of Pinay and Laniel.[5] M. Louvel, who was Minister of Industry and Commerce in both governments declared: "It is necessary first of all that the industrial sector become adapted to a modern economy. The number of firms is much too high. Only concentration of firms will be able to bring about an appreciable reduction of prices. The Government must facilitate merger operations—this concentration presupposes that certain marginal firms will disappear. This disappearance is not an evil, quite the contrary, but public and business authorities must concern themselves with the great social problems which such disappearances will engender."[6]

The policy of encouraging the concentration of industrial firms has had both political and economic consequences: politically, it has strengthened the ties between big business and the state and weakened those between small business and the state. This is of considerable importance particularly when one considers the generations during which economic policy consisted largely in catering to the small independent businessman. Economically, the push toward mergers has had the effect of encouraging a certain degree of competition and efficiency. This is because the concentration of industrial enterprises presupposes an important element of competition if only because it, initially at least, involves the big swallowing up the small. Hence, it is the clearest manifestation of the abandonment of the "live and let live" attitude that has been described as characterizing the French business mentality.

To be sure, it is important not to exaggerate the degree of competition that the process of industrial concentration entails. At the outset, competition may be very fierce, but beyond a certain point, a point which is reached when an industry becomes monopolistic or oligopolistic, the degree of competition that actually prevails may be minimal. It is at this point that the antitrust divisions become most active. But in France, as Venturini has noted, there is no antitrust tradition. As he rightly notes, "The economico-legal structure of a country is determined not only by the technical processes particular to each type of production but also by the heritage of a long past. The continuum from such a past is 'pro-

[5] Warren C. Baum, *The French Economy and the State* (Princeton: Princeton University Press, 1958), p. 236.

[6] Cited in *ibid.*, p. 237.

tectionism.' "[7] Efforts were made in the Fourth Republic to introduce effective antitrust legislation, but these generally had only
limited success. Indeed, when it became clear that parliament was
unlikely to pass any antitrust legislation, the Laniel government
issued a decree in August 1953 that sought to prohibit "bad"
cartels. However, as Baum notes, "despite the considerable weight
of evidence on the existence of 'bad' cartels, by the government's
own standard, there is remarkably little record of enforcement of
anti-trust legislation."[8]

Although there are numerous ways to measure industrial concentrations, there is little doubt that the rate of mergers in France
has matched that of other industrial countries. Venturini maintains
that this rate has been higher in France than in other European
countries.[9] A more detailed examination, by three leading French
economists, of the industrial structure concluded:

> It is difficult to compare the situation in France with that of
> the other major industrial countries, even if the comparison is
> limited to concentration at a particular date, with no attempt
> to trace movements over time. It is well known, on the other
> hand, that France has few giant industrial groups comparable
> with those in the United States, or even in Japan, Germany,
> the Netherlands, or Britain. On the other hand, apart from
> this extreme case, the degree of concentration of large firms
> does not seem any smaller in France than elsewhere.[10]

The newly embraced logic of the "industrial imperative" has
required that the state should take it upon itself to encourage the
concentration of industrial enterprises. Lionel Stoleru, one of the
chief spokesmen for the "industrial imperative," may be regarded
as expressing the official view when he writes: "In fact, the problem at this point is no longer just to stop opposing this trend but
rather to encourage it openly and actively, for the existing lag is
already disquieting."[11]

[7] V. G. Venturini, *Monopolies and Restrictive Trade Practices in France*
(Leyden: A. W. Sijthoff, 1971), p. 9.

[8] Baum, *The French Economy and the State*, p. 259.

[9] See Venturini, *Monopolies and Restrictive Trade Practices in France*,
p. 350.

[10] J.-J. Carré, P. Dubois, and E. Malinvaud, *French Economic Growth*
(Stanford, Cal.: Stanford University Press, 1975), p. 170.

[11] Lionel Stoleru, *L'Impératif industriel* (Paris: Editions du Seuil, 1969),
p. 49.

Table 9.1 shows the extent to which the largest enterprises have been involved in mergers. Table 9.2 shows that the chemical, electronics, and steel industries have had the highest rate of concentration. McArthur and Scott found in their study of the state's intervention in the key sectors of the economy that the industries concerned could be divided into three categories: a) where state influence was high; b) where state influence was moderate; and c) where state influence was low. It is interesting to observe that the state was found to have little or no influence with regard to two

TABLE 9.1

Number and Remuneration of Mergers Effected
by the 500 Largest French Enterprises

Year	No. of Mergers (Operations of Concentration)	Total Remuneration (millions of francs)	Average Remuneration of Each Operation (millions of francs)
1950	21	58.61	2.79
1951	9	2.98	0.33
1952	22	42.02	1.91
1953	41	147.96	3.60
1954	16	17.91	1.11
1955	41	45.83	1.11
1956	52	25.32	0.48
1957	36	67.31	1.86
1958	45	40.52	0.90
1959	68	101.61	1.49
1960	75	165.47	2.20
1961	70	230.29	3.28
1962	93	201.77	2.16
1963	131	298.04	2.27
1964	113	164.31	1.45
1965	96	279.16	2.90
1966	79	817.08	10.34
1967	57	759.49	13.21
1968	56	720.12	12.85
1969	72	1,287.10	17.87
TOTAL	1,193	5,466.90	4.58

Source: *Direction* (February 1970).

types of industries or firms. The first was the group of small firms. "In general, these firms knew relatively little about the shape and direction of national policy, and they expressed considerable

TABLE 9.2

Number of Mergers Effected by Private Firms, by Sector

Years	Foodstuffs	Banks, Insurance	Construction	Mechanical and Electrical Industries	Chemicals	Steel and Metallurgy	Textiles	Transport	Others	Total
1950-1960	85	183	54	181	149	98	58	41	—	849
1961	12	16	3	9	17	18	10	20	15	120
1962	17	24	3	29	30	7	4	3	10	127
1963	22	17	23	27	25	4	8	9	15	150
1964	44	49	21	46	39	20	12	7	27	265
1965	29	30	19	25	29	8	7	5	12	164
1966	33	52	11	32	28	22	13	25	33	249
1967	13	43	12	10	17	22	8	9	10	144
TOTAL	255	414	146	359	334	199	120	119	122	2,068

Source: Weber, "Fusions et concentrations d'entreprises en France," La Documentation française, 6 January 1969, p. 14.

frustration concerning their contacts with the State."[12] The attitude of the state officials toward these companies is extremely revealing:

> For their part, the Government officials we met viewed small businesses and businessmen in stereotyped and unsympathetic terms. Indeed, the role, competence, motives, and contribution of small businessmen were often regarded with considerable contempt and suspicion. Even the contributions made by the professional managers of some of the largest companies were sometimes called in question by Government and administration people. It was not uncommon for us to encounter strong value judgments in official circles about the relative social roles. Even so, there was an important difference in attitudes toward large and small businessmen.[13]

The second group of companies that the state appeared to have little interest in "comprised companies in certain industries that seemed to be regarded as falling outside the pale of twentieth-century respectability."[14] The two most important examples were textiles and food, both of which are not characterized by large-scale firms, do not have strong organizations, are internally divided, and do not attract the type of skilled management that would gain them entry into the official network.[15]

In following a policy that aims at encouraging the development of large industrial enterprises, the state believes that it encourages competition. Since mergers that lead to oligopoly often have a negative effect on competition, French policy has an inherent contradiction. However, looked at from the perspective of the goals set for French industry, competition and oligopoly may appear to be reconcilable. Stephen Cohen has observed that the concentration of industrial enterprises is seen very differently in France and the United States:

> The French attitude towards concentration and *ententes* differs from that of American economists. The American generally studies industrial concentration with the assumption that high concentration prevents competition, permits monopoly and profits and reduces competition. The French

---

[12] John H. McArthur and Bruce R. Scott, *Industrial Planning in France* (Boston: Harvard Graduate School of Business Administration, 1969), p. 391.
[13] *Ibid.*   [14] *Ibid.*, p. 392.   [15] See *ibid.*, pp. 392-401.

economist generally looks at industrial structures to see whether concentration is high enough to allow for big, efficient firms.[16]

A brief look at the oligopolistic industries where state intervention has been high shows that these industries all attempt to compete internationally. Thus, although it is often argued that economic competition is still not widely accepted in France by the business community, one must note that French industrial policy has tended to distinguish between international and national competition and has chosen to place the greatest emphasis on the former. A French economist has succinctly expressed the apparent contradiction in French policies toward mergers:

> On the one hand, the public authorities examine the market conditions, define the criteria of abuse and incriminate all those whose intention it is to interfere with competition. On the other hand, these same authorities encourage and favor the formation of large sectorial oligopolies and monopolies that can effectively meet international competition.[17]

Although it is recognized that industrial concentration limits competition within the territorial boundaries of France, it is also believed that concentration facilitates international competition.[18] McArthur and Scott observe that the political leaders of the Fifth Republic have been aware that "a strong economy depends in large measure on strong competitive enterprises. Even here, however, the idea was not so much to compete with one another as with outsiders."[19] And M. Weber notes that this policy antedates the Fifth Republic: "From a historic point of view, it seems that since the Second World War the concern for industrial policy has little by little taken precedence over the concerns relative to the advantages of a policy of competition."[20] It is striking to note how similar

[16] Stephen Cohen, *Modern Capitalist Planning: The French Model* (Cambridge, Mass.: Harvard University Press, 1969), p. 75.

[17] A. P. Weber, "L'Economie industrielle de 1950 à 1970: concentration des entreprises et politique économique," *Revue d'économie politique*, Vol. 80, No. 5 (September-October 1970), p. 770.

[18] Industrial concentration, which leads to large conglomerates with international markets also accorded well with Gaullist foreign policy.

[19] McArthur and Scott, *Industrial Planning in France*, p. 229.

[20] A. P. Weber, "Fusions et concentrations d'entreprises en France," *La Documentation Française*, 6 January 1969, p. 35. See also Carré, Dubois, and Malinvaud, *French Economic Growth*, pp. 158-176.

this is to the pattern of thinking and the pattern of policy that emerged in Japan. As Yanaga notes: "The encouragement and promotion of corporate mergers have been just as much the work of government ministries and agencies—including the Bank of Japan and the Japan Development Bank—as of private banks and private corporations. . . . [The] Bank of Japan Governor Yamagiwa [has] stated that in order to strengthen the international competitive position of Japanese industry, there was need to enlarge the scale of enterprises through mergers and agreements to meeting the existing international levels."[21]

That there has been a shift in the French state's economic policies is unquestionable. What we must now ask is, what accounts for the turnabout in French industrial policy, a policy that has shifted its preoccupation from the small businessman to the large industrial enterprise? In the first place, international prestige certainly figures as an important factor. To carry some weight and figure prominently in the diplomatic arena, De Gaulle judged it necessary to have a nuclear striking force, however small and insignificant a force this might be. Similarly, to figure prominently in the economic field it has also been judged essential to promote enterprises with an international character. If one examines the history of the Concorde project, one finds, beneath all the proclamations of "scientific progress," a fervent desire to be in the forefront of the aircraft industry. That this industry is one that has accounted for a heavily subsidized national megalomania in numerous countries only confirms the French desire to be one step ahead. In other words, it is important not to underestimate the impact of foreign-policy goals on industrial policy.[22]

Second, the Common Market has also been a key factor in influencing French industrial policy.[23] The Treaty of Rome facilitated for the other European countries their access to French markets. This made it all the more necessary for the French government to consider means to acquire markets in the countries of its European rivals. Moreover, the policy of promoting large competitive enterprises received an added stimulus from the fact

[21] Chitoshi Yanaga, *Big Business in Japanese Politics* (New Haven: Yale University Press, 1968), p. 173.

[22] Edward L. Morse, *Foreign Policy and Interdependence in Gaullist France* (Princeton: Princeton University Press, 1973), pp. 170-191.

[23] See Charles-Albert Michalet's chapter on France in, Raymond Vernon, ed., *Big Business and the State* (Cambridge, Mass.: Harvard University Press, 1974), p. 116.

that French enterprises have felt that American firms constituted the greatest threat. This was made clear in the Fifth Plan:

> The benefits of the establishment of a European Common Market will not be fully realized unless French firms participate in the construction of larger conglomerates. Such European consolidation must be all the more encouraged and aided since, in a number of cases, only they will permit resistance to the financial and technical power of the large American firms.[24]

The policy of establishing "national champions" was, if not instigated, at least supported, by the need to resist the "défi américain." In other words, French industrial policy has been aimed at developing firms that will be large enough and efficient enough to resist the American intrusion and also be able to compete with the American firms beyond the French borders.[25] To be sure, the problems posed by the multinational corporations are at once political and economic. That is, these corporations come to have an influence, sometimes more imperceptibly than directly, on the industrial and economic policy of the host country. The nature of that influence may differ depending on the economic policies of the host country and on the economic policies of the multinational corporations themselves.[26]

The third important factor accounting for an industrial policy that seeks large, internationally competitive enterprises is that this policy also facilitates the whole process of economic planning. By "planning" we refer to more than the guidelines laid down by the Plan, for the cooperation between the public and private sectors that takes place outside the Plan is perhaps of greater significance. Andrew Shonfield described the earlier period of French planning as a "conspiracy in the public interest." It was, he noted, "a very elitist conspiracy, involving a fairly small number of people. . . .

[24] Weber, "Fusions et concentrations," p. 36.

[25] Peter J. Katzenstein, "International Relations and Domestic Structures: Foreign Economic Policies of Advanced Industrial States," *International Organization*, Vol. 30, No. 1 (Winter 1976), pp. 29-30.

[26] See Raymond Vernon, *Sovereignty at Bay* (New York: Basic Books, 1971); Richard J. Barnett and R. Muller, *Global Reach* (New York: Simon & Schuster, 1974); Charles T. Goodsell, *American Corporations and Peruvian Politics* (Cambridge, Mass.: Harvard University Press, 1974); Robert Gilpin, *U. S. Powers and the Multinational Corporation* (New York: Basic Books, 1975).

It relied essentially on the close contacts established between a number of like-minded men in the civil service and in big business. Organized labor, small business, and, most of the time, the ministers of the government of the day were largely passed by."[27] Whether this has radically changed is perhaps not of crucial importance for, as McArthur and Scott note, the "important force shaping corporate strategies and strategic planning was a close relationship between business and the State." It became evident, from the outset of their investigations, that "the *state-company relationship*, and not the planning process, was the most important determinant of corporate strategic planning and strategies in France."[28] Stephen Cohen reached much the same conclusion in his study: "The *economie concertée*," he noted, "is a partnership of big business, the state, and, in theory though not in practice, the trade unions. The managers of big business and the managers of the state run the modern core of the nation's economy—mostly the oligopoly sectors."[29]

A NEW RELATIONSHIP?

The development of oligopolistic enterprises in postwar France is, as we noted above, the result of policies that the state has pursued and that have been embraced by the private sector. That this form of cooperation between the public and private sectors represents a sharp departure from previous patterns can hardly be questioned. The traditional businessman, described by Landes and others, has not disappeared, but has given way nevertheless to the manager of the large enterprise who, as in the United States, has come to fulfill the modern entrepreneurial function. The economic policies of the Third Republic, which sought above all to protect the small businessman and farmer, have been largely replaced by policies that seek to develop large, competitive enterprises. No longer can France be characterized as "La République des petits." Nowhere is this more evident than in the Fifth Republic's treatment of the small shopkeeper who, finding himself squeezed by the giants, appeals more and more desperately to the government. Because he is a part of a rather sizeable group, he is still able—mostly

[27] Andrew Shonfield, *Modern Capitalism* (New York: Oxford University Press, 1969), pp. 130-131.

[28] McArthur and Scott, *Industrial Planning in France*, p. 8.

[29] Cohen, *Modern Capitalist Planning*, p. 51.

at election times—to obtain some concessions from the government. Otherwise, he can no longer be said to figure prominently in the state's economic policies, whose aim has been to overcome its old habits and become an industrial nation. Giscard d'Estaing could declare to Roger Priouret in 1969:

> I consider that my mandate at the Ministry of Economy and Finance runs until 1976. My objective is, by that date, to bring France to an industrial level about equal to that of Germany and England. I would prefer to attain this objective without inflation. But if I have to choose, I would opt for industrial development and regard the fight against inflation as secondary.[30]

M. Priouret notes that Giscard d'Estaing was equally of the opinion that the industrialization he sought should be the responsibility of the large enterprises, whose power should remain in the hands of its directors. The extent to which the Fifth Republic has favored big business, either by passing new laws or refusing to apply old ones, is the theme of Priouret's book. Priouret cites the Belgian Baron Edward Empain, head of the giant electrical firm Jeumont-Schneider, who was summoned to the Elysée by President Pompidou. "And do you know what M. Pompidou had the audacity to tell me? That M. Ambroise Roux would like to merge Jeumont-Schneider and Alsthom. . . . That, he, the President of the Republic, would like to see negotiations begin to effect this desire so that France will have only one giant enterprise in the field of electrical materials."[31]

The drive toward industrialization has inevitably clashed with the aspirations of the sizeable number of medium and small businesses. It should not be thought that the "little man" has been totally sacrificed. He continues to obtain significant concessions from the state that seeks to protect him, or at least shelter him, from the state's policies aimed at promoting competitive conglomerates. This is the apparent contradiction that is to be found in the state's economic policies. It has put its full weight behind the large enterprises, and yet it has not been able to do what is demanded by such policies—namely, to allow the small firms to disappear. Nowhere is this better seen than in the passage of the 1973 Royer Law, which gives shopkeepers a veto power in departmental

[30] Roger Priouret, *Les Français mystifiés* (Paris: Grasset, 1973), p. 121.
[31] *Ibid.*, p. 106.

councils when the establishment of supermarkets or department stores is at issue. This extremely controversial piece of legislation reflects the corporatist policies of Vichy, in that it gives legislative powers to a nonelected body. Interestingly enough, many deputies were vehemently opposed to the law, but, although many abstained, not one deputy voted against the law.

Did the passage of the Royer Law reflect a change in attitude toward industrialization? Did it reflect a greater concern with the social costs of industrialization? Certainly, the appeal of Jean Royer, the minister after whom the law was named,[32] was to a large extent a negative one, emphasizing the social costs of modernization. But the passage of the law itself in no sense indicated a turning point. In fact, it only reflected openly what the state had continued to do, which was to subsidize an ailing sector.[33]

Insofar as elite attitudes are concerned, little sympathy is expressed for the inefficient "little man." Table 9.3 shows that the elite is by no means on the side of the small shopkeeper and businessman. The most favorable thing that could be said for him was that he should not totally disappear, but that he should "evolve." The public sector elite, if anything, shows even less sympathy for the "little man" than do his large competitors in the private sector. On the other hand, those in the public sector who express the attitude that the days of the small businessman are numbered are also those who have propped him up with subsidies, protective policies, and exceptions. They do this in part because of political pressure, and in part to justify the far greater advantages that they shower on the large enterprises. Moreover, their commitment to industrialization and economic growth is categoric (Table 9.4). Here we are referring both to a "value" and to "behavior" on the part of the elite. For those in the public sector not only accommodate themselves to a goal that they fully share with their counterparts in the private sector, but, as it must follow, they have both embraced a commitment to industrial growth.

The question may legitimately be raised as to how the restricted

[32] Royer ran as a presidential candidate in 1974 on a ticket that stressed "traditional values" and that was backed in part by small shopkeepers. He received 3 percent of the vote in the first round. See Jack Hayward and Vincent Wright, "Les Deux France and the French Presidential Election of May 1974," *Parliamentary Affairs*, Vol. xxvii, No. 3 (Summer 1974), p. 211.

[33] See Suzanne Berger, "D'une boutique à l'autre: Changes in the Organization of the Traditional Middle Classes From Fourth to Fifth Republics," *Comparative Politics*, Vol. 10, No. 1 (October 1977), pp. 121-136.

TABLE 9.3

Should the Small Businessman Disappear?

	Yes		No		He Should "Evolve"		Don't Know		Total	N
	%	No.	%	No.	%	No.	%	No.		
Public sector	51.8	29	21.4	12	25.0	14	1.8	1	100.0	56
Private sector	46.3	23	25.9	14	29.6	16	1.9	1	100.0	54

TABLE 9.4

Should the Imperatives of Technical Progress Be Accepted?

	Definitely		Probably		Probably Not		Definitely Not		Don't Know		Total	N
	%	No.	%	No.	%	No.	%	No.	%	No.		
Public sector	42.9	24	28.6	16	10.7	6	1.8	1	16.1	9	100.0	56
Private sector	38.9	21	25.9	14	11.1	6	9.3	5	14.8	8	100.0	54

number of members of the grands corps can allow these corps to continue to monopolize most of the directorial posts in both the private and public sectors, particularly in an expanding economy when the number of these posts must be increasing. Is there not a contradiction between the desire of these corps to continue restricting their membership and their desire to occupy the key posts in the public and private sectors? In effect, not only is there no contradiction between these two aims, they are perfectly compatible. This is because French industrial policy has aimed at the concentration of economic power in much the same way as political and administrative power is concentrated. Consequently, the rapidly expanding French economy has not entailed a corresponding expansion of key posts. It may, in fact, have entailed the contrary. This also helps to explain the newly established cooperation between the public and private sectors. In other words, the expanding role of the state has actually allowed the organized elites to expand their own role.

SHARED GOALS OF PUBLIC AND PRIVATE SECTORS

It is this commitment to shared goals—economic growth, modernization, efficiency, competitiveness—that represents a departure from the days of "La République des petits." While the public and private sectors may have shared different goals in the prewar period—goals that have usually been characterized as "Malthusian"—it is evident that the state has today embraced a goal that it shares with the private sector and one that is fundamentally different from the functions it performed in the prewar era. Stanley Hoffmann has expressed this clearly:

> What are the functions of the state? Today, to the earlier ones, we must add: nothing less than the transformation of society. Industrialization, the reconversion of a dwindling agricultural sector, the social-security system and policy of "social transfers," a policy of regional balance (*aménagement du territoire*), urbanization, the development of a modern network of communications and telecommunications—these are all undertaken, either under state guidance or by state agencies. There is, to be sure, a link between the old *Colbertisme* and the modern French state. But what a difference there is between state participation in developing commercial and

manufacturing activities when economic development was a side issue, and a state where economic growth is *the* collective goal![34]

It appears evident that the state's goals have changed, for the support which the state provides favors the enterprises which foster concentration rather than those which are content with their limited size. The policy of concentration applies to a number of other areas in French society. Tarrow's study of the relationship between the state and local authorities shows that the allocation of grants and loans to local authorities does not vary according to the region's class or party affiliation. He notes, for example, that "a simple class-party model cannot suffice to explain the relatively high level of subsidies received by small farm communities in Provence."[35] And he concludes that "The dominating characteristic of the French system of national-local policy allocation is that once a political choice had been made in favor of size, growth and concentration, it was difficult to reverse, either on behalf of politically friendly communities, or against the opposition."[36]

The policies aimed at fostering growth and concentration have had a profound impact on the relationship between the public and private sectors. Because elites in both sectors share a commitment to industrial growth, the relationship between the two sectors has been considerably facilitated. This comes out most clearly when one considers what the bases are for cooperation between the two sectors. We posed two questions to the elite (public and private) which tried to get at the bases for conflict and cooperation between the two sectors. One was: "In the contact between the administration and the private sector there are areas where conflicts and differences are more numerous than others. What are the areas that you see as allowing for the greatest cooperation?" The second question asked: "What are the areas that you see as causing the greatest conflict?"

The areas of cooperation are all linked to industrial growth. The state and the private sector share this goal. The latter could count on the full cooperation and encouragement of the state's financial institutions in the areas of industrial investment and export policies. Indeed, where exports were concerned, the state has taken

[34] Hoffmann, *Decline or Renewal?*, pp. 450-451.
[35] Sidney Tarrow, *Between Center and Periphery: Grassroots Politicians in Italy and France* (New Haven: Yale University Press, 1977), p. 104.
[36] *Ibid.*, p. 107.

aggressive measures (devaluation, availability of credit) to increase the volume. This is because exports were considered "le tracteur de la croissance."[37] For example, in 1970 the French government undertook an aggressive campaign to increase its share of the North American market. "The business organizations, who in the past were united by their protectionist desires, supported this effort. The one who wanted to export was really aided. Many heads of firms responded willingly to this call because they extended their horizons beyond their frontiers."[38] The results of the government's efforts were rather extraordinary: exports rose about 14 percent a year between 1969 and 1973, a higher rate than that experienced by any other industrial nation.[39] The energy crisis since 1974 has led to an even more aggressive export policy, one that seeks to export not only military equipment (though this has been the most conspicuous aspect in recent years) but technical know-how and particularly construction. The state has signed agreements to construct schools, hospitals, and roads in a number of Arab countries. All this export activity has meant that both the state and the private sector have shared very clearly discernible goals. Thus, it was possible for the presidents of industrial corporations that we interviewed to make such statements as:

> The state now has a far greater understanding of the needs of the private sector. It supports us now when we have new ideas.

> When we want to invest or when we need some help to try to break into a new market, the administration is always very receptive.

> The truth of the matter is that the administration now operates on the same wave length as we do. It's finally come to realize that we serve the national interest just as much as it does. And we do so in a more tangible way. When we want to expand, when we want to export more, what happens? We create employment and we reduce the balance of payments deficit. Who gains out of this, if not the society? And this the administration now understands.

[37] Priouret, *Les Français mystifiés*, p. 121.

[38] *Ibid.*, p. 122.

[39] See *ibid.*, pp. 122-125; Carré, Dubois, Malinvaud, *French Economic Growth*, pp. 393-416.

I would say that the greatest change in the administration's attitude has come in its desire to support more and more those who are efficient and can compete. When it concerns mergers or take-overs, we always get the full cooperation of the state. There is still quite a bit of demagoguery when it comes to "les petits commercants," but such concessions are necessary and you can't expect these people to disappear. But in the important matters—mergers, exports, expansion, relocation —it is difficult to complain about the state's attitude.

Now, the area where there remains the greatest conflict between the private sector and the state lies in price controls. The elite in the private sector was practically unanimous in condemning the controls on prices that the state continues to exercise. This understandably constitutes a restriction of freedom for the private sector, but it is a price that has to be paid for the vast areas of cooperation. In effect, price controls are part of the state's export policies, since a rise in exports depends on competitive prices. But the private sector sees the state's price control policies as interfering with its freedom which has grown so remarkably in recent years.

The commitment of both the private and public sectors to industrial growth has led to what is often described as a cozy relationship between big business and the state. But this relationship has most often been attributed to the fact that former civil servants occupy the important posts in the industrial and banking sectors. Hence, it follows, as is often argued, that there is no longer a distinction between the public and private domains. Two distinct arguments are contained here, though they are often confused. First, some maintain that France represents the epitome of a technocratic society since technocrats occupy the key positions in the public and private sectors. For many writers, this has been a key factor in French economic planning since the emphasis on rationality has been paramount.[40] For others, the movement of public officials to posts in the private sector is no more than a representation of the close link between political and financial power that now characterizes French society.[41] The argument

[40] See David Granick, *The European Executive* (New York: Doubleday & Co., 1964), pp. 147 and 72; Cohen, *Modern Capitalist Planning*, p. 75.

[41] See Jean-Jacques Servan-Schreiber and Michel Albert, *Ciel et terre: Manifeste Radical* (Paris: Denoel, 1970). See also the writings of Henry Claude, in particular, *Gaullisme et grand capital* (Paris: Editions Sociales, 1960); *La Concentration capitaliste: pouvoir économique et pouvoir gaul-*

against technocracy as it ostensibly manifests itself in the public and private sectors is most often employed by politicians. This is understandable in that it absolves them from responsibility for actions they have taken or for actions they have failed to take.[42] And one can well understand the periodic outbursts of ministers, and even of a prime minister and a president of the Republic,[43] against the technocrats whom they are supposed to control. The attack of a minister on his own "technocrats" is often an admission of a failure to control his subordinates. On the other hand, the argument that attributes the close relationship between the public and private sectors to a commonality of class interests is different in nature. It says nothing about the desire to achieve "rational," efficient goals. On the contrary, rationality and efficiency are seen as being subordinated to and defined by what serves the interests of the capitalist class. Occasionally it is argued that technocracy and class interests go together.[44]

There are strong a priori grounds for maintaining that—whether as a result of sharing a technocratic outlook, or whether as a result of sharing a common class interest—the close and cooperative relationship established between the public and private sectors in France has coincided with the predominance of members of the grands corps in both sectors. Certainly, the members of this elite are willing to acknowledge that the relationship across sectors is considerably smoother when it involves a civil servant and ex-civil servant (Table 9.5) than when it involves a civil servant and one who has never served in the public sector. This applies even more

---

liste (Paris: Editions Sociales, 1965), and *Le Pouvoir et l'argent* (Paris: Editions Sociales, 1972), and Jacques Sallois and Michel Cretin, "Le Rôle sociale des hauts fonctionnaires et la crise de l'état," in Nicos Poulantzas, ed., *La Crise de l'état* (Paris: Presses Universitaires de France, 1976), pp. 232-259.

[42] The application of J. K. Galbraith's "technostructure" to France was popularized by Edgar Faure, the politician's politician, and his analysis is often taken at face value by the French political sector. See Roger Priouret, "Face à face avec Edgar Faure," *L'Expansion*, XXII, No. 2 (September 1969), pp. 101-105.

[43] See the examples cited in Ezra N. Suleiman, "The French Bureaucracy and Its Students: Toward the Desanctification of the State," *World Politics*, XXIII, No. 1 (1970), pp. 152-153.

[44] See Jean Meynaud, *Technocracy* (New York: The Free Press, 1969), p. 175.

TABLE 9.5

Contacts With Officials in the Private Sector[1]

	Contacts Affected by Previous Administrative Experience of Interlocutor		Contacts Unaffected by Previous Administrative Experience of Interlocutor		Don't Know			
	%	*No.*	*%*	*No.*	*%*	*No.*	*Total*	*N*
Public sector	76.3	45	15.3	9	8.5	5	100.0	59
Private sector	75.0	42	14.3	8	10.7	6	100.0	56

[1] Question: When you have professional contact with a director in the private sector who has never been in the administration, do you find that your experience is different from what it is when you deal with a director of this sector who has spent time in the administration?

to membership and nonmembership in a corps.[45] This is so because "each one knows the rules of the game," or because "neither one can use facile arguments." But there is another side to this type of relationship. Since neither side can use arguments for the sake of trying to make a point, it becomes crucial from the outset, as one executive in the private sector put it, "to level with one another." Hence, there are distinct advantages for a firm to hire an ex-civil servant, if only for the easy access he has to decision-making centers in the state apparatus. But he also has to accept certain constraints, that is, he must accept the "rules of the game" which preclude the use of arguments that would not otherwise be precluded coming from a noncivil servant.

[45] Another survey has found that an overwhelming proportion of higher civil servants (87 percent) assert that they enjoy an "easy" relationship with directors of industrial enterprises, but only a third of the sample believes that the relationship is facilitated when the industrialist is an ex-civil servant. See "Les Hauts fonctionnaires et les patrons," *Le Nouvel économiste*, No. 85, June 13, 1977, pp. 35-41. The discrepancy between the findings in this survey and in our own may be explained by the more restricted nature of our sample, which included only those highest in the hierarchy of the two sectors. The term "patron" used in the *Nouvel économiste* survey has a very broad meaning. As Bernard Esambert, a member of the Corps des Mines and now a high-level official in the Rothschild Bank, says, "It's very typical of the French conception of management—on aime les patrons chefs d'état-major, pas ceux qui vont an charbon." Cited in *Nouvel économiste* survey, p. 37.

But this is not what determines the nature of business-state relations in contemporary France. The apparent degree of cohesion that characterizes the French business and administrative elites has allowed for a relatively smooth formulation and implementation of economic and industrial policies. The agreement engendered by these policies is due therefore both to the cohesiveness of the elite and to the nature of the policies,[46] that is, to the changing nature of the economy which has to operate in a more international setting than in the past. "This evolution [of the economy] has as a corollary the greater subordination of industrial decisions, as well as that of the State's intervention, to the imperatives of 'Performance' and of sanctions by the results. In addition, there is the obligation to place 'growth' at the top of the priorities both of industry and of the State's economic policy."[47]

We have, then, two phenomena occurring simultaneously: the predominance of directorial posts in the public and private sectors by an elite sharing a common training and background, and the sharing of goals concerning industrial growth. It does not follow from this that political power has now lost its independence and has become subordinated to economic power. The problem of state autonomy is more complex than it appears. In the first place, the commitment to industrial growth has allowed for the newly founded cooperation between the public and private sectors. Hence, the policy itself has brought a common aim to the two sectors, and that policy is the product of "circumstances." By that is meant that it reflects the exigencies of a specific period—roughly from the 1950s to the present. It was not always so, and it may not be so tomorrow. The state initiated the policy of growth and modernization. It sought to fashion large, internationally competitive enterprises—"national champions"—and it provided the propitious conditions under which the private sector could imple-

---

[46] See Jack Hayward, "Employer Associations and the State in France and Britain," in Warnecke and Suleiman, eds., *Industrial Policies in Western Europe*, pp. 118-147. See also Jean-Jacques Bonnaud, "Planning and Industry in France," in Jack Hayward and Michael Watson, eds., *Planning, Politics and Public Policy: The British, French and Italian Experience* (Cambridge: Cambridge University Press, 1975), pp. 93-110.

[47] Erhard Friedberg, "Administration et entreprises," in Michel Crozier et al., *Où Va l'administration française?* (Paris: Les Editions d'Organisations, 1974), p. 102. See also Jack Hayward, "State Intervention in France: The Changing Style of Government-Industry Relations," *Political Studies*, Vol. xx, No. 3 (September 1972).

ment the goals of the state. As Hayward has noted: "The new relationship is not so much one of hierarchical superior to inferior (in terms of traditional public law) as of equal partners to a bargain characteristic of civil law. The government does not (in state idealist terms) have an unchallenged status as sole exponent of the public interest and the organizations that form its environment are not *per se* advocates of sinister, sectional interests. This change in relative status has made it possible to have recourse to voluntary contractual agreements rather than statutory obligation as a way of securing the conformity of private agents to public purposes."[48]

That there are discernible "public purposes" or "state interests" is not the same as saying that there is a general interest over which the state keeps guard. It implies merely that the state itself defines its own goals, and it seeks to rally the private sector, in much the same way as it seeks to rally, say, trade unions, around these goals. As two authors have noted with regard to public-private relations in Mexico, "that which is in the interest of the state is not necessarily in the interest of the general public. By the same token, the fact that a policy is not in the interest of the general public does not imply that it is necessarily in the interest of some private group. Finally, a particular policy which is in the interest of the state may or may not be congruent with some private interest. If the latter is the case, this does not mean that the policy cannot primarily serve the interests of the state."[49] In contemporary France, "state interests" have dictated economic expansion. This goal has been pursued with singular dedication since the early years of the Fifth Republic, and it received an even greater stimulus during the period that Georges Pompidou was prime minister and president of the Republic.[50] It was nonetheless a goal set by the state and it involved the winning over of the business community. An important element in the state's decision to open the economy to international competition was that it called for important changes in

[48] Hayward, "State Intervention in France," p. 287.

[49] John Purcell and Susan Purcell, "Mexican Business and Public Policy," in James N. Malloy, ed., *Authoritarianism and Corporatism In Latin America* (Pittsburgh: The University of Pittsburgh Press, 1976), p. 198.

[50] Pompidou's links to big business, which resulted from his former position as a director-general of the Rothschild Bank, were seen as having an impact on his economic policies which favored big business. See Gilles Martinet, *Le Système Pompidou* (Paris: Grasset, 1973). Pompidou's commitment to modernization—in industry, agriculture, commerce—was unquestionable. See Priouret, *Les Français mystifiés*, pp. 104-111.

the state's manner of dealing with the private sector: "Because under the growing pressure of an open market, it is no longer so much a question of *managing* some *general regulations* as of *(re)structuring* them by exemplary and selective actions."[51] Thus, structural changes occurred on both sides so as to accommodate the goal of economic growth. As Vernon notes, "The French government, playing its role as the initiator of change and the guardian of harmony in the French economy, had long since grown accustomed to dealing with enterprises branch by branch; and where firms were relatively large, even firm by firm."[52] Consequently, when the state set itself a target, "there was no ideological barrier to singling out the firms for the chosen task," nor did the firms question the legitimacy of the tutelary ministries.[53] But even if they did have qualms about the legitimacy of the state's intervention, "they had to reckon with the fact that most of the sources of credit in the country were owned or controlled by the government, and that stringent capital controls were in effect at the French border."[54]

It follows that there is a tacit and often explicit understanding between big business and the state in France that the state will initiate and define economic objectives, and to the extent that private enterprise collaborates in the achievement of these objectives it will be adequately compensated. But this compensation ceases the moment business no longer shares these objectives. The situation is not very different in Mexico, where the government has set industrial objectives that are similar to those of the French government. As the Purcells have noted: "The government's strategy of economic development is highly favorable to private enterprise

---

[51] Friedberg, "Administration et entreprises," p. 123. Italics in original. See also Charles-Albert Michalet's chapter on France in, Vernon, ed., *Big Business and the State*, p. 116.

[52] Vernon, "Enterprise and Government in Western Europe," in *Big Business and the State*, p. 6.

[53] *Ibid.*, p. 7. Tarrow notes that the dirigisme of the French state is not evident when the state is dealing with well-organized groups or industries. On the other hand, "as its policy objectives depart from its relations with powerful economic groups and approach the grassroots, its *dirigisme* reasserts itself. . . ." See Sidney Tarrow, "Contradictions In French Industrial Policy: The Case of Fos-Sur-Mer," unpublished paper, 1976, p. 13. A different version of this paper appears in L. Graziano, P. Katzenstein and S. Tarrow, eds., *Territorial Politics In Industrial Nations* (New York: Praeger Publishers, 1978).

[54] Vernon, "Enterprise and Government in Western Europe," p. 7.

since it emphasizes a high level of profits in order to promote sav-
ings and further investment. The government sees its role as that
of encouraging private investment and business activity *as long as
it leads to economic growth.*"[55] Put simply, the relationship hinges
on the acceptance of *specific* goals which are defined by the state.

The relationship between big business and the state clearly varies
according to the type of industry involved and to the type of policy
formulated by the state. This is very clearly shown in Zysman's study
where different policies, with varying degrees of success, were applied to three different industries—petroleum, steel, and electronics. As Zysman notes, "The French state . . . has the structural
potential for autonomous action, but structure does not determine
how or whether that potential is used. A political explanation will
always be required to explain the direction of state activity."[56] It
becomes difficult to argue that the state's autonomy has totally disappeared, since there are clear instances of its having devised policies that ran counter to the interests of a particular industry. It is
true, however, as Stephen Krasner notes, that "State decisions
taken because of state interests reinforce private societal groups
that the state is unable to resist in later periods."[57] It may well
be, therefore, that the enduring consequences of the nature of the
relationship between the public and private sectors that we have
described will become apparent only at a later date. This clearly
illustrates what we suggested at the outset of this chapter, namely,
that the relation between business and the state is a dynamic one.

In this study we have observed that elites in the public and private sectors have come to be united both by their common class
origins and by their commitment to industrial policies. Enough has
been said to indicate that the policies dictated by the "industrial
imperative" have in no way been detrimental to big business. And
there is ample reason to believe that such policies have not had
the working class uppermost in their order of priorities.[58] Nor, indeed, was there for the most part sympathy for the small business-

[55] Purcell and Purcell, "Mexican Business and Public Policy," p. 198.

[56] John Zysman, *Political Strategies For Industrial Order: Market, State
and Industry In France* (Berkeley and Los Angeles: University of California
Press, 1977), p. 195.

[57] Stephen D. Krasner, "State Power and the Structure of International
Trade," *World Politics,* Vol. XXVIII, No. 3 (April 1976), p. 343.

[58] For a good analysis of the social policies of the Pompidou era, see
Priouret, *Les Français mystifiés*, pp. 48-103.

man.[59] Consequently, economic policies have been clearly favorable to big business, often to the detriment of the demand of workers and the small businessman.

From this, however, it does not necessarily follow that big business dictates economic policy. Rather, it figures most prominently in the goals which the state has set. In a not so distant past, the state showed little sympathy for competition and profits, and public goals were wholly oriented in favor of the small businessman, farmer, and shopkeeper. The working class has generally been assured of neglect, though it may be a small comfort for it to know that it shares this neglect with the farmer and the shopkeeper today. But the overwhelming commitment to industrialization has in effect led to an equation of the state interests and the interests of big business.

Is this a permanent situation? To the extent that it is based on a shared interest, the answer must depend on the endurance of this interest. The relationship between big business and the state in the United States may provide some guidance. One notices that it has had ups and downs and the nature of the relationship has varied according to the economic and political situation. However, in France, the relationship has been open to more simple explanations in view of the fact that there is an interchangeable elite in both sectors. This elite has readily accepted the new goals of the society. It has been quick to seize the task of directing the growing activities for which the state has assumed responsibility and thereby become an eloquent defender of industrial interests. As a consequence, it has successfully assured its position of dominance in the society.

[59] *Ibid.*, pp. 102-103.

Chapter Ten

CONCLUSION

THIS study has been largely concerned with the remarkable resilience and adaptability of France's elite-forming institutions. A number of general hypotheses concerning the transformation of elites can be derived from our analysis.

(i) Transformation is facilitated by the continual renewal of the elite's legitimacy.

(ii) The elite's legitimacy must be anchored in a concrete achievement which gives "charisma" to the offices occupied.

(iii) The size of the elite must remain small. This enables the elite to be well organized.

(iv) The career success of the individual members of the elite must depend to a very large extent on their corporate organizations. This ensures their loyalty vis-à-vis the group as a whole.

(v) The elite must be well trained but must avoid specialization.

(vi) The elite needs to be imperialistic. Imperialism achieves two goals: (a) it prevents the elite from becoming too narrowly specialized; and (b) it facilitates its adaptation to changing economic, political, and social conditions. In short, specialization and technical expertise lead to rigidity and hinder the elite from making concessions and compromises.

(vii) The defense of corporate interests must always take precedence over an attachment to a particular policy.

(viii) Adaptation is facilitated by the existence of some degree of intra-elite competition.

We have seen that the policies the French elite embraces achieve the twin goals of allowing its members to preserve their dominant positions and of fostering greater administrative and economic centralization. The entire elite-forming process—from initial recruitment to the mutual aid and support that members of the elite learn to give one another throughout their careers—creates a self-conscious, self-confident elite, unhampered by self-doubt.

It might be argued that all elites are equally convinced that their capacity for leadership is greater than that of the rest of the population, and that the French elite's view of itself exhibits only a self-confidence, or self-satisfaction, that is characteristic of those who enjoy positions of power and privilege. That is undeniable, but the distinguishing feature about the French elite has been its ability to preserve its dominant position despite the disappearance of its original Raison d'Être. This still leaves unexplained, however, the relationship between the elite's capacity for survival and its performance. Put simply, is the elite as good as it thinks it is, and does the society as a whole share the elite's view of itself? The problem of social mobility and democratization, which is yet another issue, needs to be treated separately.

Discussion and criticism of France's elitist institutions have always centered on the issue of egalitarianism. The grandes écoles are always praised, even by their severest critics, as institutions that train the best brains in the society. They are criticized only for being "undemocratic." Few critics of the French elitist system attack the institutions themselves or suggest that they ought to be done away with. Rather, they demonstrate their attachment to them by demanding that there be wider access to them and that they be "democratized." Nowhere is this more clearly evidenced than in the Left's timidity vis-à-vis the whole elitist structure. The Left has criticized this structure, but it has not indicated that the nation would be better served without it.

What is meant by *democratizing* institutions like the grandes écoles and the grands corps? It generally means, both to scholars and to politicians, only that these institutions should recruit a greater percentage of the children of the lower classes. The term "democratization," when applied to academic, administrative, or other institutions has no other meaning in France but a greater representation of the lower classes. To take this view is to miss the main elements of what we have characterized as elitism. Admitting a few more children of workers into ENA, or even into the Inspection des Finances (which has been singularly unhospitable to people of modest origin) would not be of much help to the working class and would not transform these institutions in any significant way. It would help, above all, to legitimize these institutions and ward off criticism against them.

The elitism of these institutions derives not so much from the disproportionate representation of the bourgeoisie in them, but from the certification of lifelong membership in the elite they accord. They also have an important negative function: they preclude other avenues for entry into the elite.[1] In depriving other institutions from acquiring a high degree of legitimacy, they come to monopolize the function of elite certification and legitimation.[2]

It is possible to preserve institutions like the grands corps, which, after all, fulfill necessary functions, without allowing them to be used as a means of identifying and legitimizing the elites in the public and private sectors. In other words, the grands corps should not be used as mere jumping-off points, or launching pads, for the most prestigious and remunerative posts in the society. The only way to prevent this—while at the same time preserving these institutions—is to restrict the leaves of absence (*détachements*) that entrants into these institutions are permitted to take.[3] As a result, the entire process of recruitment into the top posts in the public, nationalized, and private sectors would be radically altered, for it could no longer be based on membership in institutions whose main function has come to be that of nurturing and certifying an imperialistic elite. In abandoning their new commitment to the promotion of a tentacular elite, the corps themselves would be restored to their rightful and honorable place in the state apparatus.

The total absence of any serious proposal on the part of France's Left to institute such a reform may be surprising. It indicates clearly, however, that an "elite consensus" exists with respect to certain venerable institutions. The Left's loud silence is all the more surprising when it is considered that such a "simple" reform would have a far greater impact on democratizing institutions, since it would allow for the upward mobility of those who did not go through the elite institutions, than would the entry of a few

---

[1] The extent to which some of the more important positions in the society have come to "belong" to a particular elite group is seen by the example of the state-controlled oil company, EIF-ERAP. The statute for this company specifies that only a higher civil servant may be named to its presidency. Most of the top positions in EIF-ERAP are occupied by members of the Corps des Mines, and the outgoing president (Pierre Guillaumat) is a member of this corps. The statute had to be changed in order to allow an "outsider" (Albin Chalandon, a former Inspecteur des Finances) to succeed Guillaumat. See *Le Monde*, 3 and 4 August 1977.

[2] Even François Bloch-Lainé has come to the conclusion that ENA no longer makes much sense. "It is a machine for mixing and ranking." See his *Profession: fonctionnaire* (Paris: Editions du Seuil, 1976), p. 236.

[3] I have developed this argument elsewhere. See *Le Nouvel Observateur*, September 13, 1976.

more children of the working and peasant classes into the grands corps.

There is little doubt that on the level of what have now become generally accepted criteria—efficiency and merit—France's state-created elite finds itself in a practically unassailable position. Few people question, and the elite certainly does not, that to be a member of the elite one has to demonstrate a capacity for overcoming the most strenuous hurdles. The severe competitiveness that entry into the elite involves serves to a very large extent to legitimize the elite for the society as a whole. No matter how much the educational system has been questioned in recent years because of its inegalitarian consequences, the elite claims—and this claim is generally shared by the society—that merit remains a better criterion for selection than patronage, heredity, or any other criterion that relegates intelligence and talent to secondary importance. Hence, the criterion of merit, which has achieved a certain sanctity in all industrial societies, is the foundation on which the elite's structure stands in France. If the self-confidence of the British elite (administrative, industrial, financial) has faltered in recent years, it is largely owing to the fact that the process of selection of this elite never institutionalized the criterion of merit to the same degree as its French counterpart did. One has only to see how awed the Fulton Commission was by its rather cursory look into the manner in which France trains its technicians.[4] Its admiration for the training and technical competence of French government officials, exaggerated as it was, demonstrated that there were serious questions not only about the selection of Britain's elite, but also about its competence.

Competence, however, is more or less relative and requires, at the very least, some means by which it can be recognized. What the French elite has been able to do is to have its standards of competence accepted by the society. *The grandes écoles and the grands corps not only create the elite, but set the conditions that determine the recognition of the elite.* These institutions are endowed with a degree of "charisma," which has facilitated their task of determining standards of competence. Whether the French elite is highly competent in some objective sense, therefore, is not the relevant question, for what matters is exclusion of any competence

[4] The Fulton Committee, *The Civil Service*, Vol. I (London: H.M.S.O., Cmnd 3638, 1968), pp. 133-137.

that is not certified by the elite. This is the meaning of elitism rather than disproportionate bourgeois representation.

The problem that is posed for any eventual reform that would aim to preserve the high standards of institutions like the grandes écoles while allowing for less restricted movement into *and out of* the elite is linked to the concentration of power. The privileged position of the elite is closely tied to the centralization of the administrative and economic structure. The elites are fundamentally opposed to greater participation and decentralization, not so much because they are imbued with a Jacobin ideology but because their own interests and positions would be harmed by a more decentralized structure. What this suggests is that the state-created elites judge a policy not by how good or bad it is in its own right, but rather according to how it will affect their power over spheres that they now control. A particular economic or monetary policy that a corps like the Inspection des Finances is given to execute will be judged very differently by the Inspection if that same policy should call for the creation of some institution that might rival the Inspection. Bloch-Lainé is right when he suggests that decentralization would be the most effective and least traumatic way of reducing the elitism typified by the grands corps.[5] The question arises as to how this is to take place when the grands corps would themselves have to accept and to implement the dismantling of the centralized structure.

No major structural reforms have been envisaged, either by the Left or the Right, because both recognize that the elitist system is not without advantages. It provides the state with relatively competent, dedicated, and loyal servants, in the public and private sectors hence with an element of stability. It follows from this that the state-created elites that have so far served the regime of the Fifth Republic will also serve a left-wing regime if this regime does not threaten the existing elitist if and when it comes to power. When that day arrives, the Left will find itself caught in a dilemma: on the one hand, its verbal commitments from the past will require it to transform radically the elitist structure; on the other hand, it may need to sacrifice, or at least seriously compromise, these commitments for the sake of some degree of continuity and in order to gain as much confidence as possible from those on whom it has to rely (at least for the initial period upon taking power) to get its reforms implemented. Nor should it be forgotten that many of the

[5] Bloch-Lainé, *Profession: fonctionnaire*, p. 236.

Left's leaders—particularly in the Socialist Party—have long shared in the advantages which the elitist system offers and have always manifested considerable reticence about tampering with the existing structure. For the time being, the elite has succeeded in placing itself in what amounts to an indispensable position, a position that precludes replacement by a counterelite, and has succeeded in having discussions of its competence, utility, and value confined to the problem of access to elite membership. This suggests that the existing structures have more than a secure position in French society.

BIBLIOGRAPHY

Alia, Josette. "Les Agents secrets du pouvoir," *Nouvel observateur*, March 11, 1974.

Alphandery, C. et al. *Pour nationaliser l'Etat*. Paris, Editions du Seuil, 1968.

Antoni, Pascal, and Antoni, Jean-Dominique. *Les Ministres de la Ve République*. Paris: Presses Universitaires de France, 1976.

Ariès, Philippe. "Problèmes de l'éducation," *La France et les Français*. Paris: Bibliothèque de la Pléiade, Gallimard, 1972.

Armstrong, John A. *The European Administrative Elite*. Princeton: Princeton University Press, 1973.

Artz, Frederick B. *The Development of Technical Education in France 1500-1850*. Cambridge, Mass.: The M.I.T. Press, 1966.

Aulard, A. *Napoleon Ier et le monopole universitaire*. Paris: Armand Colin, 1911.

Bachrach, Peter. *The Theory of Democratic Elitism*. Boston: Little, Brown & Co., 1967.

Balzac, Honoré de. *Le Curé du village*. Paris: Garnier-Flammarion, 1967.

Barton, Allan et al. *Opinion-Makers in Yugoslavia*. New York: Praeger Publishers, 1973.

Baudelot, Christian, and Establet, Roger. *L'Ecole capitaliste en France*. Paris: Maspero, 1971.

Baum, Warren C. *The French Economy and the State*. Princeton: Princeton University Press, 1958.

Bell, Daniel. *The Coming of Post-Industrial Society*. New York: Basic Books, 1973.

Ben-David, Joseph. *The Scientist's Role in Society: A Comparative Study*. Englewood Cliffs, N.J.: Prentice-Hall, 1971.

Berger, Suzanne. "D'une boutique à l'autre: Changes in the Organization of the Traditional Middle Classes from the Fourth to the Fifth Republic," *Comparative Politics*, IX, No. 1 (October 1977).

Bernard, H. C. *Education and the French Revolution.* Cambridge: Cambridge University Press, 1969.

Birnbaum, Pierre. *Les Sommets de l'Etat: essai sur l'élite du pouvoir en France.* Paris: Editions du Seuil, 1977.

Bize, Pierre. "Nouvelles orientations intellectuelles des dirigeants des entreprises," *Sociologie du Travail* (April-June 1960).

Bloch, Marc. *L'Etrange défaite.* Paris: Albin Michel, 1957.

Bloch-Lainé, François. *Profession: fonctionnaire.* Paris: Editions du Seuil, 1976.

Boddwyn, Jean. "The Belgian Economic Expansion Law," in *Industrial Policies in Western Europe,* ed. Steven J. Warnecke and Ezra N. Suleiman. New York: Praeger Publishers, 1975.

Bodiguel, Jean-Luc. "Les Anciens élèves de l'E.N.A. et les cabinets ministériels," *Annuaire international de la fonction publique, 1973-1974.*

Boilot, Pierre. "Réflexions sur un corps," *Bulletin de PCM,* LXIV (September 1967).

Boltanski, Luc. "L'Espace positionnel: multiplicité des positions institutionnels et habitus de classe," *Revue Française de sociologie,* XIV, No. 1 (January-March 1975).

―――. *Prime education et morale de classe.* Paris: Mouton, 1969.

Bon, F., and Burnier, M. A. *Les Nouveaux intellectuels.* Paris: Editions du Seuil, 1971.

Bonilla, Frank. *The Failure of Elites.* Cambridge, Mass.: The M.I.T. Press, 1970.

Bonnaud, Jean-Jacques. "Planning and Industry in France," in *Planning, Politics and Public Policy: The British, French and Italian Experience,* ed. Jack Hayward and Michael Watson. Cambridge: Cambridge University Press, 1975.

Bottomore, T. B. *Elites and Society.* New York: Basic Books, 1964.

Boudon, Raymond. "La crise universitaire française: essai de diagnostique sociologique," *Annales,* XXIV, No. 3 (May-June 1969).

―――. "The French University Since 1968," *Comparative Politics,* IX, No. 1 (October 1977).

―――. *L'Inégalité des chances.* Paris: Armand Colin, 1973. Translated as *Education, Opportunity and Social Inequality.* New York: John Wiley and Sons, 1974.

Bourdieu, Pierre. "Reproduction culturelle et reproduction sociale," *Informations des sciences sociales*, II, No. 10. 1970.

———, and Passeron, J. C. *Les Héritiers*. Paris: Editions de Minuit, 1964.

———. *La Reproduction*. Paris: Editions de Minuit, 1971.

Bourricaud, François. "La Réforme universitaire en France et ses deboires," *Fondation Européenne de la culture*, Cahier 3, 1977.

———. *Universités à la dérive*. Paris: Stock, 1971.

Boutmy, Emile. *Quelques observations sur la réforme de l'enseignement supérieur*. Paris: Librairie de Germer Baillière, 1876.

Bowles, Samuel, and Gintis, Herbert. *Education in Capitalist America*. New York: Basic Books, 1976.

Brizay, Bernard. *Le Patronat*. Paris: Editions du Seuil, 1975.

Brunck, Robert. "L'Horizon d'un élève de l'X." *Preuves*, 4ᵉ trimestre, 1971.

Burnham, James. *The Managerial Revolution*. Bloomington: Indiana University Press, 1966.

Carré, J.-J., Dubois, P., and Malinvaud, E. *French Economic Growth*. Stanford, Cal.: Stanford University Press, 1975.

Chalendar, Jacques de. *Une Loi pour l'université*. Paris: Desclée de Brouwer, 1970.

Cheradame, R. "Les Méthodes d'enseignement dans les écoles scientifiques," *Cohesion* (November 1963).

Claude, Henry. *La Concentration capitaliste: pouvoir gaulliste*. Paris: Editions Sociales, 1965.

———. *Gaullisme et grand capital*. Paris: Editions Sociales, 1960.

———. *Le Pouvoir et l'argent*. Paris: Editions Sociales, 1972.

Closon, F.-L., and Filippi, J. *L'Economie et les finances*. Paris: Presses Universitaires de France, 1968.

Cohen, Stephen. *Modern Capitalist Planning: The French Model*. Cambridge, Mass.: Harvard University Press, 1969.

Committee for Scientific and Technological Policy. *Social Science Policy: France*. Paris: O.E.C.D., 1975.

Cot, Pierre D. "Le Rôle des Grands Corps d'ingénieurs dans la société française d'aujourd'hui," *La Jaune et la rouge*, No. 230 (October 1968).

Cremieux-Brilhac, J.-L. *L'Education nationale*. Paris: Presses Universitaires de France, 1965.

Crew, Ivor. *British Yearbook of Political Sociology: Elites in Western Democracy.* London: Croom Helm Ltd., 1974.

Crick, Bernard C. *In Defense of Politics.* Chicago: University of Chicago Press, 2nd edition, 1972.

Crozier, Michel. *The Bureaucratic Phenomenon.* Chicago: University of Chicago Press, 1964.

————. *La Société bloquée.* Paris: Editions du Seuil, 1970.

Dahrendorf, Ralf. *Society and Democracy in Germany.* New York: Doubleday and Co., 1967.

Daunesse, P. "A Propos des Grands Corps d'ingénieurs," *Association des cadres dirigeants et l'industries pour le progrès social et économique*, No. 241 (March 1969).

Debré, Michel. "Allocation de M. Debré," *La Jaune et la rouge*, No. 266 (January 1972).

————. *Réforme de la fonction publique.* Paris: Imprimerie Nationale, 1946.

De Gaulle, Charles. Speech at Ecole Polytechnique. *La Jaune et la rouge*, No. 129 (July 1959).

Delefortrie-Soubeyroux, Nicole. *Les Dirigeants de l'industrie française.* Paris: Armand Colin, 1961.

Delfau, Albert. *Napoleon 1er et l'instruction publique.* Paris: Albert Fontemoing, 1902.

De Lozère, Pelet. *Opinions de Napoleon.* Paris: Firmin Didot Frères, 1833.

Desjeux, D., and Friedberg, E. "Fonctions de l'Etat et rôle des grands corps: le cas du corps des mines," *Annuaire international de la fonction publique, 1972-1973.*

Dimock, Marshall E. *The Japanese Technocracy.* New York: Wallcer/Weatherhill, 1968.

D'Ocagne, Mortimer. *Les Grandes Ecoles en France.* Paris: J. Hetzel and Cie, 1887.

Dogan, Mattei. "Comment on devient ministre en France, 1870-1976." Paper presented at the 10th World Congress of the International Political Science Association. Edinburgh, Scotland, August 1976.

————, ed. *The Mandarins of Western Europe: The Political Role of Top Civil Servants.* Beverly Hills: Sage Publications, 1975.

Domhoff, G. William. *The Higher Circles.* New York: Vintage Books, 1971.

————. *Who Rules America?* Englewood Cliffs, N.J.: Prentice-Hall, 1967.

Drancourt, Michel. *Les clés du pouvoir*. Paris: Fayard, 1964.

Duport, Jean. "L'Administration vue par le secteur privé," *Administration et secteur privé*. Paris: Dalloz, 1973.

Durkheim, Emile. *Education et sociologie*. Paris: Presses Universitaires de France, 1960.

Ehrmann, Henry. *Organized Business in France*. Princeton: Princeton University Press, 1957.

Ellul, Jacques. *The Technological Society*. New York: Vintage Books, 1964.

Escoube, Pierre. *Les Grands Corps de l'Etat*. Paris: Presses Universitaires de France, 1971.

Faure, Edgar. *Ce que je crois*. Paris: Grasset, 1971.

Fayol, Henri. *Administration industrielle et générale*. Paris: Junod, 1920.

Ferrat, André. *La République à refaire*. Paris: Gallimard, 1965.

Fischesser, M. R., and Lafitte, M. P. "La Formation des ingénieurs du corps des mines," *La Jaune et la rouge*, No. 246 (March 1970).

Fomerand, Jacques. "Policy Formulation and Change in Gaullist France: The 1968 Orientation Act of Higher Education," *Comparative Politics*, VIII, No. 1 (October 1975).

Friedberg, Erhard. "Administration et Entreprises." *Où Va l'administration française?* Paris: Les Editions d'Organisation, 1974.

The Fulton Report. *The Civil Service Today*, Vol. I. London: H.M.S.O., 1968.

Gelinier, Octave. *Morale de l'entreprise et destin de la nation*. Paris: Plon, 1965.

Gilpin, Robert. *France in the Age of the Scientific State*. Princeton: Princeton University Press, 1968.

——. *U.S. Powers and the Multinational Corporation*. New York: Basic Books, 1975.

Girard, Alain. *La Réussite sociale en France*. Paris: Presses Universitaires de France, 1961.

Goblot, Edmond. *La Barrière et le niveau*. Paris: Presses Universitaires de France, 1967.

Granick, David. *The European Executive*. New York: Doubleday Anchor, 1962.

——. *Managerial Comparisons of Four Developed Countries: France, Britain, United States, and Russia*. Cambridge, Mass.: The M.I.T. Press, 1972.

"Les 'grosses têtes' de Mitterrand," *Le Nouvel observateur*, July 21-27, 1975.

Grunberg, Gérard. "L'Ecole Polytechnique et 'ses' grands corps," *Annuaire international de la fonction publique, 1973-1974.*

Hall, D. "L'Elite française des dirigeants de l'entreprise," *Hommes et techniques*, No. 291 (January 1968).

"Les Hauts fonctionnaires et les patrons," *Le Nouvel economiste*, No. 85, June 13, 1977.

Hayward, Jack. "Employer Associations and the State in France and Britain," in *Industrial Policies in Western Europe*, ed. Steven J. Warnecke and Ezra N. Suleiman. New York: Praeger Publishers, 1975.

———. *The One and Indivisible French Republic*. London: Weidenfeld and Nicolson, 1973.

———. "State Intervention in France: The Changing Style of Government-Industry Relations," *Political Studies*, xx, No. 3 (September 1972).

———, and Wright, Vincent. "Les Deux France and the French Presidential Election of May 1974," *Parliamentary Affairs*, xxvii, No. 3 (Summer 1974).

Herzlich, Guy. "Protéger les forts contre les faibles," *Le Monde*, April 20, 1971.

Hoffman, Stanley. *Decline or Renewal? France Since the 1930's*. New York: Viking Press, 1974.

Hughes, H. Stuart. *Consciousness and Society*. New York: Alfred A. Knopf, 1958.

Jencks, Christopher. *Inequality*. New York: Basic Books, 1973.

Kelsall, R. K. "Recruitment to the Higher Civil Service: How Has the Pattern Changed?" in *Elites and Power in British Society*, ed. Philip Stanworth and Anthony Giddens. Cambridge: Cambridge University Press, 1974.

Kessler, Marie-Christine. *Le Conseil d'Etat*. Paris: Armand Colin, 1968.

Kindleberger, Charles P. "Technical Education and the French Entrepreneur," in *Enterprise and Entrepreneurs in Nineteenth and Twentieth Century France*, ed. Edward C. Carter, Robert Forster, and Joseph N. Moody. Baltimore: The Johns Hopkins University Press, 1976.

Kosciusko-Morizet, Jacques A. *La "Mafia" polytechnicienne*. Paris: Editions du Seuil, 1973.

Krasner, Stephen D. "State Power and the Structure of International Trade," *World Politics*, XXVIII, No. 3 (April 1976).

Kuisel, Richard F. "Technocrats and Public Economic Policy: From the Third to the Fourth Republic," *Journal of European Economic History*, II, No. 1 (1973).

Lalumière, Pierre. *L'Inspection des Finances*. Paris: Presses Universitaires de France, 1959.

Landes, David S. "French Business and the Businessman: A Social and Cultural Analysis," in *Modern France: Problems of the Third and Fourth Republics*, ed. Edward Meade Earle. Princeton: Princeton University Press, 1951.

————. "Religion and Enterprise: The Case of the French Textile Industry," in *Enterprise and Entrepreneurs in Nineteenth and Twentieth Century France*, ed. Edward C. Carter, Robert Forster, and Joseph N. Moody. Baltimore: The Johns Hopkins University Press, 1976.

Lavau, Georges. "The PCF, the State, and the Revolution: An Analysis of Party Policies, Communications, and Popular Culture," in *Communism in Italy and France*, ed. Donald L. M. Blackmer and Sidney Tarrow. Princeton: Princeton University Press, 1975.

Lefebvre, Henri. *Position: contre les technocrates*. Paris: Gonthier, 1967.

Levy-Leboyer, Maurice. "Innovation and Business Strategies in Nineteenth and Twentieth Century France," in *Enterprise and Entrepreneurs in Nineteenth and Twentieth Century France*, ed. Edward C. Carter, Robert Forster, and Joseph N. Moody. Baltimore: The Johns Hopkins University Press, 1976.

Liard, Louis. *L'Enseignement supérieur en France*. Paris: Armand Colin, 1894.

Lipset, Seymour M. *Political Man*. New York: Doubleday Anchor, 1961.

Macciocchi, Maria-Antonietta. *De la France*. Paris: Editions du Seuil, 1977.

Maier, Charles S. *Recasting Bourgeois Europe: Stabilization in France, Germany, and Italy in the Decade after World War I*. Princeton: Princeton University Press, 1975.

Malek, Jeffrey L. "An Empirical Study of the Composition of French Bank Directors." Unpublished paper, 1975.

Mante, J. "Réflexion sur l'orientation du corps des ponts et chaussées," *Bulletin du PCM*, LXIV (March 1967).

Martin, Roger. "Ouverture," *La Jaune et la rouge*, No. 261 (July 1971).

Martinet, Gilles. *Le Système Pompidou.* Paris: Grasset, 1973.

Maurin, G. "Allocution prononcée devant les élèves de l'Ecole Polytechnique," *La Jaune et la rouge*, No. 2 (March 1946).

Mayer, René. *Un P.C.M., pour quoi faire?* Paris: PCM, 1970.

Meisel, James. *The Myth of the Ruling Class.* Ann Arbor, Mich.: The University of Michigan Press, 1962.

Meynaud, Jean. *Technocracy.* New York: The Free Press, 1968.

Michalet, Charles-Albert. "France," in *Big Business and the State*, ed. Raymond Vernon. Cambridge, Mass.: Harvard University Press, 1974.

Mitterrand, François. *Le Coup d'Etat permanent.* Paris: Plon, 1965.

Monjardet, Dominique. "Carrière des dirigeants et contrôle de l'entreprise," *Sociologie de travail*, Vol. 13, No. 2 (April-June 1972).

Morin, François. *La Structure financière du capitalism français.* Paris: Calmann-Levy, 1974.

Mosca, Gaetano. *The Ruling Class.* New York: McGraw-Hill, 1939.

Nora, Simon. *Rapport sur les entreprises publiques.* Paris: La Documentation Française, 1967.

Olson, Mancur. *The Logic of Collective Action.* New York: Schocken Books, 1969.

O.E.C.D. *Rapport sur la politique d'enseignement en France.* Paris: La Documentation Française, 1971.

Painé, Raymond. "Classes préparatoires et grandes écoles dans une réforme de l'enseignement supérieur," *La Jaune et la rouge*, No. 194 (June 1965).

Papon, Pierre. "Le Problème des Grandes Ecoles," *Esprit*, Special Number (May-June 1964).

Pareto, Vilfredo. *The Mind and Society: A Treatise on General Sociology.* New York: Dover Publications, 1963.

————. *The Rise and Fall of Elites.* New York: Bedminster Press, 1968.

Paxton, Robert O. *Vichy France.* New York: Alfred A. Knopf, 1973.

Perrin, René. "En marge de la réforme de l'enseignement: de

l'utilité de la formation polytechnicienne," *Bulletin de l'Association des anciens élèves de l'Ecole Polytechnique*, No. 68 (July 1957).

Peyrefitte, Alain. *Le Mal Français*. Paris: Plon, 1977.

Pinet, G. *Historie de l'Ecole Polytechnique*. Paris: Librairie Polytechnique Baudry, 1887.

Poitrat, R. "Utilité des corps," *La Jaune et la rouge*, No. 246 (March 1970).

"Portrait-Robot du P.D.G. Européen," *Expansion* (November 1969).

Poulantzas, Nicos. *Les Classes sociales dans le capitalisme d'aujourd'hui*. Paris: Editions du Seuil, 1974.

———. *La Crise de l'état*. Paris: Presses Universitaires de France, 1977.

Priouret, Roger. "Face à face avec Edgar Faure," *Expansion* (September 1969).

———. *Les Français mystifiés*. Paris: B. Grasset, 1973.

Programme Commun de gouvernement du parti communiste et du parti socialiste. Paris: Editions Sociales, 1972.

Prost, Antoine. *L'Enseignement en France, 1800-1967*. Paris: Armand Colin, 1968.

Purcell, John, and Purcell, Susan. "Mexican Business and Public Policy," in *Authoritarianism and Corporatism in Latin America*, ed. James M. Malloy. Pittsburgh: The University of Pittsburgh Press, 1978.

Putnam, Robert D. *The Comparative Study of Political Elites*. Englewood Cliffs, N.J.: Prentice-Hall, 1976.

———. "The Political Attitudes of Senior Civil Servants in Britain, Germany, and Italy," *British Journal of Political Science*, III (1973).

"A Quoi Servent les banques nationalisés?" *L'Express*, January 6-12, 1975.

Rain, Pierre. *L'Ecole Libre des Sciences Politiques, 1871-1945*. Paris: Fondation Nationale des Sciences Politiques, 1963.

Rapport de la commission d'étude des problèmes de l'Ecole Nationale d'Administration. Paris: La Documentation Française, 1968.

Renan, Ernest. *La Réforme intellectuelle et morale*. Paris: Michel Lévy, 1871.

Rongère, Pierrette. *Le Cour des Comptes*. Paris: Fondation Nationale des Sciences Politiques, 1963.

Roszak, Theodore. *The Making of a Counter-Culture*. New York: Doubleday Anchor, 1973.

———. *Where the Wasteland Ends*. New York: Doubleday Anchor, 1973.

Ruby, Marcel. *La Vie et l'oeuvre de Jean Zay*. Paris: n.p., 1969.

Sampson, Anthony. *Anatomy of Europe*. New York: Harper & Row, 1968.

Savage, Dean. "Founders, Heirs, and Managers in France: A Business Elite in Transition." Unpublished Ph.D. Dissertation. New York: Columbia University, 1975.

Schonfeld, William. *Obedience and Revolt: French Behavior Toward Authority*. Beverly Hills: Sage Publications, 1976.

Schumpeter, Joseph. *Capitalism, Socialism and Democracy*. New York: Harper & Row, 1942.

———. *Imperialism and Social Class*. New York: Meridian Books, 1971.

Servan-Schreiber, Jean-Jacques, and Albert, Michel. *Ciel et Terre: Manifeste Radical*. Paris: Denoel, 1970.

Shils, Edward. *Center and Periphery: Essays in Macro-sociology*. Chicago: University of Chicago Press, 1975.

Shin, Terry. *Savoir scientifique et pouvoir sociale: L'école polytechnique et les polytechniciens*. Paris: Presse de la Fondation Nationale des Sciences Politiques, forthcoming, 1978.

Smith, Robert J. "Normaliens of the Rue d'Ulm." Unpublished manuscript.

Stillman, Edmund et al. *L'Envol de la France dans les années 80*. Paris: Hachette, 1973.

Stoleru, Lionel. *L'Impératif industriel*. Paris: Editions du Seuil, 1969.

Suleiman, Ezra N. "The French Bureaucracy and Its Students: Toward the Desanctification of the State," *World Politics*, XXIII, No. 1 (1970).

———. "La Gauche et la haute administration," *Promotions*, No. 100 (November 1976).

———. *Politics, Power, and Bureaucracy in France*. Princeton: Princeton University Press, 1974.

Taine, Hippolyte. *Les Origines de la France contemporaine*. Paris: Hachette, 1894.

Talbot, John E. *The Politics of Educational Reform in France 1918-1940*. Princeton: Princeton University Press, 1969.

Tarrow, Sidney. *Between Center and Periphery: Grassroots Politicians in Italy and France*. New Haven: Yale University Press, 1977.

————. "Regional Policy, Ideology and Peripheral Defense: The Case of Fos-Sur-Mer," in *Territorial Politics in Industrial Nations*, ed. Luigi Graziano, Peter J. Katzenstein, and Sidney Tarrow. New York: Praeger Publishers, 1978.

Thépot, André. *Le Corps des Mines*. Thèse de Doctorat d'Etat, forthcoming.

Thoenig, Jean-Claude. *L'Ere des technocrates: le cas des ponts et chaussées*. Paris: Les Editions d'Organisation, 1973.

————. "L'Exemple français des Grands Corps." Paper presented at the 8th World Congress of the International Political Science Association. Munich, August 31-September 5, 1970.

Toqueville, Alexis De. *The Old Regime and the French Revolution*. New York: Doubleday and Co., 1955.

Touraine, Alaine. *The May Movement: Revolt and Reform*. New York: Random House, 1971.

Vaughan, Michalina, and Archer, Margaret S. *Social Conflict and Educational Change in England and France 1789-1848*. Cambridge: Cambridge University Press, 1971.

Veblen, Thorstein. *The Engineers and the Price System*. New York: Viking Press, 1921.

Vène, André. *La Lutte du pouvoir dans les sociétés par actions*. Paris: Les Editions d'Organisation, 1972.

Venturini, V. G. *Monopolies and Restrictive Trade Practices*. Leyden: A. W. Sijthoff, 1971.

Vernon, Raymond. "Enterprise and Government in Western Europe," in *Big Business and the State*, ed. Raymond Vernon. Cambridge, Mass.: Harvard University Press, 1974.

————. *Sovereignty at Bay*. New York: Basic Books, 1971.

Weber, Max. *The Theory of Social and Economic Organization*. New York: The Free Press, 1965.

Weinberg, Ian. *The English Public Schools: The Sociology of Elite Education*. New York: Atherton Press, 1967.

Wright, Vincent. "L'Ecole nationale d'administration de 1848-1849: un échec révélateur," *Revue Historique* (January-March 1976).

Yanaga, Chitoshi. *Big Business in Japanese Politics*. New Haven: Yale University Press, 1968.

Zoretti, Ludovic. *Education: un essai d'organisation démocratique.* Paris: Plon, 1918.

Zeldin, Theodore. "Higher Education in France, 1845-1945," *Journal of Contemporary History*, I, No. 3 (July 1967).

———. *The Political System of Napoleon III.* New York: W. W. Norton & Co., 1971.

Zysman, John. *Political Strategies for Industrial Order: Market, State and Industry in France.* Berkeley and Los Angeles: University of California Press, 1977.

INDEX

Index

LIBRARY OF CONGRESS CATALOGING IN PUBLICATION DATA

Suleiman, Ezra N.,
   Elites in French society.

   Includes index.
   1. Elites—France.   I. Title.
HN440.E4S94   301.44′92′0944   78-51195
ISBN 0-691-07597-2
ISBN 0-691-10071-3 pbk.